KNOW YOUR MIND

Sangharakshita

KNOW YOUR MIND

The Psychological Dimension of Ethics in Buddhism

WINDHORSE PUBLICATIONS

Published by Windhorse Publications
11 Park Road
Birmingham
B13 8AB

© Sangharakshita 1998

Cover image *Senecio*, Paul Klee 1922 © DACS 1998, photo AKG London
Cover design Dhammarati
Printed by Interprint Ltd, Marsa, Malta

British Library Cataloguing in Publication Data:
A catalogue record for this book is available from the British Library

ISBN   0 904766 79 9

The publishers wish to acknowledge with gratitude permission to quote extracts
from Herbert V. Guenther and Leslie S. Kawamura (trans.), *Mind in Buddhist
Psychology*, Dharma Publishing, Berkeley 1975.

Every effort has been made to trace the copyright in the following. If any omissions
have been made please let us know so that this may be rectified in a future edition.

Hsüan Tsang, *Ch'eng Wei-Shih Lun: Doctrine of Mere-Consciousness*
S. Dasgupta, *An Ever-expanding Quest of Life and Consciousness*

CONTENTS

About the Author

Sangharakshita was born Dennis Lingwood in South London, in 1925. Largely self-educated, he developed an interest in the cultures and philosophies of the East early on, and realized that he was a Buddhist at the age of sixteen.

The Second World War took him, as a conscript, to India, where he stayed on to become the Buddhist monk Sangharakshita. After studying for some years under leading teachers from the major Buddhist traditions, he went on to teach and write extensively. He also played a key part in the revival of Buddhism in India, particularly through his work among the ex-Untouchables.

After twenty years in India, he returned to England to establish the Friends of the Western Buddhist Order (FWBO) in 1967, and the Western Buddhist Order in 1968. A translator between East and West, between the traditional world and the modern, between principles and practices, Sangharakshita's depth of experience and clear thinking have been appreciated throughout the world. He has always particularly emphasized the decisive significance of commitment in the spiritual life, the paramount value of spiritual friendship and community, the link between religion and art, and the need for a 'new society' supportive of spiritual aspirations and ideals.

The FWBO is now an international Buddhist movement with over sixty centres on five continents. In recent years Sangharakshita has been handing on most of his responsibilities to his senior disciples in the Order. From his base in Birmingham, he is now focusing on personal contact with people, and on his writing.

Editors' Preface

For Buddhists, how the mind works has always been essentially a practical matter. When in the very first verse of one of the oldest texts, the *Dhammapada*, the Buddha says: 'Mental states are preceded by mind, led by mind, and made up of mind,' he is not airing a philosophical speculation, but expressing an insight which can guide and transform one's whole way of life.

From the Buddha's earliest pronouncements about the nature of mind has developed the field of Buddhist studies called the Abhidharma, a lineage of two thousand years of insight, experience, and scholarship, from the first Ābhidharmikas to the Yogācārins, the Gelukpas, and the Nyingmapas. Throughout the history of the Abhidharma, drifts towards scholarly abstraction have been corrected by a redirected focus on essentials. And Western Buddhists are the inheritors of the entire tradition.

The participants in the seminar from the transcript of which this book has been created were practising Western Buddhists whose concern was to experience and deal with the impact these teachings would have on their spiritual life and practice. Patiently – and sometimes not so patiently – they engaged in that near-impossible activity, thinking about the mind, with the intention of coming to understand their own mental processes so that they could direct them better. That seminar was conducted by Sangharakshita, and it was under his expert guidance that intellectual hypotheses were always, sooner or later, connected with personal and ethical implications.

For – and again this can be traced to the Buddha's first insights – our minds are not just our own affair. Consciously or unconsciously, thoughts are swiftly translated into actions; and actions have their effect, not just on those who perpetrate them but on other people, and on the world as a whole. These days we are only too aware of this in theory, but acting as if we know is still not easy. And the starting point is gaining greater awareness of how inner and outer worlds are connected. Knowing one's own mind, far from being self-indulgent, is the only means to true altruism.

Thus the Buddhist conception of psychology is that it is not a personal affair but a subject of study that has far-reaching ethical implications. The discussion of mind in this book moves from a consideration of what it is and how it works to the close scrutiny of homelier matters: positive mental states and how to develop them; and negative mental states and how to become free of them. Not just how; why. Here is unfolded a rationale for the spiritual life; for our happiness and that of others depends on our coming to know, intimately, our own minds.

In preparing this text for publication we have received a great deal of help, graciously given. Many thanks to Silabhadra, who provided the original transcripts from his store of millions of transcribed words; and to Kamalasila, Sagaramati, and Asanga, who gave us the great benefit of their knowledge of the field, and supplied many useful corrections and suggestions. Thanks especially to Asanga for checking all the Sanskrit and Pali terms, and also for taking the time to help with elusive endnote information at a time when he was hard at work on the final details of his own book. Thanks also to Shantavira and Dhivati, Windhorse Publications' remarkable copy-editors, who leave no cross-reference cryptic and no metaphor mixed. And Sangharakshita has given much of his time to checking and considering the text at various stages. As always, he has been most generous in allowing us to publish our written version of his oral teachings – the resulting style being quite different from his own preferred mode of writing – and most patient in restoring the occasional stretched point to its true proportions.

Jinananda and Vidyadevi
Spoken Word Project
July 1998

INTRODUCTION

IS THERE SUCH A THING
AS BUDDHIST PSYCHOLOGY?

IT SHOULD be admitted right at the outset that there is really no such thing as Buddhist psychology. In the West we may speak of Buddhist ethics, Buddhist philosophy, Buddhist logic, Buddhist epistemology, and so on, but the teaching of Buddhism as a whole is a fully integrated tradition. It's all of one piece, as it were; take up any one aspect of it, and all the others automatically follow. The danger of specializing in one area of study or another is that one tends to lose sight of its connections with other subjects, or even the subject from which it originally sprang – and this has indeed happened at times in the history of what I am calling Buddhist psychology.

At the same time, of course, the term is not entirely inappropriate, if one simply understands it to refer to Buddhism's teachings about the nature and functioning of the mind, especially as this has a bearing on the spiritual life in general, and on meditation in particular. Buddhist psychology is not just a descriptive science; it has no purpose other than to be put into practice. And its practical use lies in enabling us to recognize what is going on in our own minds, to discriminate between positive and valuable mental events and negative or unhelpful ones, between real vision and subjective views. It starts from the basis that we play a part in creating the world we find ourselves in, and that the only effective way to improve our situation is to take responsibility for it – which means taking responsibility for our mental states.

According to Buddhism our predicament arises out of our ignorance. Ignorance (Sanskrit *avidyā*) is traditionally likened to drunkenness, while the volitions (*saṁskāras*) that arise from ignorance are compared to actions committed whilst in a state of drunkenness. This perception of the human condition may seem extreme, but it is no more than sober fact. Sometimes we don't realize the extent of the damage we do simply because we don't know what we are doing. We initiate things, we say things, we get involved with people, and in doing so we inevitably set up problems. Although we sometimes become aware that our lives are more or less made up of the problems we create in this way, very often we don't even see them as problems – and this is a problem in itself.

Of course, there is no question of trying to stay on the safe side by putting off doing anything at all until we are Enlightened; to live, we must act, and we are therefore bound to make mistakes. But if we can understand what we are doing, we can break the reactive patterns that cause us to create the same problems over and over again. And the way to break those reactive patterns that bring us so much suffering is to set up different patterns of thought, feeling, and behaviour.

Once one sees one's predicament clearly, once one knows where one is starting from, one is in a position to perceive the choices before one, which gives one a certain degree of freedom. It isn't absolute freedom – one can't choose one's starting point – but one is free to choose what one makes of one's situation. Where one is is less important than whether or not one *knows* where one is. There is a freedom which arises out of knowing oneself and knowing the possibility of evolving beyond one's present condition.

That freedom is, however, double-edged. The mind is not a thing; it is not, as Guenther puts it in the introduction to his translation of *Mind in Buddhist Psychology*, 'a static entity or a mere state or function of consciousness'.[1] It consists solely in its activities. 'It' is therefore always changing, always moving. But it can move either creatively or reactively. At every moment the mind is confronted with the choice of repeating old patterns and going round in circles or rearranging the pattern and setting up more positive conditions for spiritual growth. At every moment there is the possibility of moving forward and also the possibility of just moving round and thus not really moving at all. We are free to develop our awareness of the spiritual path, to look for solutions; and we are also free to sink back into unconsciousness and stop asking questions. Furthermore, mental states cannot be compartmentalized. Painful and harmful states of mind cannot be shut away somewhere while we develop mindfulness, joy, and kindness. At any one time we are either encouraging positive mental states or reinforcing negative ones.

If one makes the effort to develop in a positive direction, one's life assumes a more serious meaning as one takes responsibility for it. One realizes for oneself the necessity, almost, of a certain way of living. This is what it means to follow the Buddhist path.

Buddhism is presented as a path or way, but this is only a manner of speaking. The path is a symbol, representing the fact that we can change, we can develop. If we know what we are now and what we can become, we can take steps to effect that transition. We have the capacity, and the freedom, to perceive and to realize our best interests.

According to the Pāli idiom, we *develop* the path.[2] It is not something out there, an objective thing. We *are* the path. If we think of it as something out there, like a road or track, we may get stuck with an unhelpful notion of the spiritual discipline required in order to follow it. One is not following the Buddhist path if one feels that one is being driven along it like a sheep, rather wishing one could stray off and have a nibble on some succulent wayside shrub or flower.

There is certainly an objective criterion of development which one has to understand and act upon, but the path itself is not out there; it is in here. There is no question of forcing oneself to follow a particular track or go in a particular direction. The path simply represents the individual solution to one's own particular predicament. If you know and understand yourself as you are now, that puts you in a position to develop in your own way. The path is you in the process of organizing your mental states in such a way that growth and development will take place in a positive direction.

This recognition and organization of mental states became the overwhelming preoccupation of generations of Buddhist scholars. What became known as the Abhidharma absorbed the best efforts of some of the finest minds in Buddhist history over a period of a thousand years. Although in some respects there was a degeneration into scholasticism, the zeal of these scholars for their tremendous task was very much connected with their commitment to the spiritual path. Their desire to understand mind and mental states stemmed from their commitment to following the Buddha's teaching. 'Cease to do evil. Learn to do good. Purify your mind.'[3] This was their starting point.

But what was the mind? How could it be understood? This, over centuries, they sought to fathom. They didn't just think in terms of what in the West we would call psychological health; they were inspired by the Buddha's vision of the infinite, transcendental potential of the human mind. The Abhidharma could be described as an exhaustive science of mind – although it is not really possible to speak of the mind as a subject of study like any other, because in a sense the mind doing the studying cannot be at the same time the object of that study. As we explore the Abhidharma we have constantly to take this into account if we are to derive practical benefit from it. It is true that Buddhism appeals to observation to verify its account of the nature of things, but this method of observation is not like a laboratory experiment; it always remains personal. In the case of Buddhist psychology it consists in introspection, in watching oneself – seeing how one reacts to things, for example.

So although in a sense the Ābhidharmikas were 'Buddhist psychologists', in speaking of Buddhist psychology we have to beware of limiting our conception of Buddhism. This is a real danger for the simple reason that the English language, reflecting the limitations of the general Western idea of mind, does not have words to recognize or describe higher states of consciousness (the Sanskrit term is *dhyāna*). A conscious state of mind in which there is no perception of external things, in which the senses do not function, in which there is no mental activity in the usual sense, is simply not recognized. Such states are not, therefore, included in the denotation of the term 'psyche' or 'mind'; and this means that to speak of Buddhism as a method of psychological development automatically suggests that the development one has in mind falls short of *dhyāna*.

The range of experience over and above what the term 'psychological' generally covers may be referred to by the term 'spiritual'. In this way, the 'spiritual life' comes to mean a life organized for the production of skilful mental states, especially as represented by the *dhyānas*, so as to form a foundation for the experience of Enlightenment.

We also need to find a way of referring to the distinction between states of mind which are attained temporarily, and those whose attainment constitutes a permanent change. Spiritual states of mind are not necessarily permanent; as is all too clear, one can be feeling 'spiritual' at one moment, and far from spiritual the next. It is possible, however, to achieve continuously positive and refined states of mind. At a certain point, one sustains such deep insight into the nature of reality that one's uninterrupted progress towards Enlightenment is guaranteed. This is known traditionally in Buddhism as entering the stream, an experience that may be described as transcendental. We thus have three terms – psychological, spiritual, and transcendental – to describe different phases in the development of consciousness. Although the term psychological refers to the mind or psyche, and although it is the human mind, in a manner of speaking, that experiences *dhyāna* and transcendental Insight, it may be limiting, even misleading, to refer to Buddhism as a method of psychological growth.

As well as being cautious about the use of the term psychological, we also need to be careful in using the word mind, which, in the context of the Western theistic and even post-theistic tradition, is limited in the sense that a distinction is drawn between the human mind and the 'mind of God'. According to the Buddha's teaching, however, there is no limit to the human mind, and nothing – at least potentially – beyond its reach; it has a vast, literally inconceivable, significance. For a Buddhist, the expression 'merely human' does not make sense; nor does the idea that one could have faith in a revelation on the basis that it had come from a realm beyond the compass of the human mind.

To begin an exploration of the nature of mind in Buddhist psychology, we need to remind ourselves that 'mind' and 'mental events' are concepts – concepts that may form a basis for an understanding of the reality to which they refer. Essentially, concepts arise in two ways. Firstly, one can hypothesize the existence of the thing one names on the basis of an idea or theory (this is a 'concept by postulation'). This is the starting-point of many Western philosophers, although some – Hume, for example – can be said to arrive at concepts more by the second method, which is simply to name a direct perceptual experience (this is a 'concept by intuition').[4] The concept of mind in Buddhist psychology belongs to this second category. It is arrived at not by a deduction from abstract ideas or general principles, but by way of induction from actual experience. That is, it is not a metaphysical principle (Mind with a capital 'M' – as in 'Mind over Matter'); nor does it stand for the individual ego, postulated as something distinct from the mental events it 'experiences'. In Buddhism 'mind' is conceived of in the same way that we conceive of a tree, say. Just as we experience an assemblage of sensory data – trunk, branches, leaves – and call it a tree, so we experience a range of mental events and call it 'mind'. And just as there is no meaning to the word 'tree' beyond what we can experience personally, so there is no meaning – there are no connotations – to the term 'mind' beyond what we can apprehend for ourselves.

Because mind in Buddhism refers to something that is experienced by direct perception, every point made in this book is verifiable from personal experience, provided we are prepared to examine our experience honestly. The inner tranquillity, clarity, and insight that can be developed through meditation practice is not merely helpful to this process of examination, but absolutely necessary to it. From a Buddhist point of view, to try to philosophize, or even think clearly, without getting one's negative mental states out of the way is going to be a flawed enterprise. Whatever efforts one makes to come to a true understanding of reality, if one has not given attention to the mental state with which one approaches the matter, one will inevitably see things in terms of one's own craving, hatred, fear, and delusion. In Buddhism, therefore, there is no philosophy without meditation. One has to rise above one's limited, personal, or individual standpoint, at least to some extent, and be relatively free from negative mental states, in order to see the truth.

This book has two aims: to present the picture of mind and mental events that centuries of Abhidharma scholarship brought into focus, and to act as a practical guide to mental states for meditators, showing how the various mental events may be recognized, and which are to be eradicated and which cultivated so that psychological health, spiritual insights, and ultimately transcendental knowledge may be attained.

The first part of the book is of necessity fairly theoretical; in it we trace the background of the Abhidharma, and introduce the work *The Necklace of Clear Understanding*, on which the rest of the book is a kind of commentary, before going on to look at the Abhidharma's understanding of mind and mental events. In the second part we take a fairly detailed look at the mental events themselves, and in doing so build up a picture of the kind of spiritual life needed to support the cultivation of positive states of mind.

1

THE FIRST BUDDHIST ANALYSTS

THE SPIRITUAL and scholastic undertaking represented by the term Abhidharma is very ambitious. Its origins may be traced back to the general intellectual background in the context of which early Buddhists strove to express their own distinctive vision. Of all the systems of thought prevailing at the time, that of the Sāṃkhya School of Indian philosophy is said to be the closest in spirit to that developed by the Buddha himself. Indeed, it may be significant that the Buddha was born and brought up in Kapilavastu, the city connected with the pre-Buddhist sage Kapila, who is traditionally regarded as the founder of the Sāṃkhya School.

Sāṃkhya literally means counting, numbering, or enumerating. The Sāṃkhya School tried to enumerate the elements of existence, in a way that seems to foreshadow the greatly more sophisticated and refined analysis of the Abhidharma. It was the Sāṃkhya philosophers who first, as far as we know, thought in terms of the five elements – earth, water, fire, air, and space – and conceived of the mind as a sixth sense, as well as differentiating a sort of supermind. There are some very ancient Sāṃkhya sutras (sūtra here meaning 'aphorism', not 'discourse', as it usually does in the Buddhist context) but the teaching was probably not fully systematized until a long time after the Buddha, in a work called the *Sāṃkhyakārikā*, which is attributed to Īśvara Kṛṣṇa.[5]

The adherents of the Sāṃkhya School were not the only early Indian philosophers to attempt such an analysis of the universe. It seems that it was a very strong trend in Indian thought generally to try to understand existence by breaking it up into its constituent parts. One finds the same thing in ancient Greece, in the writings of Democritus, for example. In Indian thought generally one could say that there are two major trends: a pluralistic trend which tends to be associated with the non-brahminical tradition, and a more monistic trend which tends to be associated with the brahminical tradition. Included in the pluralistic schools of thought are the Sāṃkhya, the Abhidharma in its various forms, the Jains, and also the Nyāya-Vaiśeṣika School.

In his *Buddhacarita* (an account of the life of the Buddha), Aśvaghoṣa gives a fairly detailed, although not very clear, account of the Sāṃkhya philosophy, and represents the Buddha as refuting it systematically, which would suggest that there was some danger of Buddhism's being confused with Sāṃkhya thought at the time he was writing. Some scholars have certainly seen a continuity between the Sāṃkhya School and the Abhidharma, although there are all sorts of philosophical difficulties in tracing it. The difference between the two could be said to be that the Sāṃkhya analysis is more cosmological than psychological, while the Buddhist analysis is predominantly psychological.

The classifications of the Abhidharma itself began to be compiled during the period of several hundred years after the Buddha's lifetime when his teachings were still being passed on by word of mouth. Basically, the Abhidharma began as a vast sorting-out operation. During the Buddha's life he must have given thousands, even tens of thousands, of discourses, and answered thousands of questions; and around him was always a circle of disciples who, as best they could, learned by heart whatever he said. They treasured these teachings, reflected on them, repeated them to one another, and in this way committed to memory what the Buddha had taught them. When they were old they transmitted what they had learned to their own disciples, and they to their disciples in turn. This process of oral transmission went on for at least four hundred years, and in this way the teaching was preserved for posterity.

So there was an enormous floating mass of material in existence, but to begin with it was not systematically arranged. Long discourses were mixed up with short ones, poetry with prose, teachings about the mind with teachings about the elements, teachings about cosmology mixed up with history and legend and biography. Over the years, however, some of the more brilliant scholars, those whose minds were more retentive, started to organize the teachings systematically. The result of this sorting-out process – which took hundreds of years – is what we call the Abhidharma.

One of the chief virtues of the Abhidharma was that it clarified Buddhist terminology, comparing the usage of a term in one context with its usage in another, so that a term like, say, *nirvāṇa* could be used with full confidence as to its precise meaning. This clarity of definition is one reason we still use terms that derive from the ancient Indian languages Pāli and Sanskrit.

The Ābhidharmikas also arranged all the teachings into different groupings so that they might be related to each other more easily and grasped in their entirety. It was only natural that the Buddha's followers should want to settle all the disparate points he made on various occasions into some kind of system. Thus, for example, in the *Visuddhimagga*, the 'Path of Purity', Buddhaghosa, the great Theravādin scholar of the fifth century CE, collated all the Buddha's teachings on meditation into a single clear system.[6]

This was the great achievement of the Abhidharma, which came to dominate Indian Buddhism for about a thousand years, so that an understanding of it is crucial to an understanding of Indian Buddhist thought. At the same time, it must be admitted that the Abhidharma had its negative side. One could say that it banished the human element from Buddhism, removing from the teachings all biographical and historical material, and banishing myth, legend, and above all poetry. In the Abhidharma the impersonal, the scientific, and the rational reigned supreme. (Eventually, inevitably, the banished elements reasserted themselves in what came to be called Mahāyāna Buddhism and Vajrayāna or Tantric Buddhism.)

As the Abhidharma developed there emerged two great traditions, the Theravāda and the Sarvāstivāda, each of which eventually committed to writing its own distinctive version of the Abhidharma teachings. The Theravāda version was written down in the Pāli language – so that strictly speaking we should refer to the Theravāda Abhidhamma, that being the Pāli equivalent of the Sanskrit Abhidharma – and forms part of the Theravāda Pāli Canon. The Sarvāstivāda Abhidharma, which was originally written down in

Sanskrit, is, in translation, part of the Chinese canon, the original Sanskrit texts having been lost.

Both sets of teachings consist of seven substantial books, but although there is some overlap between the two sets of books, essentially they cover different ground.[7] The Theravādins regarded the material contained in *their* Abhidhamma texts as having been preached by the Buddha to his deceased mother in the Tuṣita *devaloka*, a higher heavenly realm. Then, the tradition says, the Buddha repeated these teachings to Śāriputra, the wisest of his disciples, and in that way the Abhidharma tradition was handed down. (This claim was vigorously contested by other early Buddhist schools, notably the Sautrāntikas.) The Sarvāstivādins, on the other hand, frankly admitted that the contents of their Abhidharma texts were the work of disciples.

Not everything about the project of the Abhidharma was plain sailing. Differing interpretations of the teachings among the early schools were gathered together in the *Katthāvatthu*, the 'Matters of Discussion', which is one of the seven books of the Theravāda Abhidhamma. In the *Katthāvatthu* some views are definitely rejected, but others are left unsettled; we are just given the views of the different schools and left to make up our own minds. Both sets of teachings form one of the three *piṭakas* or 'baskets' into which Buddhist canonical literature is divided: the Vinaya Piṭaka (the 'books of the discipline'); the Sūtra Piṭaka (Pāli Sutta Piṭaka – the collection of discourses); and the Abhidharma Piṭaka (Pāli Abhidhamma Piṭaka). There is some overlap between the ground covered in the Sūtra Piṭaka and that in the Abhidharma Piṭaka. However, very early on, the Abhidharma took a direction of which the other *piṭakas* give little hint.

It wasn't long before the Abhidharma started to go far beyond its original objectives. From analysing and classifying the Buddha's teachings, it went many steps further, to start analysing and classifying the whole universe, indeed the whole of existence. For a start, the Ābhidharmikas were uncompromising in their use of language. Out went expressions like *sattva* (being), *pudgala* (person), and *puruṣa* (self), which might be taken as suggesting that the notion of a self might have some substance in reality. Through clear thinking in meditation, experience was analysed down until the irreducible elements of existence were identified. The Ābhidharmikas chose to refer to these elements, beyond which analysis could not go, as *dharmas* – a technical usage quite distinct from the usual use of the word 'Dharma' in Buddhism to mean the Buddha's doctrine or teaching.

Thus the Ābhidharmikas developed a sort of psycho-physical atomism. They conceived of *dharmas* as being a limited number of ultimately real, discrete elements which together comprehended the whole of existence – mental, physical, and spiritual, conscious and non-conscious. These elements – the Theravādins counted 170, the Sarvāstivādins 75 – included physical constituents – the elements of earth, water, fire, and air, qualities such as agility and elasticity, as well as food and other things – and mental constituents, some skilful, like faith and mindfulness, some unskilful, like anger and wrong views, and some neutral, being coloured by the *dharmas* with which they were associated.

Both the Theravādins and the Sarvāstivādins divided *dharmas* into two groups, *saṁskṛta dharmas* and *asaṁskṛta dharmas*. These terms literally mean 'compounded' and 'uncompounded', but they are sometimes translated as 'conditioned' and 'unconditioned'. According to the Theravāda there was only one unconditioned *dharma*, nirvāṇa, while the Sarvāstivāda identified three: two kinds of nirvāṇa, and space. But for both schools of the Abhidharma tradition, this distinction between conditioned and unconditioned *dharmas* was not a distinction between real and unreal. This is rather important. All these ultimate elements were thought of as being equally real, as being ultimate in the sense that no one of them could be reduced to any other of them. And this, in fact, was a kind of heresy, as we shall see.

Even this brief description should be enough to show that the Ābhidharmikas' conception of *dharmas* was very different from the fundamental particles of Western science. There is an analogy, though, in that, just as for a certain phase of scientific history atoms were held to be the irreducible 'building blocks' of which the material universe was constructed, so the Ābhidharmikas held that *dharmas* could not be broken down into further components of experience. (And, just as particle physics has come up with a completely different way of seeing things, so the Buddhist tradition later exposed the limitations of the Abhidharma's conception of *dharmas*, as we shall see.) The Ābhidharmikas went on to say that this irreducibility made *dharmas* real in a sense that what we conventionally take to be real – ourselves, tables, and so on – is not. In this way the Abhidharma came to occupy a particular philosophical position which has been called by Dr Radhakrishnan 'pluralistic realism'; and the term *abhidharma*, which originally simply meant 'pertaining to the Dharma', came to be taken as meaning 'the higher doctrine'.

The Abhidharma's starting point was the Buddha's classification of the psycho-physical phenomena of human existence. The Buddha inherited from Upaniṣadic tradition a distinction between *nāma* (name) and *rūpa* (form); and he broadened this out to analyse the whole of compounded existence into five *skandhas* (heaps): *rūpa* or form; *vedanā* or feeling; *saṁjñā* or perception; *saṁskāra* or volition; and *vijñāna* or consciousness.[8] But why did he do this?

It appears that he wanted to counteract a static view of existence and our experience of it. He wanted to break down apparently solid and stable things, not into smaller things, but into *processes*. Take, for instance, *vedanā*, 'feeling'. It is not that there is a thing called feeling that is one of five separate things that make up the human personality; *vedanā* is simply a process which, interacting with other processes, makes up our experience of ourselves.

It is important that we understand the Buddha's analysis – and the Abhidharma's analysis that followed – in this way. Otherwise, perhaps under the influence of scientific materialism, we can easily get the impression that the Abhidharma is positing a pseudo-scientific reductionism of all that is distinctively human to a collection of impersonal elements. From here we can start to imagine that reality is the dust to which we reduce everything – and this might reinforce the common, but mistaken, impression that Buddhism is nihilistic. But, on the contrary, this way of seeing things offers a vision of the possibility of human growth and development. The analysis of the *skandhas* – according to which one sees that what we think of as the self is made up of these five 'heaps', all of which are continually changing – is tremendously inspiring. If the self was really permanent and unchanging, human growth would be impossible. Only the reality of impermanence offers the possibility of change.

Having made the distinction between conditioned and unconditioned *dharmas*, the Abhidharma went on to divide conditioned *dharmas* into groups; and it was here that it departed from the sūtra tradition – that is, from the tradition of unsystematized Buddhism. The sūtras preserved the teaching of the five *skandhas*, these five 'heaps'; that was their only classification of phenomenal existence. But the Abhidharma adopted a quite different classification, positing three or four main categories of conditioned existence as an alternative to the five *skandhas*. The first category, though, was just the same as the first of the *skandhas*: *rūpa* or material form. It is the epistemological object; Guenther says '*Rūpa* ... is a name for an objective constituent in a perceptual situation.'[9] In other words, *rūpa* is 'what' we perceive in our experience. It is not matter conceived as separate from a perceiver. We are concerned simply with the fact that there is something in our experience that is intractable, that resists us in various ways.

Rūpa is traditionally described in terms of the four great elements or *mahābhūtas*: solidity, fluidity, temperature or radiation, and expansiveness or atmospheric movement. The term *mahābhūta* can also be translated as 'great magical transformation' or 'great spirit' – which, in connection with *rūpa*, reminds us that we really have no way of knowing what we are in contact with when our senses give us information about the 'objective' world. Our senses give us a sense of perception through sight, hearing, taste, touch, and smell; but we have no evidence of what may be objectively there apart from that mediated by our senses.

So in a way *rūpa* is a great mystery. One could go so far as to say that the idea that we are in contact with a thing is no more than a linguistic fiction – although the Ābhidharmikas themselves would not go that far. As the Abhidharma texts sometimes say, *dharmas* have not merely 'conceptually constructed existence' (*prajñaptisat*); they have 'more than conceptually constructed existence' (*dravyasat*).[10] So there is no need to disbelieve our senses when they tell us we are in contact with something; certainly if we walk into a door, that door is more than a 'linguistic fiction' as far as we are concerned. The point is that, while we may be in contact with something, we have no way of knowing *what* exactly we are in contact with except through our senses. Interestingly, the implication of the term *mahābhūta* is that we are in contact with something living rather than inert physical matter. Apparently one should understand the Abhidharma's idea of the four elements not as a primitive attempt at science but as referring to living symbols representing different manifestations of energy.

Of course, for the Abhidharma the elements of earth, water, fire, and air were just four of the kinds of the *dharmas* they identified as *rūpa*. According to the Theravāda, there were twenty-eight such *dharmas*, while in this first category the Sarvāstivāda placed just eleven *dharmas*. The second and third categories posited by the Ābhidharmikas as an alternative to the five *skandhas* are what we are concerned with in this book; here is where the Abhidharma's analytical philosophy became an analytical psychology. The second category is mind or consciousness (*citta*), and the third consists of mental concomitants or mental events, functions associated with mind (*caitta* in Sanskrit, the equivalent of the Pāli *cetasika*).

So far the Theravādin and Sarvāstivādin traditions were in agreement. However, they differed when it came to the way they classified mind and mental events. As far as the second category is concerned, the Theravādins thought in terms of 89 different *cittas*, including *kuśala* (skilful), *akuśala* (unskilful), and *avyākṛta* (neutral) mental states. As for the third category, mental events, they listed 52 *cetasikas*, considering each type of *citta* to be characterized by a particular combination of mental events. The Sarvāstivādins, on the other hand, while identifying 46 mental events (*caittas*), recognized only one single *citta*, arguing that mind is essentially one, because although there are many mental states, they are all phenomena of consciousness itself; they are not independent.

For the Theravādins, these three categories covered the whole of conditioned existence comprehensively, but the Sarvāstivādins came up with a fourth category, *cittaviprayuktasaṁskāra*, 'factors dissociated from mind', which basically consists of all those factors that do not fall under the other three headings; it includes, for example, a list of the various possible kinds of conditionality, or causal relationship.

Altogether the Sarvāstivādins identified 72 compounded *dharmas* and three uncompounded ones – that is, two types of nirvāṇa (before and after *parinirvāṇa*) and space – while the Theravādins enumerated 169 compounded *dharmas* and one uncompounded one. Most of these *dharmas* are mental, because the whole project of the Abhidharma was geared to the spiritual purpose of meditation. However, all of them, whether compounded or uncompounded, were supposed to be equally real, inasmuch as together they made up the irreducible building blocks of existence. On this basis the Abhidharma embarked on a massive cross-referencing operation.

Abhidharma literature was by no means confined to the two sets of seven books; those constituted only a beginning. Subsequently hundreds of other works were produced, but among all the writers of Abhidharma texts two in particular stand out, both of them belonging to the fifth century CE. On the Theravādin side was the great scholastic commentator Buddhaghosa, author of the *Visuddhimagga*, the 'Path of Purity'; he was a native of India but lived and worked in Sri Lanka. And among the Sarvāstivādins was Vasubandhu, the author of the *Abhidharmakośa*, who lived and worked in north-west India, and – as we shall see – in his old age became a follower of the Mahāyāna.

Some of the discussions and classifications of the Abhidharma are very helpful, but others are less so. We must therefore study it in the analytical and critical spirit of the Abhidharma itself – not swallowing it whole, as it were. If we were to swallow everything indiscriminately, perhaps with the attitude that everything that comes out of India or Tibet or Japan must be wonderful, we would probably get intellectual, spiritual, or aesthetic indigestion. We need to learn to discriminate – which will mean seeking good advice.

In the Pāli Canon the Buddha tells a story to illustrate the danger of imitating Enlightened behaviour without Enlightened experience. He says there were once some elephants who pulled up lotus stalks from a pond and washed them carefully before eating them – and those elephants thrived. But some younger elephants, uninstructed by their elders, went to the pond and ate the roots just as they were, covered in mud. 'That was not good for either their looks or their health, and they incurred death and deadly suffering because of that.'¹ The moral of the story is, of course, that we mustn't follow even a good example unthinkingly.

It was this critical spirit that led to the arising of a new phase of the history of the Abhidharma which swept away many of the earlier ideas. This new initiative was part of the Mahāyāna tradition of Indian Buddhism, which arose in order to counter the increasingly narrow focus of some of the schools subsequently characterized (though not by themselves) by the term Hīnayāna, 'the Lesser Way'. The Mahāyāna gave a fresh emphasis to Buddhist practice – to devotion, metaphysics, and meditation, and to making the Dharma available to everyone, whether monk or lay-person. And when it came to philosophy, the Mahāyāna flatly denied the reality of *dharmas* as ultimately existent entities. Just as the self was empty, so, the Mahāyānists insisted, were *dharmas*. Anything we think we can identify as real is in reality empty of self-nature (*svabhāva*).

That the earlier schools should have gone so far as to assert the existence of a certain fixed number of material and non-material elements, themselves irreducible, to which all the phenomena of existence were capable of being reduced, was a very serious thing. Central to Buddhism from the very beginning had been the doctrine of *anātman* – 'no-self' – which denied that in the absolute sense there existed in any object, whether transcendental or mundane, an eternal, unchanging principle of individuality or selfhood. As we have seen, it was in order to counter the wrong belief in absolute selfhood that the

Buddha himself analysed the so-called person into the five *skandhas* (*khandas* in Pāli), showing that apart from these psycho-physical phenomena, which were in a state of perpetual flux, there existed no unchanging psychic substratum corresponding to the *ātman* as conceived by certain non-Buddhist schools.

Ironically, although it was the Buddha's analysis of existence into the *skandhas* that the Ābhidharmikas made it their special business to develop, the analysis they ended up with in fact contradicted the *anātman* doctrine. While they still maintained that the *pudgala* (person) or *ātman* (self) was nothing but an assemblage of evanescent parts, as we have seen, they saw the parts themselves as being real – as being, in fact, absolute realities. This was a deviation from orthodoxy of the most disastrous type. As the Mahāyānists saw, it was in effect a repudiation of the doctrine of *anātman*, for the conception of permanent individuality had not been superseded, but simply transferred from the whole to its parts.

In order to counteract this tendency to deviate into the heretical extreme of eternalism (*saśvatavāda*), the Mahāyānists brought forward their doctrine – in reality a reversion to the Buddha's own position – of *sarva-dharmāh-śūnyatā*, 'emptiness of all *dharmas*'. *Dharmas*, they said, not being self-existent, but arising in dependence on conditions, could not rightly be regarded as absolute realities, any more than the self.

The link between the earlier 'Hīnayāna' Abhidhamma and the Mahāyāna's development of Abhidharma doctrine is Asaṅga, who lived in north-western India in the fourth or fifth century CE. His *Abhidharmasamuccaya*, 'Collection of the Abhidharma',[12] is an abridgement of the first two chapters of his *Yogācārabhūmi*, which harnesses the Sarvāstivāda – i.e. Hīnayāna – Abhidharma teaching to the 'Greater Way' of the Mahāyāna. As we will see, the *Abhidharmasamuccaya*'s analysis of mind and mental events differs slightly from the Sarvāstivādin classification, producing a different and slightly longer list of mental events (51 instead of 46).

While Asaṅga was always a Mahāyānist, his older brother Vasubandhu came to the Mahāyāna point of view rather later in his Buddhist life. He had become the greatest teacher of the Sarvāstivāda School, and had compiled the major work of Abhidharma in Sanskrit, the *Abhidharmakośa* or 'Treasury of Abhidharma',[13] when Asaṅga persuaded him to take up the practices of the Mahāyāna. Vasubandhu's major work is the product of this transition; he wrote a commentary on his own *Abhidharmakośa*, the *Abhidharmakośabhāṣya*, criticizing the Sarvāstivādin view from a Sautrāntika position. Vasubandhu subsequently became a great teacher of the Yogācāra School of the Mahāyāna, second only to Asaṅga himself.

The Yogācāra is one of the two major schools of the Indian Mahāyāna tradition, the other being the Madhyamaka; but the two schools are closely interconnected, the difference really amounting to predominant emphasis. Very broadly, one might say that the Yogācāra took a more psychological approach, while the Madhyamaka was more logical, metaphysical, or even dialectical. The Yogācāra was more closely concerned with meditative experience, one could say, whereas the Madhyamaka's preoccupation was with abstract truth.

The Madhyamaka School probably began around the first or second century CE with Nāgārjuna, who tried to show the non-reality of what we take to be real by exposing its contradictory nature. He gave sound logical reasons why it cannot possibly exist, proving that every formulation we construct to describe or identify the nature of reality is riddled with contradictions – including even the categories of Buddhist thought. He demolished everything except for *śūnyatā* – *śūnyatā* stripped, that is, of any conceptual content. It has to be admitted that some of Nāgārjuna's 'sound logical reasons' have been shown to be fallacious, but his was an audacious project. Perhaps one could say that the only Western philosophical method that compares with what he tried to do is the Eleatic method of Parmenides. But whereas Parmenides embarked upon this spiritual exercise in the interests of absolute being, Nāgārjuna did so in the interests of *śūnyatā* or 'emptiness'.[14]

Nāgārjuna, therefore, and the adherents of the Madhyamaka School with him, while they certainly meditated, relied on the whole upon sustained philosophical thinking. The Yogācāra, on the other hand, although it had a strong philosophical basis, relied upon meditation. The very name Yogācāra means the practice of yoga in the sense of meditation. The philosophy that emerged out of the meditation of the Yogācārins was established upon the idea of *cittamātra* or 'mind only', which in some respects comes close to the immaterialism of Bishop Berkeley, the British eighteenth-century empirical philosopher.

Cittamātra denies the reality of matter as a separate category from mind. What we perceive are not external objects as such, not objects as opposed to ourselves, the subject. We perceive 'mental impressions', that is all. The significance of this insight is that if you remove the notion of an object, you also effectively remove the notion of a subject. There can be no sense of a subject without the sense of an object, and *vice versa*. In this way you break down the notion of a self that is separate from the world, to be left with 'mind only'. This 'mind only' is, by definition, not 'mind' as opposed to 'matter', and thus not mind in the limited way we usually understand the term.

So, over centuries, the scholars of Mahāyāna Buddhism developed and refined the Abhidharma vision of the universe which the Theravādins and Sarvāstivādins derived from their own understanding of the Buddha's teaching. If one looks at, say, the *Abhidharmakośabhāṣya*, in which Vasubandhu comments on the discussion by other scholars of his own verses, his quotations from different teachers and schools give an impression of a vigorous discussion that carried on for centuries. The Abhidharma is known as 'the delight of the learned' because if one is an academically-minded individual one can happily spend a lifetime immersed in one branch or another of this kind of study. One hardly notices the years passing, the decades rolling by, as one burrows deeper and deeper into one's favourite Abhidharma topic. Some at least of the scholars of the Abhidharma certainly meditated on what they studied, and their contributions to the debate embodied real spiritual insight. But the danger is that the Abhidharma becomes a delightful hobby, an end in itself, and one loses sight of the Abhidharma's original spiritual purpose.

In Tibet, the Yogācāra and the Madhyamaka were brought together, and lamas of all schools have always studied works from both traditions. It is generally difficult to compartmentalize Tibetan Buddhists – and this is true, too, of the later phases of Indian Buddhism. Very often monks would devote many years to studying the Abhidharma and logic, say, and then just take off to become wandering yogis and practise Tantric disciplines. However, within a general free flow of ideas, certain patterns may be discerned.

Of the two main schools of Tibetan Buddhism, the Geluk and Nyingma Schools, it could perhaps be said that the Nyingmapas, founded by Padmasambhava, are the heirs of the Yogācāra tradition, inasmuch as they emphasize meditation and direct experience. The Gelukpas are more influenced by the Madhyamaka tradition, and tend to regard the Yogācāra as, in a sense, a slightly lower truth, a sort of preamble to the full truth of the Madhyamaka system.

There is, therefore, no separate school of Yogācāra Abhidharma in Tibetan Buddhism. However, although it is evident that the Nyingmapas take their inspiration from the Yogācāra, of the two schools the Geluk tradition is the more closely connected with the original Indian Buddhist literature, including the Yogācāra literature. The Gelukpas go in for the study of the sūtras, the Abhidharma, the Vinaya, logic, and epistemology, while the Nyingmapas concentrate on the tantras, the *ter-ma* literature, and the writings of the teachers of their own school.

It is no surprise, therefore, to find that Yeshe Gyaltsen (1713–93), the author of the text on which this commentary will be based, *The Necklace of Clear Understanding*,[15] is a Tibetan Buddhist of the Geluk School. But he does not offer any particular line of Gelukpa interpretation. Though he includes quotations from Tsongkhapa (the founder of the Gelukpa tradition) and from Tsongkhapa's disciples, he is clearly at pains to interpret faithfully the original Yogācāra Abhidharma tradition as expounded by Asaṅga in the *Abhidharmasamuccaya*. Basically, he follows the Yogācāra tradition with regard to mind and mental events only so far as it is more or less in tune with the Madhyamaka.

In its form, *The Necklace of Clear Understanding* follows a pattern quite commonly found in Buddhist literature. The author writes a series of verses that express what he has to say as concisely as possible (for purposes of memorization, perhaps) and then explains each verse with a prose commentary. As it is a commentary on his own work, it is called an autocommentary. No doubt it would be possible to offer a further commentary on his autocommentary, but for the purposes of introducing the basic outlines of the Abhidharma this would probably be counter-productive. I shall therefore simply base my comments on the overall layout and scope of Yeshe Gyaltsen's work, drawing on his quotations and comments as appropriate, together with an occasional reference to other works. *The Necklace of Clear Understanding* is quite elementary and therefore a good introduction to what is probably the most important and useful part of the whole subject.

Of course, Yeshe Gyaltsen himself was in the position of being able to draw on what by his lifetime amounted to two thousand years of Abhidharma tradition. He himself writes very much in the spirit of the earliest Ābhidharmikas, always focusing on the practical spiritual import of the teaching, and avoiding getting into detailed discussion of abstract matters.

There is one other work from which I will draw a number of definitions and explanations: the *Ch'eng Wei-Shih Lun*, or 'Doctrine of Mere-Consciousness',[16] which is the basic text of the Chinese branch of the

Yogācāra. It was written by the Chinese pilgrim, translator, and scholar Hsüan Tsang, and consists of a set of thirty of Vasubandhu's verses on the Vijñāvāda/Yogācāra teaching, explained and commented on by Hsüan Tsang. In Sanskrit, Vasubandhu's text is known as the *Vijñapti-mātratāsiddhi-trimśika*, the 'Treatise on the Establishment (or Proof) of Vijñāpti-only'. Hsüan Tsang's commentary on Vasubandhu's work is based on ten Indian commentaries, but relies mainly on that of Dharmapāla, who was abbot of the great Indian Buddhist university Nālandā in the sixth century CE, and upon whose interpretation of the Yogācāra Hsüan Tsang established the Fa-hsiang School when he returned to China.

Just to complete the picture of the lineage of this teaching, I should add a word or two about the context in which *The Necklace of Clear Understanding* has been translated by Dr Guenther and Dr Kawamura. Until fairly recently, Dr Guenther was labouring in the field of Buddhist psychology virtually single-handed. Today, however, important new texts are becoming available in translation almost every year, and this process will no doubt go on for quite a few more decades. The impact of Buddhism on the intellectual and spiritual life of the West in the twentieth century has already been quite dramatic, and the publication of more difficult texts, like those which deal with the Abhidharma, should begin to deepen that impact.

Although a lot of useful academic work has been done in Tibetan studies over the last few decades, pioneered especially by Japanese scholars, what is required now is a sifting process to isolate the really useful texts from those which are less so. Practically speaking, we don't really need so very many Buddhist texts. We don't need to master the entire field of Buddhist literature in order to practise Buddhism. Take Buddhist logic, for example: however interesting a development it might be from an academic point of view, it is questionable whether it really has any relevance for practising Buddhists in the West.

A creative response to this influx of Buddhist literature into Western culture is therefore required. The only period in Buddhist history to which we can look for a parallel to the present one is the time when Indian texts first started to be translated into Chinese, and the Chinese literati were having to try to get to grips with this mysterious new literature, adjusting to it and assimilating it as best they could. The Tibetans, by contrast, had no highly developed pre-Buddhistic civilization to enable them to make the kind of evaluation or response to

Buddhism that was made in medieval China, and which is being made in Europe today.

However, the unsophisticated acceptance of Buddhism by the Tibetans had some obvious spiritual advantages. The danger of the sophisticated response to Buddhist teachings in the West is that it trivializes them: Zen, for example, becomes – as a friend of mine observed, writing about London Buddhist circles in the early 1960s – 'the witty word among the teacups'.

Another danger, already hinted at, is that the whole teaching becomes psychologized – that is, its reference point becomes psychological in the restrictive sense rather than spiritual and transcendental. There is no foolproof safeguard against this; the unenlightened mind will always find a way. The best we can do is to develop a tradition of study and interpretation to ensure that texts are not just left at large, so to speak, for anybody to misunderstand. What we need to keep in view is the essentially practical nature of the Abhidharma, both in aiding meditation practice through enabling us to discriminate between skilful and unskilful mental states, and in helping us to realize that what we usually think of as our self is just an ever-changing combination of mental states – a realization which is, for any Buddhist, of supreme importance.

2

ANALYSING THE PATH TO ENLIGHTENMENT

IN THE INTRODUCTION to his translation of *The Necklace of Clear Understanding*, Dr Guenther chooses to introduce the Buddhist path, or 'the "way"', as he calls it, not in terms of the most universally known formulations, but according to a more obscure one: the path of five stages. This is a Sarvāstivādin formulation which was taken up by the Mahāyāna. (Vasubandhu outlines it in his *Abhidharmakośa*.) Instead of the eight limbs of the Noble Eightfold Path, or the basic threefold analysis of Buddhist practice into ethics, meditation, and wisdom, we have the five stages of the path – or, more literally, the five paths. According to some later commentators all Buddhist practices and teachings can be accommodated within this framework. Although such an enterprise would probably be a little over-ambitious, the five *mārgas* certainly provide an illuminating breakdown of what Buddhists are trying to do with their lives. The five stages are: the path of accumulation or preparation; the path of practice or application; the path of insight; the path of transformation; and the path of no more learning.[17]

In the first stage, the path of accumulation (*sambhāramārga*), one establishes a foundation of relative integration by accumulating certain moral, intellectual, and spiritual qualities. This accumulation stage basically consists of three degrees of intensity. The first is represented by the practice of the four foundations of mindfulness. This involves being constantly aware of one's body – its position and movement; of one's feelings, pleasant, painful, and neutral, and one's emotions; of one's thoughts as they arise; and of ultimate reality. This last aspect of mindfulness involves developing a general awareness of ultimate reality by, for example (to take the method proposed by the Abhidharma), analysing things into their constituent *dharmas*.

According to the 'Hīnayāna' tradition this practice is a self-sufficient path to Enlightenment, but the Mahāyāna saw the notion of trying to go the whole way by force of mindfulness as a bit dry. For the Mahāyāna, mindfulness is therefore the key practice only at the most elementary level of one's spiritual career. This is not at all to suggest that mindfulness can be dispensed with once one has progressed beyond the nursery slopes of the spiritual life; it is more that a deep and full experience of mindfulness requires the support of other practices.

It is sometimes suggested, particularly in Theravādin literature, that if one just observes an unskilful mental state, it will eventually disappear; but anyone who has tried this will know that it doesn't work. However, one can take a more active approach, represented by another aspect of the path of accumulation, the four right efforts. These are: to remove the unskilful states that have arisen in one's mind; to prevent further unskilful mental states from arising; to maintain and develop skilful states of mind; and to bring into being further skilful mental states.[18]

With the practice of mindfulness one is just observing what is going on, but when one takes up the four right efforts as a practice one works much more dynamically with one's mental states. No longer the passive observer of one's own mental processes, one actively works to change them. It is said that by means of this practice one will establish a connection with the purely spiritual stage of the path in one's next life. Whether or not it is necessary to have this kind of sense of a continuity of lives in order to follow the path, we will consider later.

A prime example of the practice of the four foundations of mindfulness is the meditation called the mindfulness of breathing, while another basic Buddhist meditation practice, the development of loving kindness (*maitrī bhāvanā* in Sanskrit, *mettā bhāvanā* in Pāli), is clearly representative of the Four Right Efforts.[19]

The practice of mindfulness is powerful, and the development of positive emotion is even more radical and effective. But one can go even further, to tap the energy which becomes available when one has gone beyond the conflict involved in weeding out the unskilful and cultivating the skilful, to gain access to energy that was previously caught up in negative emotions. Having got rid of unskilful mental states, or at least held them at bay, the victory is virtually won when one moves on to the four *ṛddhipādas*, the 'bases of psychic power'. These are: *chanda, vīrya, citta,* and *mīmāṁsā.*[20]

Chanda means 'thrust, urge, desire'; it is the whole force of one's will bent in a certain direction. With the development of *chanda*, one's interest in the path is fully aroused. With the second *ṛddhipāda, vīrya* or energy, one brings all one's vigour into play; one's energies are fully aroused. When one establishes the third *ṛddhipāda, citta*, which means 'mind' or 'heart', one really put one's heart into what one is doing. And with the fourth, *mīmāṁsā* or 'investigation', one goes into the matter thoroughly; one is fully alert.

With this level of integration one begins to develop an effective measure of transcendental insight. The different traditions are not clear about whether or not one's contact with the transcendental becomes irrevocable at this point, but one certainly makes some sort of connection with it, by way of what is called the linkage or *gotrabhū*. This is a rather obscure aspect of the path of the five stages. It represents the point at which one becomes involved with a particular spiritual lineage; that is, when one determines which particular aspect of the transcendental path one will be following – whether that of the Arhant, the Pratyekabuddha, or the Bodhisattva.

Having traversed the path of accumulation, one is ready to undertake the path of practice – *prayoga-mārga*. By now it is no longer a struggle – one is in a position to meditate effectively, and to bring one's energy to bear on something – so one applies oneself to penetrating the Four Noble Truths, or any of the basic doctrinal formulations. Then one enters into a sub-stage of the path of practice, that of 'meditative heat'. Heat is generated by energy, and the intensity of one's practice generates, in the course of one's meditation, a sort of inner or psychic heat called *tapas*. The term comes from a root meaning 'glow' or 'burn', and it is the oldest Indo-Aryan, Vedic word for what we now call spiritual practice or discipline. This psychic heat has a sort of melting effect, melting the hardness and rigidity of one's whole mental structure, softening it, making it more pliable.

At this point the five spiritual faculties come into play. One develops faith, energy, mindfulness, meditative absorption, and a modicum of wisdom, or *prajñā*.[21] Finally one experiences what is called the supreme worldly state, the highest mundane realization. One has gone as far as one can possibly go in terms of mundane development, in terms of human health in the ordinary sense.

As a result of the path of practice, one has a flash of pure Insight, which can gradually be increased. Having mobilized all one's energies and become more open and pliable, one enters upon the path of seeing (*darśana mārga*), in which one has some direct vision of the truth. One has a detailed Insight into the Four Noble Truths, and into the nature of the mind and mental events.

In the light of that breakthrough into the transcendental, a gradual transformation of one's whole being takes place. This is the path of cultivation (*bhāvanā mārga*), and according to Mahāyāna tradition it takes a very long time indeed to follow this path to the end. Paul Williams says, 'All the remaining nine Bodhisattva stages, as well as the other perfections, occur during this path [i.e. the path of cultivation] which (short of adopting Tantric practice, which can lead to Buddhahood in one lifetime) is said to take aeons of compassionate activity and striving to follow to its end.'[22] But eventually, however long it takes, one experiences a permanent transformation of oneself, at every level and in every aspect, in accordance with that vision. And as one works to reorganize one's existence, that experience of Perfect Vision continues to develop until one gains full Enlightenment, when one has no more to learn.

It might be objected that this last stage, the path of fulfilment or 'no more learning', cannot be counted as a stage in any meaningful sense, since it is the goal itself. However, this is to take the idea of Enlightenment too literally. In reality it is not a full stop. Enlightenment abounds in compassionate activities that are completely spontaneous. You don't just settle down and twiddle your thumbs. In fact, the stage of no more learning is called by the Tibetan teacher Gampopa, in the *Jewel Ornament of Liberation*, the stage of Buddha activity.[23]

In this way the path as a whole is laid out in regular steps, as five distinct stages. In practice, as with other formulations of the path, most people approach it in a more irregular way. Perhaps one starts – never having given the spiritual life any serious thought – with a flash of Insight – that is, with stage three. One may even try to move on to stage four and embark on the path of transformation; but one will find that the vision and the transformation are not sufficient to sustain one at this level, so that one will need to go back and start at the beginning. One may not necessarily start with the path of accumulation, but one will have to go back to it at some point in order to consolidate the attainments that technically belong to the more advanced stages of the path.

In the end one needs to follow what I have sometimes called a path of regular steps. This is where discipline comes in. Unfortunately, the word discipline has negative connotations for many people. Most of us don't like the idea of submitting our unique individuality to someone else's notion of what is good for us. However, without in any way condemning a healthy resistance to pressures imposed by others, it is true to say that those who can remain positive, inspired, and spontaneous through following their own natural inclinations without the need for any discipline, whether imposed by others or by themselves, are very rare indeed. Most people, if they allow themselves to do what they please, do nothing very constructive, and end up feeling dull, listless, and uninspired.

In a sense, it comes down to energy. If our energies are unintegrated, they work against one another; galvanizing them, getting them working in harmony together, requires some element of discipline, of imposed order. Paradoxically, inspiration and spontaneity are the product of discipline and regular practice. There is a gradual build-up of energy which gains momentum until finally we break free of all habits whatsoever, whether negative and unconscious, or positive and disciplined. It is only at this point that the need for conscious regular effort in our practice drops away. When our energies are integrated without depending on discipline to bring them together, when integration is our normal state, when our energies are always immediately available – that is when we can be simply spontaneous.

The nature of the path of five stages gives some idea of the need for the study of mind and mental events which was the preoccupation of the Ābhidharmikas, and which the present work will consider. If, for example, one is to remove unskilful mental states and develop skilful ones, one needs to be able to distinguish skilful from unskilful, to recognize exactly what is going on in one's own mind.

But first, of course, one needs to feel inspired to do so. The very fact that our energies are not integrated means that we are certain to be in conflict about how much effort we want to put into spiritual practice. Our inspirations are all too likely to be sabotaged by something in us that says 'Why bother?' To keep ourselves inspired to follow the path of regular steps, we need constantly to remind ourselves of why we are following the path, of who we can become if we work on our minds in this way.

Such a need for inspiration is acknowledged by Yeshe Gyaltsen at the very beginning of *The Necklace of Clear Understanding*. He begins the text with some 'verses of veneration and intention', which put him, and the reader with some understanding of the Buddhist tradition, directly in contact with his sources of inspiration, historical and archetypal exemplars of how to follow the path.

Crucial to all study of the Dharma is the way we approach it, our attitude and our intention. There is only one real reason for studying the Dharma, and this needs to be acknowledged right at the start, particularly in the case of the Abhidharma, where one can all too easily lose sight of the wood for the trees. So one needs to be clear about one's motivation; and one may purify one's motivation by establishing a devotional attitude. Here are the verses with which Yeshe Gyaltsen does so.

I bow with folded hands to him who is inseparable from
Lord Mañjughoṣa, the reverend and excellent teacher.
And I pray that he may accept me in his love for all times.

I bow to the supreme protector, Śākyamuni,
Who illumines the world where he looks
By his Omniscience from which all obscuring darkness
Has gone and who has fulfilled the two requisites
By the power of his spirituality.

From the bottom of my heart, I fold my hands devotedly
To the invincible Lord, Buddha's representative,
Known as Maitreyanātha in all the three times
Because he showers his love on all beings.

I bow to the most supreme leaders from among the
Six ornaments of India, renowned as the Great Charioteers
Who, having been predicted by the Sugata himself,
Illumined the auspicious Buddha Teachings, profound and vast.

I bow to 'Jam-mgon Lama worthy of praise
Like the Buddha-sun to unfold again and let bloom forth
The forest of Sūtras, Tantras, and commentaries,

Like the thousand-petalled lotus, in this country
Surrounded by snow-capped mountains.

May the light of the sun-like reverend Guru
Reside forever in the petal of the lotus-like heart
Brightening the mental eye
That views the auspicious path
By merely seeing a ray of his charismatic activity.

Even if others do not benefit from talk by people like me,
I am dealing here with the mind and mental events
Because I have been urged by others and because
I want to increase the training of my own mind.[24]

So here, in a manner very typical of the Tibetan tradition, our author shows his respect and love for his teachers and inspirations, both historical and archetypal. Mañjughoṣa, the first named, is a manifestation of Mañjuśrī, the Bodhisattva of Wisdom. *Mañju* means 'gentle', 'soft', or 'auspicious', and *ghoṣa* is 'speech' or 'voice', so Mañjughoṣa is 'he of gentle voice'. There is a softness about him – a spiritual softness, a gentle glow – no hardness, no rigidity. 'He of gentle voice' is, however, an embodiment of transcendental wisdom, and in his right hand he holds aloft a flaming sword – an apparently violent appearance which doesn't seem to go with his gentle name. But this contrast itself directs us to think again about the true nature of wisdom.

When I was seven or eight I went to see a film about the Crusades. It was rather a corny film, I seem to remember, but there was an episode in it which made a strong impression on me. This was the scene in which Richard the Lion Heart meets Saladin and wishes to demonstrate his great prowess with the sword to the Saracen prince. He calls for a great log of wood to be brought in; it is placed across two trestles, and with a single blow of his sword he cuts it in two. But Saladin just smiles and calls for his own sword. Then, unsheathing it, he orders that a piece of silk should be tossed up into the air and allowed to fall across the blade. And of course the sword is so sharp that the piece of silk falls on either side of the blade, severed in two.

So we don't have to think of Mañjuśrī cutting through all delusions by ferociously swinging his sword and bringing it down with a crash, like Richard the Lion-Heart cutting through his log. The kind of wisdom he represents is much more subtle and gentle – and devastating – than that.

Mañjuśrī is also called Kumārabhūta: 'he who has become a youth' or 'he who is youthful'. There is a definition of beauty in Sanskrit poetics: 'Beauty is like that which, from instant to instant, is always new.'[25] Mañjuśrī is represented as being beautiful and never growing old because the experience of wisdom is like that: it is always fresh, always new, always young. The experience of Enlightenment never grows old or stale. One never grows tired of it; it renews itself from moment to moment. The beauty, the magic of it, never fades away.

In this first verse the author bows to 'him who is inseparable from Mañjughoṣa' – that is, the author's own teacher, though we are not given his name. He is saluted as the living embodiment of Mañjughoṣa because he is a Geluk teacher. Mañjughoṣa is a particularly important figure for the Gelukpas, and they all regard the founder of their school, Tsongkhapa, as a manifestation of Mañjughoṣa. Indeed, Mañjughoṣa is the inspirational source of the whole Madhyamaka lineage, in the same way that the Bodhisattva Maitreya is particularly associated with the Yogācāra lineage.

Next, Yeshe Gyaltsen pays his respects to the Buddha Śākyamuni, the historical Buddha of our own era. He refers to Śākyamuni as being omniscient, but the word should not be taken literally; the historical Buddha claimed omniscience only with regard to what constituted the path to Enlightenment and the obstacles to that path.[26] The 'two requisites' are *puṇya* (merit) and *jñāna* (wisdom). To understand this, one has to appreciate another of the paths delineated by the Buddhist tradition – this time by the Mahāyāna. This is the path of the Bodhisattva. The Bodhisattva is said to practise six *pāramitās* or perfections: giving, ethics, energy, patience, meditation, and wisdom. The first five perfections represent the accumulation of merit, while the sixth, *prajñā*, is said to represent the accumulation of wisdom.

Mundane perfection, in other words, is represented by the first five *pāramitās*; one could even say that they represent the fullest possible psychological and spiritual development. The sixth, on the other hand, represents comprehensive transcendental insight, beyond mundane, psychological, and even spiritual perfection. So *puṇya* and *jñāna*, the two 'requisites' or 'accumulations', represent a twofold perfection made up of the consummation of the mundane and the consummation of the transcendental, united in the person of the Buddha, Śākyamuni. Iconographically, *puṇya* is symbolized by the halo around the Buddha's body and *jñāna* by the halo around his head.

Now Yeshe Gyaltsen turns his devotional attention to Maitreya-nātha, 'the invincible Lord, Buddha's representative'. Who exactly he is referring to is a moot point. Some would say that the reference is to Asaṅga, generally regarded as the founder of the Yogācāra School. According to tradition, Asaṅga received his inspiration from Maitreya, the Bodhisattva who is said to be waiting for the right moment – when all record of the Dharma has been lost – to take his last rebirth on earth, in which he will gain full Enlightenment and reintroduce the Dharma into the world. He is waiting in the highest of the heavens of the world of form, the Tuṣita ('contented') heaven, which is where Bodhisattvas are born before their final human rebirth. It is said that the five books of teachings written by Asaṅga were not just inspired by Maitreya, but actually revealed to him by the Bodhisattva. The books, therefore, naturally became known as the 'Five Books of Maitreya'. Some Western scholars are unable to give credence to this account of the originator of the tradition, and suggest that this Maitreya must have been a human teacher who later became confused with the Bodhisattva of that name. Dr Guenther sorts the problem out with a neat theory of his own, which is that this accredited author is in fact Asaṅga himself, because some texts refer to the author not as Maitreya but as Maitreya-nātha: 'he whose master (*nātha*) is Maitreya'. In this way Guenther comes to the conclusion that the 'Five Books of Maitreya' were authored by Asaṅga under the inspiration of Maitreya.

However, this is a controversial view which would find little favour in some quarters, particularly those of the Tibetan tradition. According to tradition, we are looking at a Bodhisattva here – whether Maitreya or Maitreyanātha – rather than Asaṅga or any other human teacher. We cannot discount the possibility that Maitreya or Maitreyanātha was in actuality a human teacher. But the fact that Asaṅga is referred to in the next verse rather counts against the likelihood that his is the true identity of Maitreyanātha – at least as far as the author of this text is concerned.

The 'Six Ornaments of India', often depicted in Indian paintings as three sets of pairs, are Nāgārjuna and Āryadeva, Asaṅga and Vasubandhu, and Dignāga and Dharmakīrti. They are all great teachers: Nāgārjuna and Āryadeva of the Madhyamaka tradition; Asaṅga and Vasubandhu of the Yogācāra; and Dignāga and Dharmakīrti of the tradition of Buddhist logic that grew out of the Yogācāra.[27]

They all embody an aspect of the Bodhisattva ideal that is sometimes overlooked: the idea that the Bodhisattva should be able to teach and convert all beings – that is, rid them of their wrong views. To this end it was necessary – in the highly sophisticated intellectual climate of the Indian Middle Ages at least – to be well-versed in logic and rhetoric. In fact, for more than a thousand years, Indians of all schools, both Buddhist and non-Buddhist, engaged in great public debates with each other, a ding-dong battle that ended only with the disappearance of Buddhism itself from the soil of India.

The only comparable intellectual era is the scholastic period of medieval philosophy, which was much more short-lived. And it would be fair to say that the Indian thinkers conducted their debates at a much more rigorous, exacting, and sophisticated level than that achieved by the medieval schoolmen of Christendom in their controversies, tightly disputed as these were. In this milieu the possession of a finely-honed command of logic became so important that it eventually became an end in itself – thus setting up an inevitable reaction, which to some extent arose in the form of the whole Vajrayāna movement. The Vajrayāna reasserted the primacy of direct spiritual experience and stressed the importance of meditation as the most direct means to that end, while tending to dismiss logic almost entirely. Even so, the old debates continued to be rehearsed. Right down into the nineteenth century Tibetan Buddhist teachers were still busily refuting the views of medieval thinkers, both Hindu and Buddhist, who had been dead for up to a thousand years, such was their determination not to let a wrong view pass uncorrected.

Just how many people are capable of deriving real spiritual benefit and inspiration from the cerebral path carved out by the formidable intellects of the Six Ornaments of India is hard to say. What one can count on throughout the writings of Nāgārjuna, Asaṅga, and Vasubandhu is a definite and powerful overall spiritual orientation, however much the traditions they seeded may have degenerated later on. From that point of view, rather than reading modern interpreters and commentators on, say, the Madhyamaka, one might be better off reading the original works, just plunging straight into Nāgārjuna's *Madhyamakakārikās*,[28] the key work of the whole Madhyamaka tradition, perhaps balancing it with Śāntideva's *Bodhicaryāvatāra*[29] for something a bit more practical, and looking to Nāgārjuna's *Ratnāvalī*[30] for a general survey of the Mahāyāna. However, it has to be said that some Madhyamaka works, including the *Madhyamakakārikās* themselves, are extremely obscure; to make sense of them, one may need the help of modern commentaries, some of which are very good.

The Six Ornaments of India are 'renowned as the Great Charioteers', that is, the charioteers 'of men who are ready to be tamed'. This is the sense in which the word appears as one of the Buddha's titles in the *Ti Ratana Vandana*, the 'Salutation to the Three Jewels'. They are 'predicted' by the Sugata (another title of the Buddha) in the sense that the Buddha has, according to followers of the Mahāyāna, especially in Tibet, predicted their coming in certain sūtras. Nāgārjuna, for example, is said to be referred to in the *Laṅkāvatāra Sūtra*, though the word that bears the weight of this interpretation (it appears in the *Sagāthakam* section) is actually Nāgāhvaya.[31]

'Jam-mgon means 'Mañjunātha' – 'he whose master is Mañjuśrī' – by which the author designates Tsongkhapa, whose voluminous writings explain and clarify the sūtras, tantras, and Indian commentaries. Tsongkhapa never left Tibet to visit India, as many other teachers did, so he did indeed produce all this work 'surrounded by snow-capped mountains'. Tsongkhapa is singled out here because he is the founder of the Geluk School, which is the dominant tradition of Tibetan Buddhism.

Through these verses of veneration, our author generates in himself – and us, he hopes – a sense of intention, a wish to emulate those whose spiritual greatness he celebrates. We ourselves will be able to find our own ways of doing this, whether by contemplating those qualities of Buddhas or Bodhisattvas to which we are drawn, or by deriving inspiration from our friends and spiritual teachers. But dwelling on such sources of inspiration is not the only way to move us to follow the spiritual path. There is another; and it is to this that Yeshe Gyaltsen now turns, in his introduction to *The Necklace of Clear Understanding*: 'Introduction to Mind and Mental Events'.

3

WHAT'S THE POINT?

HAVING CALLED upon the sources of inspiration as an incentive to embark on the Buddhist path, Yeshe Gyaltsen now turns to another strong motivation for spiritual practice. To begin with, he distinguishes between two kinds of people: those who think only of this world and this life, who are content with acquiring material things and pursuing mundane goals, and those who take into account the implications of the law of karma with regard to a future life, and on the basis of this consideration start thinking in ethical and spiritual terms. This is the traditional assumption with regard to what motivates people in their practice of Buddhism: that what one is seeking is a good rebirth, and that spiritual practice will be a means to that end.

This, of course, would have been the prevailing view in India at the time of the Buddha; but in the modern West we are not necessarily going to find it easy to go along with it. In fact, the Buddha himself does not seem to have put the kind of emphasis on karma and rebirth that so many Buddhists did later on. This is understandable. He had already gained Enlightenment, and his disciples were eager to do the same. If one's aim is to gain Enlightenment, a state beyond the conditions of life and death, there is little need to consider future lives.

The great Tibetan yogi Milarepa attained Enlightenment in one lifetime, though in his case it was not that he did not consider the long view, but that he could not afford to take it. Having lived a wicked and murderous life before he converted to Buddhism, he perceived that no accumulation of merit he might gather in the life he had left could outweigh his evil actions sufficiently to divert his course away from a rebirth in the hell realms, where he would probably have remained for aeons upon aeons. His only hope was to gain Enlightenment in one lifetime, starting from scratch.

It was assumed by many that he must have practised all sorts of virtues and perfections over many, many lifetimes, but he himself always insisted that he began his spiritual practice with no merit to his credit at all. So although Milarepa himself had a powerful appreciation of the implications of karma and rebirth, he does at the same time provide a model for anyone who has difficulty with these ideas.[32]

In fact, there is no need to assent to the idea of karma and rebirth in order to be a practising Buddhist. Any account of Buddhism as traditionally handed down tends to bring it in at some point, but there are plenty of texts and teachings which present the path simply as the path, making no reference to karma and rebirth at all. If the Buddhist tradition holds good, then as one's understanding deepens the truth of karma and rebirth will presumably become clearer. After all, Buddhists have disagreed over many things, but no teacher of any school or sect has ever suggested that belief in karma and rebirth might be a wrong view – except in the sense that time itself, mundane existence itself, is not ultimately real. The idea of rebirth, one could say, follows logically upon the fundamental tenet of Buddhism that actions have consequences. However, one doesn't have to be completely logical in order to follow the Buddhist path, and it is possible to draw motivation for one's practice by considering the operation of karma in this life without necessarily taking rebirth into account.

Of course, however logical belief in it may be, rebirth is not the only possible answer to the universal question 'What happens when we die?' For many people the Buddhist conception of rebirth seems more or less self-evident. But there are, obviously, other views on the matter. In fact there are three, or possibly four, views to choose from. The Christian view is that one will exist after death – in heaven or elsewhere, though not again on earth – but that one did not exist before this life. At least, that is the view which has been held almost universally throughout Christian history. One or two of the early Greek

Christian scholars, like Origen, did believe in some sort of pre-existence before physical birth. Their idea was that the soul, which one inherited from one's parents, ultimately came from Adam. This belief – which amounted to a belief in a sort of group soul of which one's individual soul is a part – was known as Traductionism (because one's soul is 'traduced' or conveyed from Adam).

Christian opinion is more divided on what happens after death. Some believe that the soul created by God is immortal, and that it eventually goes to heaven or hell – or, in the case of unchristened babies, to Limbo – for all eternity. Others take the view that the soul is created mortal and dies with the death of the body until it is revived, either shortly after death or – according to, for example, Seventh Day Adventists and Jehovah's Witnesses – at the time of the Last Judgement. Then one goes either to heaven or to hell – though the Seventh Day Adventists replace eternal torment with a much kinder final solution for the condemned, which is that God simply annihilates them.

This, in brief, is the Christian view. The second possible view is the strictly materialist one: the belief that there is just this life with no kind of existence whatsoever before or after. The third possible view is purely theoretical; it would be the view that there is just this life and one single previous life – but no one, to the best of my knowledge, actually holds this view. Finally, the fourth possible view is that there is a past life or lives, a present life, and a future life or lives.

Most people find that one of these views seems more satisfactory than the others. No one view is altogether free from difficulties; but personally I have come to the conclusion that the idea of rebirth fits best. And the most telling confirmation of its likelihood would seem to lie not in some objective intellectual demonstration but in a feeling – a quite definite and powerful feeling – that develops through one's life.

This is something one can't appreciate when one is young, unless one is rather exceptional. But as one gets older, one starts seeing that one's whole life has had a certain clear direction or tendency which cannot be accounted for fully by any accumulation of circumstances within this present life, but which definitely seems to originate from what one can only assume is a previous life. Furthermore, one gets a strong feeling that this trend isn't just going to stop, but will continue after one's death. If one is relatively observant and reflective I think one cannot but entertain quite seriously the idea that one has come into this life with a propensity, even an agenda, already in place and that one will project it – project oneself – beyond the conclusion of one's life.

One can get a sense of this from telling one's life story to a friend or friends. This is a useful and powerful practice which often brings to the surface half-forgotten aspects of one's life and allows one to discover patterns in one's experience. And one theme that frequently emerges as one tells one's life story is a sense that in the business of growing up something important has been lost along the way. Quite a number of people have this feeling, that when they were young, before they got caught up in worldly responsibilities, they really did have a sense of what life was all about, before it all got overlaid by the dense complex of adult experience. It's as though we lose contact with our true feelings, our true self, even – not just in a psychological way that requires some psychotherapeutic solution, but in a definitely spiritual way.

In our early years many of us have experiences or feelings that seem to belong not to this world but elsewhere – or that even seem to indicate that we *belong* elsewhere. A few years later, when one starts to think and feel as an individual without yet being weighed down with responsibilities, one wants to find one's way back to one's origins, back to a truer, more innocent experience, and take that as one's starting point.

All this is not to suggest that there is some kind of primeval innocence about a child, or that children are in some way in touch with the Absolute. Unfortunately, one can get a sentimental and mistaken impression of this sort from some of the English poets: Vaughan, for example – 'Happy those early days when I / Shined in my Angel-infancy';[33] or Wordsworth –'trailing clouds of glory do we come / From God who is our home'.[34] Wordsworth himself is a very clear, though unusual, example of someone who achieved a true vision in early adolescence which he managed to sustain well into his thirties. William Blake is another – indeed, he never really lost contact with his childhood. Though he was a very mature person he never grew up at all in the sense of becoming corrupted with (in Traherne's phrase) 'the dirty devices of the world'.[35]

There will always be people who say that it is a necessary part of one's development to taste something of the dirty devices of this world, but this is a wrong view. Ideally, one should try to remain an adolescent in this positive sense for as long as possible. One should seek to deepen one's vision, to mature it – but not to lose it. To return to the idea of rebirth, it's as though when we are young we are in touch with something from a previous life. One may not be aware of it as a small child, but as one comes up to adolescence one becomes old enough to have a sense of it – though not, perhaps, old enough to appreciate how precious it is, or how easily it is lost.

Such experiences lead many people to see the idea of rebirth as quite reasonable, even obvious. However, if we find it difficult to take it to heart as our Tibetan author would like us to, we do not thereby lose our motivation for the spiritual life – at least, not necessarily. In fact, in some Buddhist countries the doctrine of karma and rebirth sometimes provides an excuse for postponing any real spiritual effort. It is even said that it isn't possible to gain Enlightenment any longer – the Buddha lived so long ago and there aren't any Enlightened teachers around any more – so our best bet is to accumulate merit, hope for good rebirths, and wait a few thousand years for the next Buddha to reappear, in the hope that we will get a chance to become his disciples. That will be the time to make an effort to gain Enlightenment. So some people believe – but it is a disastrously wrong view. It is better to disbelieve in karma and rebirth and follow the path anyway than to believe in karma and rebirth and make that one's excuse for not following the path here and now.

Yeshe Gyaltsen's assumption that it is concern for one's future rebirth that motivates one to take up Buddhism is simply not the way most people think in the West today. People tend to become interested in Buddhism, or start practising meditation, because it seems to offer a solution to psychological problems, or an intellectually respectable alternative to a purely materialist philosophy. Many practising Buddhists may be said to take a frankly agnostic or even sceptical attitude to the idea of rebirth. The very survival of human life on this planet is an issue that seems to many of us more pressing than any consideration of future rebirths.

Nowadays we can see things happening much more quickly than people could in more traditional and stable societies. It seems as though the whole process of life has speeded up, so that we can see the results of karma in this life itself. We are continually made aware through the media that we are teetering on the edge of global catastrophe, and this deepens our sense of responsibility. Never mind future lives; if we don't act now something terrible will happen in *this* life. (Of course, one can also think in terms of the consequences of our actions for future generations.) On a more personal level, too, one may conclude that only through some kind of spiritual development will one be able to transcend one's immediate painful conditions in this life. In these ways it is possible to accept the principle of karma within the much narrower context and more limited timescale of a single lifespan. Some people derive sufficient inspiration from thinking in terms of transforming their lives and the world around them, without needing to consider a long view of futurity at all.

Alternatively, one can take a completely opposite, more positive, perspective to that recommended by our author. Within the framework of karma and rebirth one is usually thinking in terms of escaping from something. Some Tibetan lamas teaching in the West make a point of describing in vivid detail all the different hells and heavens that await us – what will happen to you if you do this, what will happen to you if you do that – and this uncompromising, even dogmatic laying down of traditional doctrine evidently has a strong effect. But many Buddhists see this approach as unnecessarily fundamentalist. For them the spiritual life has its own intrinsic appeal which overrides the fear of any unpleasant contingencies attendant upon the worldly life, whether here and now or in the future. This innate love for the spiritual life should be encouraged. There are people who do not need to be told that they will suffer if they follow the worldly life, because they see spiritual development as good in itself.

Of course, the doctrine of karma and rebirth need not be intimidating. Some people are positively invigorated by the prospect of practising the spiritual life for life after life after life, gathering momentum over aeons of time and visiting all sorts of Buddha-worlds as described in the Mahāyāna sūtras. That others will find the mind-boggling duration of three *asaṁkheyyas*[36] of lifetimes simply depressing testifies to the necessity of developing an appropriate motivation of one's own.

But whatever we think about rebirth, we can still take karma seriously. Karma, it should be noted, is only one of the five levels on which conditionality operates. This is an aspect of the teaching that is not always made explicit in the Mahāyāna, although it is standard Theravādin teaching.[37] (Indeed, not all Mahāyāna Buddhists would even agree that conditionality is multi-faceted in this way; in some Mahāyāna traditions karma has become very dominant indeed.) But taking the Theravādin line on this, we can say that everything that happens does so as the result of a network of conditions, involving causal links which can be of a physical, biological, psychological, karmic, or transcendental nature. While karma – the level on which our skilful actions bring happiness for us and our unskilful actions bring suffering – is a causal factor in our lives, it does not follow that everything that happens to us is a result of our karma. Nonetheless, an understanding of the karmic level of conditionality is crucial to us because it is something on which we can rely. If we act skilfully, joy is sure to follow; if we act unskilfully, we are letting ourselves in for suffering we could have avoided.

This insight can be traced back to the very earliest Buddhist teachings, to the first few verses of the *Dhammapada*, which say:

[Unskilful] mental states are preceded by mind, led by mind, and made up of mind. If one speaks or acts with an impure mind suffering follows him even as the cart-wheel follows the hoof of the ox.

[Skilful] mental states are preceded by mind, led by mind, and made up of mind. If one speaks or acts with a pure mind happiness follows him like his shadow.[38]

So, as these verses make clear, there is a connection between our mind and the nature of our future life or lives. According to the doctrine of karma and rebirth, our actions have a direct effect on our own being by modifying the patterns of habit, the conscious and unconscious volitional drives, which constitute the most essential part of us. This 'essential nature' is not unchangeable; on the contrary, it can change in any direction at any time. It carries on through death and into another rebirth, in accordance with the karma that has accumulated during the previous life.

To delve briefly into the implications of this as outlined in Buddhist tradition, we can say that these volitional drives, modified by karma, take an appropriate physical embodiment. For a predominantly human consciousness, this will be a human form; for an angelic consciousness it will be the form of a god; for an animal consciousness, an animal form, and so on. Of course, the new form one assumes is not 'off the peg', as it were. There are said to be innumerable classes of beings – Buddhists in Eastern countries have had no difficulty with the notion of the existence of all kinds of what the scriptures call 'non-human beings' – but the variety of beings even within each class that we know of is enormous. More than that, each individual living being is in some way unique, and has a unique history and future. And to the extent that they are unique, to that extent individual living beings have the potential to modify the habit-volitions that make them up in order to promote their growth towards higher levels of consciousness. As human beings we are able to do this through various practices known collectively as the Dharma, or the way to Enlightenment, or Buddhism. Some forms of living beings, like animals, are in no position to take advantage of these practices; beings that are in a good position to do so may be said to have a precious opportunity which should not be thoughtlessly squandered.[39]

> As long as there is the belief in the *skandhas*,
> There will come from them a belief in a self.
> When there is a belief in an ego, then there is *karma*.
> From this, there will come (re)birth.[40]
> Nāgārjuna

Here Yeshe Gyaltsen brings in the first of his many quotations from the Mahāyāna tradition. And with this little verse from the sage Nāgārjuna he plunges us into deep water – or, at least, into a more Abhidharmic perspective on rebirth.

The *skandhas* are, as we have seen, the five constituents making up the psycho-physical organism that we call the self. They are: form, feeling, perception, volition, and consciousness. The Buddha exposed the insubstantial nature of the self by analysing one's experience of oneself into these five heaps or aggregates. But here Nāgārjuna points out that one should take care not to make the mistake of regarding the *skandhas* themselves as being substantial. To do this is to take something that exists merely empirically to be ultimately and permanently existent, effectively rebuilding a false belief in the self. So long as there is that fixed point of reference in the form of an ego, there will be an indefinite repetition of the pattern in the form of rebirth.

The whole process can also be seen at work within this life itself – indeed, within each minute of our lives. We are constantly reaffirming our belief in the discrete and substantial existence of the *skandhas*, thus giving rise to a self which acts in a particular way, as a result of which our present ego-ridden existence undergoes a manner of rebirth from instant to instant. This mistaken assumption – that the self, comprising the physical body, feelings, perceptions, impulses, and consciousness, is a real entity – gives rise to behaviour which in turn supports that mistaken assumption, until the adoption of positive conditioning eventually unravels all conditionings whatsoever, and we are able to see things as they really are.

The root of *saṃsāra* is motivation.
Therefore, the wise do not make plans.
The unwise, therefore, become agents
Because they see only unwiseness.[41]

This verse from Nāgārjuna's *Madhyamakakārikā* is not as contentious as the translation makes it appear. What Nāgārjuna says in fact is that the root of saṃsāra – compounded existence – is the fourth of the five *skandhas*, the *saṃskāras*, more straightforwardly rendered as volitions, impulses, or karma formations. They are only 'motivations' inasmuch as they are based on a belief in a fixed self. So it is not that 'the wise' do not make plans (which is simply untrue) but that they do not set up *saṃskāras*. The wise do not make plans only in so far as plans are the production of a rigid mental attitude, where the framing of that plan and the projection of its realization fulfils some neurotic need, so that one is unable to adapt or adjust it in the light of changed circumstances. The wise are fully equal to each and every situation as it arises, so the plans they make are always provisional.

The seeds for the possible worlds are concepts.
The objects are their field of activity.
Āryadeva, *Catuḥśataka*

The Buddha himself said, 'Thus, all terror
And also the countless frustrations
Come from the mind.'[42]
Śāntideva, *Bodhicaryāvatāra*

In these terse statements is contained an immense idea: that w' atever world we find ourselves in owes its origin to ideas in the mind. Hence the overwhelming importance of the study of mind and mental events for the spiritual welfare of all beings – because mind and mental events are what constitute karma. This is the traditional and appropriate motivation for the study of the Abhidharma: the fact that mind and mental events together with the law of karma determine one's whole future, both in this life and throughout future lives.

One could say that everything that happens in the universe – from a personal point of view – can be divided into two great classes: things that happen to us and things we do. Many of our experiences come into the first category. It rains, for instance, and we just experience the rain. We have nothing to do with making it rain; it just happens to us.

Then, secondly, there are things we do: things we initiate, things in respect of which we are active rather than passive.

The Buddhist viewpoint ties these two categories together by saying that what happens to us, our present *vipāka* (*vipāka* means 'fruit'), is the product of things we have done in the past – that is, the product of past karma. This term *vipāka* (or *karma-vipāka*) is of crucial importance to any discussion of mind and mental events. The symbol known as the Tibetan Wheel of Life, but more accurately called the 'Wheel of Becoming' (*bhāvachakra*), gives a graphic illustration of the workings of karma and *karma-vipāka*. The outer rim of the wheel illustrates what are known as the 'twelve links' (*nidānas*) of compounded existence. Although these links are popularly associated with the symbolism of Tibetan Buddhism, in fact they derive from the Buddha's own description of the insight he gained into the nature of human existence. We are reminded not to take this idea of twelve 'links' too literally by the fact that the Buddhist tradition also enumerates other combinations of links, sometimes five, sometimes ten, to describe the same process. The Ābhidharmikas themselves, as we shall see, came up with a rather different – though related – picture, with their classifications of mind and mental events. However, the twelve links do give a clear and useful idea of the way life unfolds.

We have already come across the first two links of the chain – ignorance (*avidyā*) and 'karma formations' (*saṃskāras*). These refer to the past life, reflecting the process by which, acting on the basis of ignorance, we formed the karmic propensities that have shaped our present life. The next eight links show the process of this life. The karma of our past life bears fruit (*vipāka*) in the form of consciousness (*vijñāna*), in dependence upon which arise the five *skandhas*. From the *skandhas* come the six senses (*ṣaḍāyatanas* – the mind being considered as a sixth sense), in dependence upon which arises contact (*sparśa*); and this in turns leads to feeling (*vedanā*). These five links are all *karma-vipāka*; they are all 'things that happen to us' in the sense that we have no choice about their arising – they arise in dependence upon our past karma.

But the next link is different. At this point we do have a choice. On our response depends the future course of events; we are back in the realm of 'things we do'. At this point we can create fresh karma by craving (*tṛṣṇā*) which leads to grasping (*upādāna*) and becoming (*bhāva*). The momentum of this karmic process leads to a future rebirth – hence the last two links of the chain, birth (*jāti*) and decay-and-death (*jarāmaraṇa*), a compressed and therefore grim snapshot of one's future life.

Alternatively, if we can learn to respond to pleasant feeling without craving and to unpleasant feeling without aversion, we set up fresh karma which will ultimately lead us beyond the wheel of life and death altogether, towards Enlightenment. Through the 'things we do', in other words, we can direct the 'things that will happen to us' in the future. And from a Buddhist, and especially an Abhidharmic, perspective, it is the things we do with our minds – in other words, our mental events – that make all the difference. All this it will be the concern of this commentary to explore in some detail.

However, as we have seen, not everything we experience is the *direct* result of things we have done. According to the doctrine of the five *niyamas*, whatever happens to us may be the result of a combination of five types of conditionality, only one of which consists of our ethical choices. The others represent the conditions that obtain within the general context of human existence.

Many of the things that happen to us simply arise out of the environment in which we find ourselves. Suppose, for example, that bad weather is preventing one from doing something one really wants to do. The rain is not necessarily the karmic consequence – the *vipāka* – of one's having once stopped somebody else from doing what they wanted to do, perhaps in some previous existence; that would be to take the law of karma too literally.

However, although what happens to us may do so as a result of physical, biological, psychological, or even transcendental factors, as well as arising from our karma, one could argue that these other factors have, indirectly, a karmic origin. For example, if bad weather sometimes stops one from doing what one wants to do, one could say that this is a result of one's having been born as a particular psycho-physical organism inhabiting a particular kind of world in which it rains from time to time. And how has one come to be in possession of this particular psycho-physical organism? Because of previous karmas one has performed. According to this line of reasoning, one could conclude that everything we experience *is* in fact a *vipāka* of previous karmas, though not in a literal 'eye for an eye, tooth for a tooth' sense.

This indirect karma could also be called collective karma; though this term has no traditional provenance, the Sarvāstivādin texts make it clear that such karmic concatenations occur.[43] One could even go as far as to say that a world comes into existence, so to speak, because a number of beings have performed the same kind of actions, thereby setting up the same kind of results. This congeries of common *vipāka* constitutes their world, which they also – broadly speaking – perceive in common. The same principle applies in the case of a Pure Land: by virtue of his infinitely powerful volition a Buddha is able to set up a whole ideal environment single-handedly, but others who have managed to 'tune in' to this Pure Land can also be reborn into it.[44]

The fundamental implication is that volition is a creative force that is capable of producing what we would call objective consequences. Expressions such as 'It's only a thought' are simply not Buddhistic. A thought is, in a sense, everything. Thought is a force; thought is a power; thought is an energy. But what exactly is it that this energy produces? What do we mean by the objective consequences produced by volitions?

We cannot say that thought creates matter. What we can say is that thought produces *rūpa*, 'the objective content of a perceptual situation', as Guenther puts it.[45] So while we may say that our experience has an objective pole, just as there is a subjective pole, we should not go as far as to think in terms of an object which is actually out there waiting for us to perceive it.

One may also create karma with regard to specific individuals. The Jātaka tales suggest as much, anyway. When the Buddha relates one of these stories of something that is supposed to have happened millions of years ago, he says that such-and-such a figure was himself, that another was Ānanda (the Buddha's companion), and yet another was Devadatta (the Buddha's opponent on many occasions). So the same dramatis personae are presented in each story. They travel down the ages together, appearing in different guises but standing in much the same relation to one another as they do in their historical incarnation. Devadatta, for example, is for lifetime after lifetime trying to kill the Buddha. It is as though he couldn't leave the Buddha alone. The Buddha was always there in his thoughts, so Devadatta always got reborn along with the Buddha. They somehow got tangled up together, for one rebirth after another.[46] The idea behind the Jātaka tales perhaps provides an explanation for the feeling one gets with certain people that one is picking up threads that were dropped a long time ago (though one wouldn't want to press this point towards unduly romantic conclusions).

The main point to be drawn from all this is that as one's mind is, so is one's karma. As one's karma is, so is one's rebirth. As one's rebirth is, so is one's happiness or one's suffering. And ultimately, with the attainment of Enlightenment, one is freed even from the alternation between happiness and suffering. The Buddhist tradition sums the whole matter up in one key phrase – actions have consequences; and, if we are uncomfortable with the notion of rebirth, we can readily see the truth of this even within our present life. All this depends on the mind and mental events. But what is the mind, and what are mental events? To these questions Yeshe Gyaltsen now turns his attention.

4

THE NATURE OF THE MIND

THE YOGĀCĀRA BACKGROUND

Our ordinary experience is firmly and securely based on subject–object dualism. All our knowledge, all our thinking, takes place within this framework – subject and object, me and you, 'me in here' and 'the world out there'. But the Enlightened mind, we are told, is completely free of such dualism. This, at least, is one of the key doctrines of the Yogācāra: *cittamātra* – 'mind only'.

Between the experience of non-duality and our ordinary, everyday dualistic consciousness, there is obviously a great gulf; and to move from the one experience to the other will entail a complete and absolute reversal of all our usual attitudes. This reversal, this great change – this great death and rebirth, even – is what the Yogācāra terms the *parāvṛtti*. Sometimes *parāvṛtti* is translated as 'revulsion', but this is not really satisfactory because it implies a psychological process rather than a spiritual and metaphysical one. It is much better to use the literal translation of *parāvṛtti* – 'turning about'.

As we have seen, *The Necklace of Clear Understanding* is more or less based on the Yogācāra tradition's understanding of how the mind works. Before plunging with Yeshe Gyaltsen into the distinction between mind and mental events, therefore, we will look a little more closely at the Yogācāra's conception of mind, on which Gyaltsen's commentary largely rests.

Basically, the *cittamātra* doctrine denies the reality of matter as a separate category from mind. The objects of our perception, it says, are not external objects as such, not objects as opposed to ourselves, the subject. We perceive mental impressions, that's all. The significance of this insight is that if one removes the notion of an object, one also effectively removes the notion of a subject. In this way one breaks down the notion of a self that is separate from the world, to be left with 'mind only'. This 'mind only' is not mind as opposed to matter, but a completely different conception of mind.

We have already come across the teaching of the five *skandhas*, which states that our experience can be analysed into five heaps or aggregates: form (*rūpa*), feeling (*vedanā*), volitions (*saṁskāras*), perception (*saṁjñā*), and consciousness (*vijñāna*). Contradicting the standard Abhidharma teaching, the Yogācāra made the bold statement that there is really only one *skandha*, *vijñāna* or consciousness, the other four being manifestations of *vijñāna*. (In consequence, the Yogācāra School is sometimes called the Vijñānavāda.) Having established this metaphysical position, the Yogācārins drew attention to its practical consequence: if you think in terms of an object, you will grasp at that object, they said; but if you see that what appears to be an object is in fact a transformation of mind, your experience is like someone who dreams that they are about to eat a delicious fruit. When they wake up, they realize that the fruit is just a product of their own mind, and they forget about it – the grasping is gone.

So, rather than being able to make a sharp distinction between subject and object, all one can really say is that there is a 'perceptual situation' (to use Guenther's expression) comprising two opposite poles. One pole is the experience of what I call myself, together with everything I have under my immediate control; that is the 'subjective content' of the perceptual situation. And then, at the opposite pole, there is everything and everyone that is independent of my direct control – the 'objective content' of the perceptual situation. When one becomes Enlightened, that perceptual situation still occurs, but one no longer identifies oneself with its subjective content, which means that the whole perceptual situation is expanded, clarified, illuminated, enlightened.

The Yogācāra interpretation is not so much that there is a thing called 'mind' and a thing called 'matter', and that the thing called matter is discovered actually to be mind. It's not like discovering that what one thought was a jug is in reality clay. It's more that *citta* or mind is the term applied to that undifferentiated substratum which has been polarized into subject and object, mind and matter. Mind and matter are just symbols for the two poles of the one perceptual situation, and it's sometimes very difficult to tell where one ends and the other begins. If one can attenuate that subject–object polarity a little, for example in meditation (the Yogācāra, remember, came out of meditative experience, not philosophical reasoning), then one's experience is transformed.

There is of course the question of how we all come to share more or less the same 'objective content'. The general, though perhaps rather implausible, Yogācāra view is that we have a common perception to the extent that we have a common karma – to the extent, that is, that we share a common mental outlook. The 'objects' more or less coincide because the 'subjects' more or less coincide. This consensus reality, however, is real for practical purposes only.

When you attain Enlightenment, the element of resistance to the objective content of the perceptual situation is no longer there. You no longer have a will that is separate from that of others. It's as though you utterly identify with others, and with what they are doing. You no longer want one thing while they want another, or want something from them that they are unwilling to give. What they want, you want; what you want, they want. You don't experience another person as a sort of brick wall that you are coming up against, and you no longer experience yourself as a separate and conflicting solid force. You experience others in a completely different way: they become diaphanous or transparent, because your will is not coming into collision with theirs. This completely different, more relaxed, lighter, and freer attitude, taken to the *n*th degree, is something of the nature of Enlightenment. The world is the same but you see it differently. Perhaps one could say that it's like what happens when you fall in love, only much more so. Even though everything is there as before, the world looks almost physically different.

The Yogācāra describes the process of becoming Enlightened in terms of the transformation of what it calls the eight *vijñānas* into the five *jñānas*. *Vijñāna* is usually translated as 'consciousness', but that is not exactly accurate. The prefix *vi-* means 'to divide' or 'to discriminate', and *jñāna* means 'knowledge' or 'awareness', so we can translate *vijñāna* as 'discriminating awareness'. *Vijñāna* therefore refers to awareness of an object not just in a pure mirror-like way but in a way which discriminates the object as being of a particular type and belonging to a particular class, species, or whatever. The first five *vijñānas* are the five 'sense *vijñānas*', the modes of discriminating awareness that operate through the five senses – through the eye with respect to form, the ear with respect to sound, and so on.

Guenther uses the term 'perception' where other translators use 'consciousness', so that, for example, instead of 'eye-consciousness' we have – more correctly, in my view – 'visual perception'. In his commentary, Yeshe Gyaltsen classifies perceptions according to the sense organ through which they function or take place. And the sixth of the six categories is – perhaps surprisingly to anyone schooled in Western ways of thinking – mind itself. In Buddhism, mind in the everyday sense is classified as a sort of sixth sense; it doesn't have a special elevated position above the five sense consciousnesses. The word being translated as mind here is *mano-vijñāna*, which Guenther translates as categorical perception. This is the mind as the simply mechanical or reactive process of perceiving mental objects (as opposed to *manas*, the mind as – so to speak – the seat of ego identity).

The idea of the mind as a sense organ is a necessary corollary to the Buddhist conception of what Guenther terms the perceptual situation. The conventional Western view is that thoughts remain part of oneself as a subject set against a separate world of objects. But this is a limited viewpoint. It is akin to what William Blake calls the *ratio* of the senses, the split-off intellect, representing a process of induction from a narrow field of experience: you observe, you classify, you generalize, from the limited field of sense experience. When you look out, you construe a world of actually existing objects, and when you look within, you construe an actually existent self. Blake contrasts this ratio with Imagination, which is based upon, or is the expression of, the experience of the whole person.[47]

In other words, the Buddhist viewpoint recognizes thoughts as objects of perception along with any other objects. Just as objects flow through one's visual field, so do objects flow through one's cognitive field. One could even say that, in a sense, one's thoughts are even less a part of oneself than the objects of the other five senses, because it would seem that one has rather less control, generally speaking, over what one thinks than over what one sees, hears, tastes, smells, and feels. It seems unreasonable to identify oneself with a realm of experience over which one seems to have so little control.

According to Yogācāra philosophy there are two aspects of *mano-vijñāna*. The first of these is awareness of what we might describe as ideas of sense – in other words, the mind's awareness of impressions presented to it by the five senses. The second aspect is awareness of ideas that arise independently of sense-perception, out of the mind itself. This latter aspect of *mano-vijñāna* is of three kinds. First of all, there are the ideas and impressions that arise in the course of meditation, as when one experiences light that doesn't have its origin in any sense impression but comes from the mind itself. Then, secondly, there are functions such as imagination, comparison, and reflection. If, for example, one's immediate impression of someone was that they were untrustworthy, this might be a subtle sense impression, but on the other hand it might be that one has in the past met someone who resembled this person in some way and who turned out to be untrustworthy. In this latter case one's impression would come under the heading of categorical perception (*mano-vijñāna*). Thirdly, there are images perceived in dreams, which again come not from sense impressions but directly from the mind itself. Categorical perception, in short, covers any perception that does not come in through the physical senses. It is the perception of all kinds of mental operations, including recollections of experiences that originally came through the senses and also things that were never experienced through the senses at all.

The seventh consciousness or *vijñāna* is the *kliṣṭa-mano-vijñāna*. *Kliṣṭa* means 'afflicted' or 'suffering', and also 'defiled', defilement being a source of suffering; it has also been translated as 'tainted'. This mode of awareness, therefore, is afflicted, defiled, or tainted by a dualistic outlook. Whatever it experiences, it interprets in terms of a subject and an object – subject as self, and object as world or universe. Everything is seen in terms of pairs of opposites: good and bad, true and false, right and wrong, existence and non-existence, and so on. Of course, this dualistic mode of discriminative awareness or consciousness characterizes the way in which we usually live our lives.

The eighth consciousness is called the *ālaya-vijñāna*. *Ālaya* literally means a repository or store, or even treasury – as in 'Himalaya', which means 'repository of snow'. This store consciousness, one could say, has two aspects, the 'relative' or 'tainted' *ālaya* and the 'absolute' or 'pure' *ālaya*. This is not, however, a traditional Yogācāra distinction; for Paramārtha (499–569CE), for example, the distinction was between the *ālaya-vijñāna* (by which he meant what I am calling the relative *ālaya*) and a ninth consciousness, the 'immaculate consciousness' (*amala-vijñāna*).[48]

The relative *ālaya* consists of, or contains, the impressions left deep in the mind by all our previous experiences. Whatever we have done or said or thought or experienced, a trace or residue of it remains there; nothing is absolutely lost. The Yogācāra School conceives of the impressions that are deposited in the *ālaya-vijñāna*, the consequences of our various thoughts and deeds, as being like seeds (*bījas*). In other words, these impressions are not passive; they are not like the impression left by a seal in a piece of wax. They are *active* impressions, left like seeds in the soil, and when conditions are favourable they sprout and produce fruits.

This subconscious collectivity of seeds sown by previous actions fructifies and evolves eventually into the six sense perceptions, plus the *kliṣṭa-mano-vijñāna* or ego-consciousness; and all these seven *vijñānas* together comprise the evolving consciousness which produces the illusion of the world as we know it. It is this *kliṣṭa-mano-vijñāna* , often referred to simply as *manas*, 'mind' or 'ego-consciousness', that interprets the impressions it receives from the other six *vijñānas* as representing an objectively existing external world, and at the same time interprets a reflection in itself of the *ālaya-vijñāna* in terms of a separate, real self.

The *ālaya* in its absolute aspect is Reality itself, conceived of in terms of pure awareness free from all trace of subjectivity and objectivity. It is a pure, continuous, and non-dimensional – or even multi-dimensional – awareness in which there is nothing of which anyone is aware, nor anyone who is aware. It is awareness without subject and without object – something which it is scarcely possible for us to imagine.

The *asraya-parāvṛtti*, the 'turning about in the deepest seat of consciousness', is brought about, according to the Yogācāra, by the accumulation of impressions – seeds – in the relative *ālaya*. Through spiritual practice, more and more pure seeds are gathered in the relative *ālaya*, and as these pure seeds accumulate, they put pressure on the impure seeds until in the end the impure seeds are pushed right out of the *ālaya*; it is this that constitutes the *parāvṛtti*. When the *parāvṛtti* occurs, the eight *vijñānas*, the eight modes of discriminating awareness, are transformed into five *jñānas* – five modes of pure, that is, non-discriminating, awareness or wisdom.

These five modes of pure awareness are represented in Mahāyāna iconography by five archetypal Buddhas, the five Buddhas of the mandala. The first five *vijñānas*, the sense consciousnesses, are transformed into the all-performing wisdom of the green Buddha, Amoghasiddhi. The *mano-vijñāna*, the mind consciousness, is transformed into the distinguishing wisdom of the red Buddha, Amitābha. The *kliṣṭa-mano-vijñāna* , the defiled mind consciousness, becomes the wisdom of equality of the yellow Buddha, Ratnasambhava. The relative *ālaya* is transformed into the mirror-like wisdom of the dark blue Buddha, Akṣobhya. And the absolute *ālaya*, of course, does not need to be transformed at all; it is equivalent to the wisdom of the Dharmadhātu, the wisdom of the universe perceived as fully pervaded by Reality, the wisdom of the white Buddha, Vairocana.[49]

The doctrine of the *ālaya-vijñāna* provides an explanation for how it is that we take illusory things like the self and the world to be real. According to Maitreyanātha, Absolute Mind is the sole reality, but its radiance is obscured by its own dynamic, or potentially dynamic, principle, the *abhūtaparikalpa* or unreal imagination.[50] This dynamic principle comprises two aspects: the relative or tainted *ālaya-vijñāna* or store consciousness, and the *pravṛtti-vijñāna* or evolving consciousness.

Whether or not one accepts the idea of the *ālaya-vijñāna* depends, traditionally, on whether one takes it to be an explicit teaching or an implicit teaching. The distinction here is between those texts that have to be interpreted (*neyartha*) and those that can be taken literally (*nitartha*). Some teachers say that the word of the Buddha is at all times quite explicit and never requires any interpretation to bring out its real meaning. They say that reading something other than the explicit meaning into it falsifies it. The Yogācārins do not go this far; they accept the presence of implicit statements in the teachings. For example, according to the *Samdhinirmocana Sūtra*, an important scripture for the Yogācāra, the Perfection of Wisdom sūtras and the *Madhyamaka* itself should not be taken literally; the teaching of emptiness as presented in these texts is a skilful means.[51] But as far as the *ālaya-vijñāna* is concerned, the Yogācārins posit it on the basis of what they take as explicit statements in the teachings. It is on this basis that they declare the whole of reality to be 'mind only'.

The Madhyamaka School, by contrast, explains away references to the *ālaya-vijñāna* by saying that it is not to be understood explicitly; it is not to be taken in a strictly literal, philosophical sense. Indeed, the Madhyamaka goes one step further than the Yogācāra, saying that even mental events – or what we think of as mental events – are illusory, just logical fictions.[52] On the other hand, texts which teach the universal emptiness of inherent existence are, for the follower of the Madhyamaka, to be taken literally, while the Yogācārin would have seen this – perhaps with good reason – as tantamount to nihilism.

In *The Necklace of Clear Understanding* Yeshe Gyaltsen chooses not to go into the seventh and eighth *vijñānas*; for practical spiritual purposes his main concern is with the first six, as we shall see. In his brief chapter on mind, however, he notes simply that one can gain Enlightenment by following either the Madhyamaka or the Yogācāra.[53] Though they are different teachings – different ways of looking at things – they lead ultimately to the same goal.

This serves as a reminder that all this analysis is intended for a practical purpose. Given the way things are – given that we see things dualistically, through the lens, as it were, of the defiled mind consciousness – we can learn to discriminate between positive, skilful mental states, which are to be cultivated, and negative, unskilful mental states, which are to be dropped. This is very basic Buddhism. In the Buddha's teaching of the seven factors of Enlightenment,[54] for example, the second factor (after mindfulness or awareness) is *dharma-vicaya*, investigation of mental events. The Abhidharma project developed this idea further by identifying and classifying a definitive range of positive and negative mental events. It is these that are the subject matter for the main body of Yeshe Gyaltsen's commentary.

First, though, he chooses to explore a crucial distinction: the difference between mind and mental events.

MIND AND MENTAL EVENTS DISTINGUISHED

Yeshe Gyaltsen begins his discussion by singling out a quotation from the *Madhyāntavibhāga*, one of the five books of Maitreya that Asaṅga taught to his brother Vasubandhu, who wrote notes and commentaries on all five books. This is the quotation:

Seeing a thing belongs to mind.
Seeing its specific characteristic belongs to a mental event.[55]
Madhyāntavibhāga

In his translation of the *Madhyāntavibhāga*, Stcherbatsky renders Vasubandhu's explanation of this statement as follows:

This means – the Mind (itself, i.e. pure sensation) apprehends the Thing alone, (i.e., the Thing-in-Itself, the pure object). The mental phenomena, such as e.g. feelings (pleasant and unpleasant) etc., apprehend its qualities, (i.e. the qualities of the Thing, pleasant or unpleasant) ... (Vasubandhu says) 'among them the Mind apprehends the Thing alone.' Here the word 'alone' serves to exclude (every kind) of definiteness.[56]

In other words, mind is awareness of what Guenther calls facticity: awareness of the unique specificity of an object or, more simply, awareness that it is there. This does not include an awareness of any qualities as such, even qualities that differentiate that thing from other things. All this comes under the heading of mental events. As defined here, mind is a general, even vague, awareness. But it is vague only in cognitive terms. Though it does not assign the object to any particular class, it has a clear, direct apprehension of the object as being there. To put it another way, mind is the perception of what Guenther calls the haecceity of a thing. Haecceity is a term derived from scholastic philosophy which means 'this-ness' in the sense of the specific character of a thing – that it is this particular thing – rather than the this-ness of any particular quality. It is a clear perception without conceptualization. It is almost as though one has an instant, a bare instant, of pure awareness before the mind starts to function with respect to what one perceives.[57]

Just occasionally one becomes aware of a slight extension of that bare instant. For example, sometimes first thing in the morning when one wakes up, mental events can be quite slow to arise, and in the meantime one perceives without interpreting for a minute or two before mental events start coming into operation. In the usual course of things we swiftly move away from this experience, but it can be developed. In meditation one may move *towards* this quality of almost pure perception, which would seem to show that the potentiality of an experience of pure mind is already there, already functioning, if only in a very minor way.

Having apprehended an object, the mind tends to become involved with it in certain specific ways. It is interested in it or otherwise; it likes it or dislikes it, accepts it or rejects it; it is pleased or angered by it; it compares it with other things – and so on. These specific ways in which the mind becomes involved with an object are called in Pāli *cetasikas*, which means 'connected with the mind', and in Sanskrit *caittadharmas*, 'that which pertains to the mind': i.e. 'mental events' or 'mental concomitants'.

If I look at and become aware of a person, this is mind. But if I then start thinking, say, 'He's a bit taller than that other fellow' or 'I don't like the look of him,' these are mental events. It's possible, of course, for more than one mental event to be present at the same time; there can be whole complexes of them. Indeed, as we shall see, there are five mental events that are 'omnipresent'. Mental events arise as one engages oneself with the object more specifically and begins to apprehend or cognize its distinguishing qualities. One may wonder, though, how this interpretation of one's experience, this idea of a kind of hiatus between mind and mental events, squares with Yeshe Gyaltsen's next quotation, which appears authoritatively to contradict it:

> The mind and mental events are certainly together.[58]
>
> *Abhidharmakośa*

I have suggested that it is possible for there to be awareness of an object without mental events coming into play. This does not, however, appear to be the conclusion we are being offered here. These two statements can be reconciled by the introduction of a third term: 'mind as such'. But why do we need this? Why can't we just say that mind is sometimes associated with mental events and sometimes not? The simple answer is that while one can have mind without mental events, one cannot have mental events without mind; and the mind one gets with mental events is different from the mind without them.

It's as though when mental events cease, mind in the sense of the mind that accompanies mental events also ceases. What one is left with then is mind as such. If mind and mental events were twins, when one twin disappeared, the remaining twin would no longer be a twin. If mental events cease to exist – or have not yet arisen – mind is no longer what it was; it 'becomes' or 'is replaced by' 'mind as such'. The term 'mind as such', incidentally, is not an Abhidharma expression, but translates *sems-nyid*, a term coined by the Tibetan Nyingmapa philosophers who studied the Abhidharma and developed their own perspective on it.

Yeshe Gyaltsen goes a little further than the *Abhidharmakośa*, saying that 'mind and mental events arise together, as far as time is concerned, and are of one and the same stuff'.[59] To say that mind and mental events are of the same stuff is to say rather more than that they are certainly together. Vasubandhu probably didn't feel that it was necessary to go as far as that. It is enough to assert that – because they are concerned with the same object at the same time – mind and mental events are certainly together.

For a further perspective on this, we can look to Dr Guenther's introductory notes to the text.[60] Here Guenther suggests that the relationship between mind and mental events is like that between a father and his sons. The sons have a 'symmetrical' relationship to each other, whereas their relationship with their father is 'asymmetrical'. That is, if David is John's brother, then John is David's brother – the relationship is symmetrical. But if Peter is James's *father*, it does not follow that James is Peter's father; in that case the relationship is asymmetrical. So the mental events or concomitants stand in a symmetrical relationship to one another, because they all pertain to one and the same mind, but they all stand in an asymmetrical relationship to mind itself.

It would be a mistake to gather from this, however, a notion of mind as a sort of stable centre or ego around which mental events come and go. It's not that first of all you get mind in its pristine glory and then mental events come along. Mind – in the sense in which the term is being used here – and mental events arise together; generally speaking, in the instant one perceives an object the mental concomitants are there. In this sense the mind itself is a mental event – an elder brother, if you like, rather than a father. The 'father' is not mind but what Guenther calls the 'x factor', in relation to which mind and mental events stand in a symmetrical relationship between themselves.

The x factor is mind as such, or mind as pure fact; this is the point of reference for both mind and mental events. If mind as such can be represented by the image of a lake without any ripples, the ripples that arise can be said to have two sides to them (mind and mental events) which necessarily arise and cease at the same time.

So although we naturally tend to think of mental events as arriving subsequent to a kind of constantly present mind, in fact there is no real difference between mind and mental events: they simply perform different functions within the process of subject–object interaction. Mind can just as well be spoken of as itself a mental event. Following the Yogācāra's relational approach, we may even question whether mind exists at all. We may indeed ask this about all the terms we are using. 'Mind' and 'mental events' are useful ways of describing the process we experience; they are not to be taken as a fixed and final description.

Mind, in short, cannot really be described at all, and to try to do so is to falsify it, although trying to describe it does provide a means of coming to an understanding of its true nature. The term 'mind as such' is metaphysical or epistemological rather than psychological, referring to mind undescribed and thus unfalsified. We could therefore regard 'mind as such' or 'mind as pure fact' as an operational concept that guards against our mistaking mind for some permanent and unchanging ego. It is the existence, so to speak, of mind as pure fact which prevents us from absolutizing mind as described fact, i.e. taking it too literally. As nothing may be said about mind as pure fact, what we talk about when we speak of mind is termed described fact. In other words, described fact is no more than our falsifying attempt to describe mind as pure fact.

To go with pure fact and described fact, we have *vidyā*, or wisdom, and *avidyā*, or ignorance. *Vidyā*, which Guenther translates as 'pure awareness' or 'appreciative discrimination', is what perceives pure fact; it is as though wisdom is mind as pure fact in action. *Avidyā*, or 'absence of pure awareness' (usually translated as 'ignorance') is what perceives described fact. As ignorance is classified among the mental concomitants, the mind itself, in a state of ignorance or lack of awareness, is also a mental concomitant.

Indeed, to take this very complex matter to its conclusion, the fact that we distinguish between mind and mental events at all is an instance of that ignorance which is itself a mental event. So the distinction between mind and mental events is not an absolute distinction, but an operational concept. One can't chop reality into mutually exclusive little bits and then put them together again to get at the truth. The only way to get at the truth is to stop cutting reality into little bits altogether.

But wasn't the whole method of the Ābhidharmikas to chop reality into bits in just this way? We have to be careful – and one could perhaps say that the Ābhidharmikas themselves weren't ultimately quite careful enough about this – not to take this whole question of analysis too literally. Is it really possible to divide one part of a thing from the others, or is the division only notional? You can divide your nose from the rest of your face, but where does your nose end and the rest of your face begin? Is there an actual point? And if not, is not the division of the nose from the face arbitrary, at least to some extent? Or take time: we divide time into minutes, but is time really divided into minutes?

If you divide things, there is always a problem of how to put them together again. One can't help making these divisions for practical purposes, but it is dangerous to take those divisions as actually corresponding to realities. It is the mind that chops things up into bits; but reality does not consist of bits strung together. At the same time, we can't say that things are completely continuous, because we do see, if not differences, at least corrugations, so to speak, in reality. All we can do is use these concepts of continuity and being made up of parts appropriately.

From this perspective we may view the Abhidharma simply as playing with operational concepts for a certain practical purpose. It's an example of what the Tantrics call 'using dirt to get rid of dirt'. It is the mental concomitant of 'lack of pure awareness' that makes the distinction between mind and mental events; but by making this distinction, we can classify and sort out skilful mental events from unskilful ones. Living our spiritual life on that basis, we eventually go beyond unskilful mental events. Then we go beyond skilful mental events as well, and finally we go beyond the distinction between mind and mental events altogether.

It is highly questionable whether the Ābhidharmikas themselves would have looked at what they were doing in quite this way. Guenther, who looks at things very much from the Nyingma point of view, is at pains to point out that we have the Nyingma philosophers to thank for this perspective, for making a living experience of the Abhidharma tradition.[61] One might say that this perspective takes us a bit beyond the Abhidharma proper, but if it does, it does so quite justifiably.

Through spiritual practice, particularly with the development of *dhyāna* – *dhyāna* being a state of higher consciousness reached through the practice of meditation – the mental events become purer and fewer, until eventually, when one enters the realms of the *arūpa* or 'formless' *dhyānas*, one is left with the singleness of mind without any defilements whatsoever. This mind is not pure in the sense that the mental concomitants have dropped away. It is more that they have been absorbed and fully integrated. All the energy that had been bound up in those mental concomitants passes into mind itself, which remains as the pure perceiver. Nothing has been lost: it is a singleness of richness rather than poverty.

This singleness is reflected in the experience of the four *arūpa-dhyānas*. When one enters the first of them, the sphere of infinite space, it is not as if one perceives an object out there called space. It's more that the mind proceeds without resistance or impediment. The usual interpretation of the second *arūpa-dhyāna*, the sphere of infinite consciousness, is that in order to traverse infinite space, mind must itself be infinite. But it is perhaps more accurate to say that in this state of consciousness one becomes aware of the infinite range of the mind's activity. With the third *arūpa-dhyāna* one begins to doubt whether there is an object at all, and also, therefore, whether there is, in a sense, a subject either. In this way one enters the sphere of 'no-thing-ness'. Finally, the sphere of neither perception nor non-perception carries this process a stage further. This is the 'highest worldly attainment' of the path of practice. One can enter the path of vision from any of the *dhyānas*, but the higher the *dhyāna*, the more concentrated energy there is behind the penetration that leads to vision.

THE FIVE FUNCTIONAL CO-RELATIONS

As we have seen, it is in the nature of mind to have attendant mental events. The Abhidharma, as one might expect, goes into the specifics of this relationship, and it does so by enumerating five 'functional co-relations', as Guenther rather awkwardly translates them (Hopkins gives 'five similarities' or 'five samenesses').[62] Correspondingly, it is in the nature of mental events to arise in conjunction with mind – and again, this happens through the five functional co-relations. According to the *Abhidharmakośa* they are: 'alike basis, alike objective reference, alike observable quality, alike time, [and] alike stuff'.[63]

So firstly, 'alike basis'. To understand this, we have to recollect the idea that in Buddhism the mind is regarded as one of the six senses – the others being, of course, taste, touch, smell, sight, and hearing. The six sense faculties (which include the mind) are the means by which the mind perceives; there is no sense perception without a perceiving mind. The sense faculties therefore depend upon the mind in the same way as do mental events. Hence there is a common basis – an alike basis – for the senses (including the mind considered as a sense) and the mental events.

'Alike objective reference' means that mind and mental events refer to the same objects. 'Alike observable quality' refers to the fact that when the mind is aware of the existence of a blue object, say, the mental events are concerned with the specific qualities of that same blue object. 'Alike time' means that the mind and mental events refer to objects simultaneously.

As for 'alike stuff', this functional co-relation emphasizes that the mind which is associated with mental events is never pure mind. It bears a residue from previous situations (whether remembered or forgotten), a residue that has not exhausted itself within those situations, and which therefore goes on looking for a new situation into which it can project itself. Guenther helps to make this clearer by translating mind in this context as 'mental attitude'. It is this aspect of mind that the Theravāda School addresses in its enumeration of the 89 *cittas*, the states or moods of the one original, pure *citta*.[64]

This perspective of the Theravādins helps to make sense of 'alike stuff'. If one perceives something with anger, for instance, then all the mental events that arise in that situation will also be imbued with anger (as it were). That is, if one looks at someone with anger, various mental events will arise – 'How ugly, how stupid, how unpleasant he is' – which will be of the same nature or 'stuff' (not a happy expression, this). If the object is coloured by the mind, it is coloured more specifically by the mental events or functions. This goes for complexes of emotions as well: if the mind is one of mixed feelings, then the mental events will be of mixed feelings. However, whereas the Theravāda focuses on the different forms the mind appears in – whether it be as mind-with-anger, mind-with-craving, or mind-of-the-plane-of-form, or even mind-of-the-formless-plane – the Sarvāstivāda and Yogācāra Schools are more concerned with the oneness of the mind.

The author of the *Abhidharmasamuccaya*, Asaṅga, comes up with a slightly different list of functional co-relations, replacing 'alike basis' with 'alike spheres and levels'.[65] 'Alike spheres and levels' refers to the possibility in meditation of moving into higher realms that are qualitatively different from everyday experience. If one's mind is dwelling in one realm, mental events proper to a different realm cannot also be present. When one is in a state of meditative absorption, say – and thus dwelling in the *rūpadhātu* (world of form) or the *arūpadhātu* (world of no-form) – then certain kinds of mental events like anger or craving will simply not arise. They can only arise in connection with an angry or craving mind, and the moment an angry or craving mind develops one falls back into the *kāmadhātu* (world of desire).

This is not to say that an unpleasant experience may not arise from time to time even in higher states of consciousness. Such an experience may constitute *karma-vipāka* – that is, it may be the result of the karma of, say, anger in the past. But if one does not react to that experience, not experiencing further anger in consequence of that unpleasant experience, and therefore not setting up fresh karma, then one's sphere or level of consciousness is unaffected by it.

This discussion of spheres and realms plunges us into an area of Buddhist thought that so far we have encountered only briefly. The notion of different realms of experience or existence is one that can be taken literally, metaphorically, or even psychologically. For a literal depiction we can look again at the Tibetan Wheel of Life, which illustrates six different realms: the human realm, the animal realm, the realm of the gods, the realm of the warlike titans or *asuras*, the hell realm, and the realm of what are called hungry ghosts.

Buddhist cosmology envisages these realms as actually existing, and encompasses the possibility that one might be reborn in any one of them. One can equally think of the realms as symbolizing different mental states, our inner states being reflected in our experience of the external world – so that, for example, if we are very angry or miserable, the world seems a hellish place, while if our experience is refined and blissful, that will be reflected in an experience of the world that is similarly pleasurable and beautiful. As Milton's Satan says in *Paradise Lost*, 'The mind is its own place, and in itself / Can make a heaven of hell, a hell of heaven.'[66]

As the depiction of the realms in the Wheel of Life suggests, held as it is in the grip of the devouring monster called Time, these realms are not permanent. There are no such things as eternal damnation or everlasting paradise in the Buddhist scheme of things. Our birth into a realm is the result of our past karma, and our life in that particular realm will last only until that *karma-vipāka* is exhausted.

Another traditional classification of realms is threefold: the *kāmaloka* or *kāmadhātu*, the realm of sensuous experience or desire; the *rūpaloka* or *rūpadhātu*, the realm of (archetypal) form; and the *arūpaloka* or *arūpadhātu*, the 'formless' realm or sphere. The *kāmaloka* is the world of our ordinary experience; the *rūpaloka* and *arūpaloka*, which in Buddhist tradition are called 'god realms', relate to the experience of higher states of consciousness. So there is a correlation between this idea of realms and meditative experience; again, the connection is through mental states. We will go into this more in the next chapter when we consider the mental event termed 'feeling-tone'.

Returning to the two differing lists of functional co-relations between mind and mental events, it may seem as if Asaṅga's 'alike spheres and levels' amounts to something very different from the functional co-relation it displaces, 'alike basis'. However, I would suggest that they are, in fact, the same thing. What we have with the different spheres and levels are different levels of sense perception.

On the level of the *kāmaloka* the physical senses come into play; in the *rūpaloka* it is the subtle senses; while in the *arūpaloka* there are, in a way, no senses at all. So 'alike basis' and 'alike spheres and levels' represent, perhaps, just different ways of looking at the same thing.

MIND

So far, the main thing we have gathered is that mind in Buddhism is not a thing, an entity, but a relational term. Mind is a relationship with an object, an awareness that an object is there and that this object is a particular object. So mind or *citta* is not a passive registering or mirroring of things; it is a reaching out, as it were. This is one of the key insights of the Abhidharma.

Now, having set out the distinction between mind and mental events, Yeshe Gyaltsen goes on to reflect further on the nature of mind. He begins with three definitions of perception from the Mahāyāna tradition:

> What is perception? It is a distinct awareness of what is before the mind.
> Pañcaskandhaprakaraṇa

> Perception is a process of singling out.
> Abhidharmakośa

> The individualizing perception by means of being aware of the mere factual presence of an object is the defining characteristic of the mind.[67]
> rGyal-tshab

This statement by rGyal-tshab (one of Tsongkhapa's disciples) corresponds to Yeshe Gyaltsen's own definition: 'To be aware of the mere facticity and haecceity of an object is mind.' 'The individualizing perception' is a perception that singles out a particular object – *this* man, say, rather than man in general. So the term mind here is not used with regard to just a general awareness of things – to what psychologists call 'breadth of field awareness'. It refers to the process of singling out, when one's attention focuses on to just one thing.

It's as though when we perceive things in general we are in some sense passive, and what we register in this way is *vipāka*. We are born with senses as a result of karma, and the sense organs themselves are therefore *vipākas*, as are the experiences conveyed by those sense organs in the form of general perceptions. The general field of potential sense-objects that surrounds us at any given moment – our world – represents the fruit of previous karma. But once one starts singling out (and this is a conclusion of my own, not one to be found in the Abhidharma as far as I know) then some kind of motivation necessarily comes into play. This is the first stirring, as it were, of fresh karma.

So here again we see that mind is an activity. The mind that is associated with mental events is not a passive, mirror-like reflection of what is there. It is not, as the English philosopher John Locke has it, a *tabula rasa*, a blank wax tablet upon which objects of perception impress themselves. It is never like this; there is always a bit of movement here and there until our attention is seized by a particular object.

It is the adverting of the mind to a particular object that leads directly to what the Theravāda terms the *javana*,[68] the stage of volition; and it is at the *javana* stage of the perceptual process that karma is produced. Every process of perception includes these two elements: a stage of turning towards a particular object and, in dependence upon this, the *javana* at which volition or karma enters in. Where that singling out process ends and karma proper (in the sense of *javana*) begins it would be hard to say.

MENTAL EVENTS

They are whatever correspond to the mind.[69]
Pañcaskandhaprakaraṇa

So mental events are whatever are in accordance with the general nature of the mind. In a way, they share that general nature. As the mind is, so are the mental events.

No list of mental events can be exhaustive; nor are the boundary lines between them always fixed. Any classification of them is solely to provide a tool for spiritual practice, allowing one to give provisional labels to one's experience, and thereby enabling oneself to transform one's life. This needs constantly to be borne in mind. As we have seen, the Sarvāstivādins number 46 mental events, while the Theravādins distinguish 52; but the Yogācārins, whose classification we will be following here, identify 51 different mental events, divided into six categories: five omnipresent mental events, five object-determining mental events, eleven positive mental events, six basic emotions (primary negative mental events), twenty proximate emotions (secondary negative mental events), and four variable mental events.[70] It is with the nature of these mental events that the second part of our commentary will be concerned. I will be referring to them according to Guenther's translations from the Tibetan, as well as adding alternative translations where appropriate. I will use the Sanskrit terms, not the Tibetan as in Guenther's text, simply because the main authority the Tibetan author cites for his definition of each mental event is Asaṅga's *Abhidharmasamuccaya*, which is written in Sanskrit.

5

THE PERCEPTUAL SITUATION

LOOSELY SPEAKING, in every situation in which the mind not only
perceives an object but, as it were, moves towards it, these five mental
events are present. To be more accurate, one could say that the presence of the five omnipresent (*sarvatraga*) mental events is implicit in
the very definition of what it means to experience an object. It's not
that when one experiences an object these mental events are present.
It's the other way round; when these mental events are present, one
is experiencing an object.

We must go further: it cannot be asserted that there is an object there
at all, nor a subject (oneself) to perceive it. All we can say is that a sort
of network of these five mental events constitutes a perceptual situation within which there is a subjective content and an objective
content. This is the case at all mundane levels of experience, including
the higher states of *dhyāna*.

The five omnipresent mental events are: feeling (*vedanā*), recognition
or identification (*saṁjñā*), directionality of mind (*cetanā*), contact
(*spārśa*), and what Guenther calls 'egocentric demanding' (*manaskāra*),
also translated as 'mental engagement' or 'attention'. So there is some
overlap between the Abhidharma's analysis and earlier Buddhist
classifications. Well, given that the entire Buddhist tradition is in

agreement that the whole of mundane, compounded existence can be analysed into the five *skandhas*, there would have to be some correspondences.

From the Abhidharma's perspective, *rūpa* (form) is the objective content of the perceptual situation, which would leave the other four *skandhas* as constituting its subjective content. *Vijñāna* (consciousness), as we have seen, corresponds to mind; the illustration for the five *skandhas* on the Tibetan Wheel of Life is a boat with four passengers and a fifth person – representing *vijñāna* – steering.

Among the omnipresent mental events we encounter two more of the five *skandhas* – *vedanā* (feeling) and *saṁjñā* (recognition), as well as *cetanā* (directionality of mind), which is roughly synonymous with *saṁskāra* (volition), the fifth *skandha*. To add to these three omnipresent mental events we have *spārśa* (contact), which also features as one of the twelve links of the Wheel of Life, and *manaskāra* ('egocentric demanding').

1. FEELING-TONE (*VEDANĀ*)

Yeshe Gyaltsen begins his discussion of 'feeling-tone' with a quotation from the *Abhidharmasamuccaya*:

> What is the absolutely specific characteristic of feeling? It is to experience. That is to say, in any experience, what we experience is the individual maturation of any positive or negative action as its final result.[71]

The second part of this description indicates that *vedanā* is the feeling-tone of our experience of *vipāka*, which is what we experience as the result of karma. That is, whatever one experiences, pleasant, painful, or neutral, represents – directly or indirectly – the maturation or result of skilful or unskilful action, whether of body, speech, or mind. In short, *vedanā* constitutes the final result of action.

The first part of the *Abhidharmasamuccaya*'s definition of *vedanā* is less helpful; 'It is to experience' is something of a tautology. But is it really possible to define feeling? We all know what feeling (as distinct from thought) is, but it would be impossible to communicate what feeling is like to someone who had never experienced it. Feeling cannot be described in terms of something else.

Conceptual terms can be used to communicate feelings in the sense that one can use concepts to indicate to someone something in their experience which is analogous to something one has experienced oneself. But it is impossible to communicate the feeling itself. My feeling is mine and your feeling is yours. All one can say is that one experiences the same *kind* of feeling that someone else experiences. If you stick a pin in yourself you feel something and perhaps you say 'ouch'; if you stick a pin into someone else and they make the sort of sound you made, you can infer that they have had a feeling of the kind that you had. You don't directly perceive their feeling, nor do they directly perceive yours.

It is important to distinguish feeling from emotion, though of course they are connected. One could say that feeling is the raw material out of which emotion is produced. The seventeenth century Dutch philosopher Spinoza discusses this. If one has a feeling of pleasure, he says, and that feeling is accompanied by the idea of the external cause of the pleasure, then one feels an emotion of love towards the cause of that pleasure. If one has a feeling of pain and that feeling is accompanied by the idea of the cause of that pain, then one feels hatred towards the cause of the pain.[72]

The point to be emphasized with regard to emotions is that they are not produced automatically. We actively manufacture them out of the raw material of our feelings; they are actions of the mind. If one has a painful experience, one can choose whether or not to manufacture hatred out of it. And if one chooses to do so, one has performed another unskilful karma which will make one liable to further painful sensations in the future.

As well as being one of the five *skandhas*, *vedanā* is one of the links of the chain of conditionality that binds us to the Wheel of Life from one life to the next. The crucial link or *nidāna*, the one that keeps the whole cycle of birth and death going, is the one following *vedanā*: *tṛṣṇā* or 'craving'. While *vedanā* is something that happens to us, *tṛṣṇā* is something we do. We are presented with feelings, but what we do with those feelings – whether we manufacture positive emotions or negative ones out of them – is our own choice. Feeling is passive, but emotion (as the word itself suggests) is active.

It is the possibility of responding creatively to our experience that gives us the opportunity of coming off the Wheel of Life. For example, in the meditation practice called the *mettā bhāvanā*, one develops a response of loving kindness towards oneself and towards a good friend, and one then brings that naturally positive response to bear upon someone one ordinarily has little regard for, either positive or negative. In this way one starts to shift one's habitual reaction to other people in a more positive direction. One begins to develop genuine *mettā*, a response of warmth and care which is not simply the product of attachment.

When the mind is sufficiently imbued with *mettā*, even when one introduces the thought of someone one dislikes, this thought will not be unpleasant, even though it would normally give rise to an unpleasant feeling and therefore to hatred. So one can then proceed at least comparatively easily to develop *mettā* even towards this person. Eventually, when one attains real insight into the true nature of things, it becomes impossible for an unskilful mental state to arise in dependence upon a painful feeling.

Feeling is a conditioned phenomenon. It arises in dependence upon conditions and disappears when those conditions are removed. This has the important corollary that we can create or abrogate our own feelings by manipulating our impressions. If, for example, one feels depressed, one may know from experience that a day in the country will put one in a much more positive mood, that pleasurable feelings will arise in dependence upon some space and fresh air. So our feelings are to some extent under our control.

However, the feelings that arise as a direct result of karma are not altogether under our control. Unless circumstances are such that we are able to produce a counteractive karma we may simply have to bear that particular *vipāka*. If one takes adequate measures to change the circumstances that appear to be giving rise to one's discomfort and those measures fail to work, it may make sense to conclude that a particular unpleasant feeling is a direct result of karma.

Feeling is classified in several different ways: according to whether it is pleasant, unpleasant, or indifferent; according to whether it is a physical or a mental feeling; according to whether it is subjectivistic or transpersonal; according to which sense organ is involved; and, finally, according to whether it sustains attachment to or disentanglement from mundane existence.

First, Yeshe Gyaltsen tackles the question of pleasant, unpleasant, and indifferent feelings:

> 'Pleasant' is that which one would like to feel again (when the original feeling is over). 'Unpleasant' is what one would like to get rid of when it is present. 'Indifferent' is where neither of these two desires occur.[73]
>
> Pañcaskandhaprakaraṇa

Striking as this statement is, things are not, of course, as simple as this. The myriad degrees of pleasure (*sukha*) and pain (*duḥkha*) we are subject to elicit more than just commensurate degrees of one and the same response. Different degrees of pleasant feelings elicit responses that range from 'Wouldn't it be nice if that happened again' to 'Let me make sure that happens again as soon as possible' and even to 'I must have another of these right now even though I haven't finished the first one yet.'

However, it is true that by and large the desire to repeat a pleasant experience takes place after the event whereas with unpleasant feelings there is generally no question of waiting until the unpleasant feeling is over and then thinking 'Well, I wouldn't want that to happen again': one wants to be rid of it as soon as it starts. But again, our response to unpleasant experiences is not quite as straightforward as this. There are experiences that may be more troublesome to get rid of than to endure, so that one doesn't really think of getting rid of them (in which case, although they might feel unpleasant, they count as 'indifferent feelings' according to the criteria employed here); and at the other end of the scale there are feelings that are so unpleasant that, in order to be rid of them, one is prepared to put up with a lot of other disagreeable feelings – which again would have to be classed here as indifferent feelings.

Of course, in the end we want to be rid even of pleasant feelings. The physical organism has its limitations. If one has had a good meal, for example, one doesn't want to repeat the experience immediately. At more refined levels of sense experience, including some states of meditative concentration, one can sustain pleasant feelings for longer: one can perhaps enjoy listening to music, for example, for hours at a time. But a pleasant experience, at whatever level of refinement, if prolonged to the point where the psycho-physical organism can no longer sustain it (if only because it needs to sleep), will gradually diminish in intensity and may even turn into an unpleasant experience.

This can also happen the other way round: one can get used to some unpleasant experiences to the point that one feels quite indifferent to them. Not just indifferent: with acquired tastes – tea, wine, modern art, and unfamiliar music, for example – very unpleasant experiences can subsequently change into very pleasant ones. Even extreme pain does not stay the same, and may, in some circumstances, change into pleasure. And in some very stressful situations, one can experience such a rapid alternation of pain and pleasure that it is hard to know which is which. People who have experienced the break-up of a sexual relationship sometimes say that there is an intense sense of loss, but at the same time there is an equally intense sense of relief at being free of all the insecurity and conflicts that the relationship entailed. In some circumstances at least, it is as if one is a switch flicking madly back and forth, from joy to sorrow and back again in a moment. At such times it is possible to see that pleasure and pain are, in a sense, the same thing. A change in attitude, and the one becomes the other. The switch is oneself and the flick is the change of attitude.

So pleasure and pain are both in the end rather elusive. Pleasure is here defined as that which one wants to feel again, and it is that very wanting to feel it again which changes the pleasure into pain. As far as we are concerned, the problem usually seems to be how to get hold of whatever it is that provides the pleasant feeling, but it isn't really. But – as we realize if we examine our experience closely – it is wanting to get hold of the pleasure in the first place that starts to vitiate the very pleasure we crave. The more we grasp hold of pleasure, the more we find that what we are holding on to is pain. The solution to the paradox is to let go of pleasure as it comes to you:

> He who binds to himself a joy
> Does the winged life destroy
> But he who kisses the joy as it flies
> Lives in Eternity's sunrise.[74]

The ancient Greek philosopher Epicurus maintained that the pursuit of pleasure was the only rational purpose in life – in his conception, the highest pleasures being those of the mind: art, friendship, conversation, and so on.[75] It seems quite an attractive idea, but it doesn't work, because one becomes subject to the law of diminishing returns. If one devotes oneself to pleasure one ends up with nothing to enjoy, because in the end pleasure is really a by-product of something else. Certain things give us pleasure, but it is self-defeating to get involved in situations simply on account of the pleasure – even the refined pleasure – that they give us, regardless of any other value or interest they may have. The world may provide all sorts of conditions and supports for the attainment of satisfaction of one kind and another, but the real source of satisfaction is within oneself. Our own happiness depends on our overall attitude towards things, and what we ourselves do.

With awareness it is possible to enjoy pleasant feelings without allowing craving to arise. If one is sufficiently mindful while, say, eating good food, so that the pleasant feeling does not give rise to a desire to repeat that experience, then one will not be creating fresh karma. So being mindful does not involve starving out pleasure. It *is* possible, if one is mindful enough, to enjoy an experience without wanting it to continue or be repeated. Clearly one is on a knife-edge here and one has to find one's balance as one may – but becoming non-attached certainly does not mean losing one's feelings.

Feeling is, after all, an omnipresent mental event. If one is going to experience anything at all, there has to be feeling of some kind in that experience. And a certain amount of pleasure acts as a tonic for the system. One can enjoy the pleasure of the sunshine, the atmosphere of the early morning, or a walk in the forest, and feel a sense of openness, expansion, and liberation that goes beyond pleasure, in the ordinary sense at least. But one shouldn't just be trying to squeeze pleasure out of the situation; that would be counter-productive. And experience teaches us to keep mindfully aloof from situations in which pleasure is sooner or later connected with painful or unskilful mental states.

With pain, the same thing applies in reverse: the desire to be rid of pain actually contributes to it. If one is mindful of this fact, developing sufficient equanimity so that one no longer contributes to the pain in this way, one is also no longer creating karma (which doesn't necessarily mean that the pain goes away).

As for indifferent or neutral feelings, there is the possibility of some confusion here. The word being translated as 'indifferent' or 'neutral' is *upekṣā*, but *upekṣā* has a variety of meanings. The same word is used to describe the culminating phase of the seven factors of Enlightenment, in which context it can be translated as 'non-attachment', 'equanimity', or even 'the higher indifference'; and we will also be discussing *upekṣā* as a positive mental event (see page 148), in which context it is considered as a factor of meditation.

There is a great difference between *upekṣā* as an aspect of the feeling-tone that accompanies sense experience – Lama Govinda terms it 'hedonic indifference'[76] – and *upekṣā* as a factor of Enlightenment or a positive mental event. 'Hedonic indifference' is a sense experience that is neither particularly pleasant nor particularly unpleasant, that one is bothered neither to prolong nor to get rid of. With *upekṣā* in the more positive sense, one is likewise concerned neither to prolong nor to get rid of the feelings one experiences, but this is not because the feelings themselves are neither pleasant nor unpleasant. That kind of *upekṣā* is not determined by sense experience at all. Pleasure and pain, however intense, do not impinge upon it.

Furthermore, it is not arrived at by getting rid of all pleasant and painful feelings. In fact, it arises out of the development of pleasant feeling – or rather, it arises as the culmination of the conscious development of positive emotion that has pleasant feeling as its fruit. *Upekṣā* in this sense is the mind poised in a collected and deeply happy state that is unaffected by pleasure and pain. As a positive mental event it represents the full development of positive emotion, a deep emotional stability that is connected with the development of the fourth *dhyāna*. And as the culminating factor of the seven factors of Enlightenment, one could even say that it is synonymous with Enlightenment itself.

This is not, obviously, what is meant by *upekṣā* as a kind of feeling-tone. It is important to be clear on this point; indeed, perhaps the most useful thing to be said about this third category of *vedanā* is that it represents the sort of feelings which can easily be mis-identified in various ways. Whether one can in fact classify indifferent or neutral feelings as a properly separate category on a par with pleasant feelings and painful feelings is of course questionable. All experience, all thought, is feeling-toned, even emotionally-toned. If pleasant feelings are those one wants to have repeated and unpleasant feelings are those one wants to be rid of, then a third category has to be introduced to represent feelings that fail to elicit either of these responses. But this suggests that indifferent feelings are either simply not intense enough to qualify as pleasant or unpleasant, or else consist in a rather complicated mix of pleasure and pain so that the two feelings cancel each other out and leave one at an emotional standstill. This kind of state is certainly not to be thought of as non-attachment – although it often is.

Another class of indifferent feeling that can be confused with non-attachment could be termed 'alienation'. This is a superficial, even superimposed, indifference where one doesn't allow oneself fully to experience a strong feeling or emotion because it doesn't fit in with the idea one has of oneself. If one were to acknowledge that one experienced such a feeling, one might have to acknowledge also that one was, for example, not as spiritually developed as one would like to think. So the kind of feeling that does not go with one's ideal picture of oneself gets locked away, and because this happens unconsciously, the energy caught up in that feeling gets locked away as well. Alienation from feeling and emotion is thus also alienation from energy. Though it is not an obviously strong feeling it is, in a way, much more dreadful than straightforwardly unpleasant feelings. The unpleasant or unacceptable feeling has not gone away; it is still there and still wielding its influence, but – being unconscious of its real nature – one is unable to do anything about it.

These three categories of feeling (pleasant, unpleasant, and indifferent) are further divided in terms of whether they are physical or mental. As far as physical feelings are concerned, Yeshe Gyaltsen chooses to illustrate the operation of the visual faculty, and by extension all the other physical sense faculties, with a quotation from Āryadeva's *Catuḥśataka* which offers an analogy with the faculty of touch:

Darkness is everywhere just as the skin covers the whole body.[77]

We inhabit a realm of sense perception called the skin, within which we experience particular physical feelings pertaining to the sense of touch when we come into contact with objects impinging on that particular realm of sense perception. Similarly, the realm of eye perception is the whole visual field; and a physical feeling pertaining to the sense of sight is whatever is experienced visually with regard to any object within that visual field. Āryadeva's usage of 'darkness' is somewhat obscure, but we can perhaps take it to mean the potential for light and visibility. 'Darkness is everywhere' in the sense that we are surrounded by a seamless visual field like a skin, which extends wherever the eye perceives. A visual feeling can presumably relate to the whole of this visual field or to any part of it.

Visual consciousness arises in dependence on the interaction of subject with object, of eye with visual form. This meeting of subject and object provides the field of operations, so to speak, where physical feeling takes place, whether that feeling be touch, sight, sound, smell, or taste. It is a particularly positive way of regarding our physical and sensory interaction with the world because it proposes not so much that objects are 'out there' as that we ourselves are 'out there'. The suggestion is that we need not think of our experience as wholly taking place within our fleshly envelope, that we have other, different kinds of sensory 'skin', so to speak. This enables us to realize a closer involvement with the objective world, carrying our experience of our subjective world beyond the crude confines of the flesh. It helps us to see that what we think of as object is, in fact, subject, or at least an extension of what we think of as subject. In short, it helps to break down the hard and fast distinction we maintain between subject and object.

Feelings may further be categorized as being either subjectivistic or transpersonal. This classification distinguishes between what we are all able to recognize as feeling, and a kind of feeling which is outside commonly accepted notions of what feelings are. 'Transpersonal' feelings do not include a sense of possession; they are not felt as one's own because they are felt where there is no idea of a fixed, unchanging self. They are in some way equivalent to 'mind as such', the suggestion being that mind as such has a sort of feeling tone or feeling value. In other words, there can apparently be feelings around without there being anyone around whose feelings they are.

But can we relate this to anything in our own experience? It's rather like picking up the atmosphere of a place, where one feels something that is not one's own, making contact with feelings that one has not produced oneself. But the idea of transpersonal feelings goes further than this. Perhaps one could say that one gets a sense of it in the *mettā bhāvanā* meditation practice, the development of loving kindness. In the final stage of this practice one develops – or rather, one makes contact with – an 'impersonal *mettā*', a positive emotion that one has not actually produced, that is not a personal feeling.[78] It's like a stream or current of something out there which one is able to channel through oneself. This isn't quite the same as the profundity of feeling that accompanies mind as such, but perhaps it gives us a clue as to what is meant by 'transpersonal feeling'.

One might still wonder, though, what on earth a transpersonal unpleasant feeling might be. This would be an unpleasant feeling experienced by an Arhant or even a Buddha as a result of unskilful actions committed prior to attaining Enlightenment. It is possible to have quite different feelings occurring at different levels at the same time. One can, at the same time as one stubs one's toe or traps one's finger in the car door, be overjoyed by some other event. Physical pain does not necessarily preclude joy in the mind. But in the case of the Arhant who experiences the inner bliss that arises out of being free from the delusion of an ego, any headache he experiences is also unconnected with an ego. It is just there: it could be anybody's headache. It certainly does not diminish that inner bliss.

Conversely – to take the Mahāyānist viewpoint – just as the Arhant's suffering is not experienced as his own personal suffering, so the Bodhisattva experiences the suffering of the world as if it were his or her own suffering. Where there is no distinction between subject and object there is no distinction between one's own suffering and that of other people. At the same time, there is no diminution of the Bodhisattva's own inner bliss. The result is, in Tennyson's words, 'painless sympathy with pain'.[79]

The important point to take from this particular classification of feeling is that from the spiritual point of view we are trying to realize the experience of non-self rather than the experience of pleasant feelings. In a sense, the experience of non-self is pleasant – but only in a sense. One can have that experience of non-self around any combination of pleasant, unpleasant, and neutral feelings; it doesn't matter. Whether those feelings are one's own or other people's doesn't matter either. One will try to get rid of the unpleasant ones and cultivate the pleasant ones, but whether one succeeds or fails doesn't make any difference to one's fundamental experience of non-selfhood – which in another sense, or on another level, has its own very refined positive feeling value.

Feeling is further classified according to which particular sense organ is involved in giving rise to the feeling by making contact with its object. In this context the mind itself counts as a sense faculty (associated, of course, with mental feelings). Finally, feeling is classified according to whether it sustains attachment to, or disentanglement from, mundane experience. Yeshe Gyaltsen terms these 'a sustaining feeling of addiction' and 'a sustaining feeling of realization'. He goes on to say:

> The sustaining feeling of addiction occurs on the level of desiring sensuous things of this world. The sustaining feeling of realization is to turn away from being addicted to these things and occurs on the level of ... the first meditative stage.

> This division into two kinds of feelings is made here for the purpose of knowing how the strength of feeling itself may ... bring to light an existing desire or bring about detachment from this addiction through ... meditative concentration. But if one wants to know this more deeply, one should look up the *Abhidharmakośa*, the *Abhidharma-samuccaya*, and also the *byang-chub lam-rim* in order to prevent the three feelings of pleasure, pain, and indifference from becoming the cause of the three poisons.[80]

The three poisons are ignorance, craving, and hatred. In the iconography of the Tibetan Wheel of Life they are represented by the pig, the cock, and the snake which circle endlessly at the very hub of the wheel. These three poisons arise from feelings of indifference, pleasure, and pain when these feelings lead to an addictive response – that is, attachment – 'on the level of desiring sensuous things of this world'. This 'level' is more literally a 'realm': it is the *kāmaloka*, the realm of sensuous desire, which is where we are when the mind is functioning in the ordinary way. The *kāmaloka* is what we might call the objective correlative of the experience of sensuous desire, just as the *rūpaloka*, the realm of form (or of archetypal form, as it is sometimes translated), is the objective correlative of the meditative experience. The 'experience' and the 'realm' are the same thing seen from different perspectives – subjective or objective. Like the term Pure Land, the idea of a realm need not be taken in a purely literal sense, but neither can it be simply reduced to a subjective experience.

A feeling of addiction is what sustains our existence on the *kāmaloka*. And this addiction is not just to pleasant feelings; it is the *strength* of our feelings – whether of pleasure or pain or dull indifference – that sustains our attachment. We cannot enjoy something intensely, flinging ourselves ravenously at it and really wallowing in it, without feeling intense craving. We cannot wallow in our own pain without indulging a corresponding degree of hatred. And we cannot sink into dull indifference without sinking into ignorance.

However, strength of feeling does not necessarily reinforce attachment. Once the feeling exists, it can go in either of two directions. It can deepen our involvement in the *kāmaloka*, in which case it is 'a sustaining feeling of addiction'. On the other hand it can be led into the *rūpaloka*, in which case it is 'a sustaining feeling of realization'.

This category is introduced, as Yeshe Gyaltsen says, because a distinction needs to be drawn between a feeling that is associated with an experience of the *kāmaloka* and a feeling – which may not otherwise be any different – experienced by someone who is developing feelings appropriate to the *rūpaloka*. One can't really turn away from the grosser pleasures of the senses unless one has had some taste of the pleasures of meditative concentration. One can hold oneself off from sense pleasures by force of will as a disciplinary measure, but in the end one has to find something better; and until one has had some experience of meditative pleasure one doesn't have anything better (unless one finds it in the realm of aesthetic experience).

If one applies oneself to meditation, one will relish ordinary pleasant feelings less, at least as long as one can sustain some degree of meditative absorption. For example, one would experience a good meal as pleasant, but only at a certain level. In comparison with the pleasure of the *rūpaloka* it would, in a sense, not be a pleasure at all. Experienced in this way such a feeling would be a 'sustaining feeling of realization' rather than a 'sustaining feeling of addiction'.

2. RECOGNITION (OR CONCEPTUALIZATION) (SAMJÑĀ)

It is to know by association.[81]

Abhidharmasamuccaya

This is *samjñā*, the second omnipresent mental event. The term is often translated as 'perception', but in fact it refers to a certain phase within the process of perception, which involves an act of cognition, a sort of mental labelling, that arises in dependence upon sense perception of an object. So *samjñā* is perception, but perception of a particular kind. It is not perception *of* something, but perception that something is this or that, which is quite a different matter. One perceives the characteristics of an object, and then makes a judgement based on pre-existing conceptions, labels, or names as to what those characteristics represent. So *samjñā* may be defined as 'judgemental perception' or simply 'apperception'. Its two aspects can be described thus:

a. Naming: Directly perceiving and simply naming the characteristics of an object without fitting those perceptions to a pre-existing proposition.

b. Defining: Identifying those characteristics that define or specify the object, and enable one to make a proposition as to what it is.

According to Yeshe Gyaltsen, 'The former deals with the specific characteristic of an apparent object in a conceptless perception and the latter deals with the specific characteristic of an apparent object in a judgemental perception.'[82] On the one hand one perceives and recognizes characteristics possessed by an object; on the other, one perceives characteristics that the object shares – or does not share – with certain other objects. This second aspect is to do with definition in the sense of binding a thing to its correct genus and species (logically rather than biologically speaking). When one sees a chair or a leopard and recognizes what it is because one has seen one before, or identifies it from one's knowledge of domestic furniture or natural history, one is recognizing or identifying the 'specific characteristics of an apparent object in a judgemental perception'. One has seen the characteristics of the object and they correspond with an abstract, already labelled, idea in one's mind.

However, when in the Middle Ages Europeans saw an animal that looked like a cross between a lion and a panther and they called it a leo(*lion*)pard(*panther*), they were simply naming characteristics without having a pre-existing idea of the object perceived. Although the animal had some recognizable qualities, it did not conform to any pre-existing proposition in the mind by which they could recognize or identify it. Similarly, when one identifies a colour, there is no proposition to be applied to the perception.

It wouldn't be quite correct, though, to describe this sort of conceptualization as a conceptless perception as opposed to a judgemental perception. Perceived characteristics of whatever kind are of course concepts, and identifying them requires judgement. The difference is that in the one case one is just labelling characteristics, while in the other one is labelling characteristics by which one is able to identify or recognize what something is. In both categories of *saṁjñā* one is dealing with concepts and making judgments; the difference is in the kind of mental activity involved.

If we attempt to describe how *saṁjñā* takes place, we need to bear in mind Dr Guenther's careful terminology in order to avoid conveying an assumption that there is necessarily an ontological, ultimately real object that corresponds in some way with the epistemological object, the object we know about. Hence the term 'apparent object'. The way Guenther puts it, where there is a perceptual situation, a subjective constituent that we call the mind perceives an objective constituent that we call the object. So, you understand the proposition 'This is a leopard'; you know what it means. Then within the perceptual situation there is an objective constituent with certain qualities, and you, the subjective constituent, proceed to apply your proposition to this object. But those qualities belong to the objective constituent of the perceptual situation, not necessarily to an objectively existent object. And the same thing goes for you, the perceiver: you cannot infer from the fact that the perceptual situation has a subjective constituent that this refers to an objectively existent subject. What we conceive to be the case is not necessarily the same as what is really the case.

The four bases for saṁjñā
We have already been introduced to these in effect, but Yeshe Gyaltsen makes things clear with a list, which can be summarized thus:

a. What is perceived in immediate sense perception.

b. Trustworthy information as to what an object is.

c. Recognizing the characteristics of an object.

d. Understanding a proposition in such a way as to be able to apply it appropriately to a particular object.[83]

The six forms of sense base for saṁjñā
As *saṁjñā* arises on the basis of sense perception, it may be classified according to which of the six senses is involved in making contact with the object. You name or recognize or identify something from seeing, hearing, smelling, tasting, touching, or thinking it. In the case of the last of these – which Guenther terms ideational perception – the object of perception is of course thought itself of some kind: you define or identify or recognize a thought; 'Ah, that's the same thought I had last week', or 'I had that same thought in my dream.'

Levels of saṁjñā
Yeshe Gyaltsen goes on to list six 'levels' of identification, depending on the state of consciousness in which the object is perceived. First there's the level of conceptual understanding involved in *saṁjñā*. This has three strata: identification that accurately applies names to objects, identification that includes a reflection on the impermanence of the object, and identification that clarifies one's insight into the impermanence of the object. These three correspond to the 'three levels of wisdom': listening, reflecting, meditating.

Then there's a corresponding level of conceptual *mis*understanding involved in *saṁjñā*: that is, three bands of false identification corresponding to those of conceptual understanding.

Thirdly, there is limited *saṁjñā*: identification taking place on the level of the *kāmaloka*, the realm of sense desire, which is our normal, everyday experience. Here, one's identification has a range limited to that of the five senses and the ordinary mind.

Fourthly we have *saṁjñā* involving an aesthetic perspective; and fifthly, identification involving an infinite or unlimited viewpoint.

Sixthly, there is identification 'which is nothing whatsoever ... the idea of an experience which one would objectify as nothing'.[84]

So the field of one's identification or conceptualization progressively broadens out as one steps back from the narrow viewpoint of the *kāmaloka*. Once one has taken this step, one is able first to look at things from the aesthetic perspective, which involves a refinement and intensification of sensory perception and a condition of appreciative awareness, developing into a state of meditative concentration or *dhyāna*. The word 'aesthetic' has quite a broad range of connotations in English, but in this context the level of aesthetic perception could be said to comprise the *rūpa dhyānas*, the levels of meditative absorption corresponding to the plane of archetypal form.

On the basis of the fourth *rūpa dhyāna*, the four *arūpa* or formless dhyānas may be developed. The infinite viewpoint mentioned here would appear to refer to the first two of these *arūpa dhyānas*, the sphere of infinite space and the sphere of infinite consciousness. It would then be an obvious step to take 'identification of an experience which one would identify as nothing' as referring to the third *arūpa dhyāna*, the sphere of no-thing-ness, in which one does not discriminate one thing from another. Whether it refers as well to the fourth *arūpa dhyāna*, the sphere of neither perception nor non-perception, it is hard to say. It may be that there is no exact correspondence here. Indeed, it may well be that the infinite viewpoint refers to the *arūpa dhyānas* generally, and that the sixth level of identification refers to an experience beyond them. Guenther habitually translates *śūnyatā* as 'nothing' or 'nothingness', so it is perhaps justifiable to assume that 'the idea of an experience which we would objectify as nothing' refers to the transcendental experience of *śūnyatā*.

At this point we have to address something of a conundrum. *Saṁjñā* is presented here as an omnipresent mental event, which implies that it is present in all states of consciousness. But this seems to contradict the teaching of the five meditation factors outlined by Buddhist tradition. In his *Visuddhimagga*, Buddhaghosa lists these as applied thought, sustained thought, rapture, bliss, and concentration.[85] All these factors need to be present if one is to enter into meditation in the full sense of the development of states of higher consciousness (the *dhyānas*). But according to tradition, as one progresses through the *dhyānas* these factors cease to be part of one's experience. So, when one moves from the first to the second *dhyāna*, the first two factors – applied thought (*vitarka*) and sustained thought (*vicāra*), sometimes translated as 'apprehension of an object' and 'investigation of an object' are no longer present. Furthermore, 'apprehension and investigation of an object' sounds more or less synonymous with *saṁjñā*. Does this mean that if *vitarka* and *vicāra* are no longer present, *saṁjñā* is not after all an omnipresent mental event?

To address this question, it would seem reasonable to assume that there *is* a form of identification in the higher *dhyānas*, but that it is too subtle and refined to come within the definition of *vitarka* and *vicāra*, which represent a comparatively coarse kind of mental functioning.

It's as well not to take the notion of identification in too crude a sense. Perhaps *saṁjñā* is capable of degrees of refinement that are difficult for us to conceive of. One may not, upon entering the third *dhyāna*, actually say to oneself 'bliss, bliss', as do monks recorded in the Pāli suttas, but one is certainly able to identify one's experience as being blissful. Otherwise, how would one know afterwards what one had experienced? There must be some subtle thread of identification connecting one's *dhyāna* experience with one's everyday conceptualizing mind.

One must assume that the same goes for deep sleep. It seems that when one emerges from a state of higher consciousness or from sleep, one is able to haul back an impression of what was going on in that state which enables one to know that one was in *dhyāna* or asleep. If one has an experience of *dhyāna* which one never had before, one may, if one has a book on meditation, be able to say 'Ah, the experience I've had corresponds to the level of *dhyāna* described on page 64,' say.

For a further perspective on *saṁjñā* we can consider the sequence of twelve positive links that describe the spiritual path as it spirals away from the Wheel of Life towards Enlightenment. This positive spiral is mentioned in the Pāli Canon but on the whole it is an aspect of the teaching that has been much neglected.[86] It starts from the point at which, rather than allowing feeling to turn into craving or aversion, one takes what could be called the spiritual initiative, recognizing that one's desires cannot be fulfilled in the mundane sphere. Out of this experience of unsatisfactoriness arises faith, in dependence upon which joy, rapture, calm, bliss, and concentration successively arise. On the basis of concentration arises knowledge and vision of things as they really are – which we can call Insight, for short.

The arising of Insight – the eighth link – is the beginning of the transcendental part of the spiral; once one has attained it, one has built up an unstoppable momentum towards Enlightenment. Then follow the stages called withdrawal, disentanglement, and freedom. (I am, of course, merely sketching the outline of a process about which much can be said.) From the point of view of understanding *saṁjñā*, the interesting link is the last one, which is synonymous with Enlightenment itself. It is called the knowledge of the destruction of the *āsravas* – that is, one recognizes that craving for sensuous pleasure, craving for existence, and ignorance, have been destroyed.

But this attainment certainly does not involve identification in the sense of *saṁjñā*. The Sanskrit term for it is *āsravakṣayajñāna*. *Jñāna* is usually translated as 'knowledge' but in this context it's more like an instantaneous and direct awareness: you just see. It's not that a quick mental reckoning takes place and you realize 'Ah! the *āsravas* aren't there any longer. Excellent!' You simply see the empty space, so to speak, where the *āsravas* were. This recognition is not *saṁjñā*. The point is that *saṁjñā* is an aspect of all *mundane* experience, not transcendental experience.

Incidentally, what happens cognitively when one perceives the non-existence of something is exhaustively discussed in Indian logic. In the period after the demise of Buddhism in India the adherents of the ancient Nyāya School of Indian – mainly Bengali – logic were considerably exercised over questions about absences and their ontological status. For example, what exactly is the object of one's cognition when that object is the absence of, say, a pot? It can't be the pot, because it isn't there. But how can one recognize a 'not-pot'?[87]

In the Buddhist tradition the Enlightenment experience is often described in negative terms: as an absence of the *āsravas*, say, or an experience of *śūnyatā* (emptiness), which is often described as the absence of inherent existence/self-nature (*svabhāva*) of entities. Such expressions help to minimize the possibility of mistaking Enlightenment for some kind of conceptual perception. It is in the very nature of the experience that it is inconceivable: you don't know what you have experienced in the way you do when you have experienced *dhyāna*, say.

However, we can still refer to the Enlightenment experience in conceptual terms. If you were to ask the Buddha 'What is your experience?' and he said 'It is *śūnyatā*,' he would have communicated at least something of the nature of the experience of Enlightenment by means of conceptualization or identification. Thus while the 'experience which one would objectify as nothing' remains ineffable, the *idea* of that experience comes within the bounds of *saṁjñā*.

3. DIRECTIONALITY OF MIND (CETANĀ)

It is a mental activity that propels the mind forward.
Abhidharmasamuccaya

Just as iron cannot but be attracted by a magnet, so also the mind
cannot but be set on an object by this mental event.[88]
Yeshe Gyaltsen

The Sanskrit term for this omnipresent mental event, *cetanā*, is roughly
equivalent in meaning to two other terms: *karma* and *saṁskāra*. The
saṁskāras are one of the five *skandhas* or heaps making up the totality
of the human personality. The *saṁskāras* heap is the one which, under
the law of karma, leads to a particular rebirth; it is defined by the
commentators as *karma-cetanā*, volitional action. At the same time, the
Pāli texts say that *cetanā* equals karma.[89] Karma is that which produces
consequences in the form of pleasant or painful experiences. *Cetanā*,
one could say, is the same thing viewed from a less existential, more
psychological viewpoint.

Cetanā is sometimes translated as 'volition' or 'will', but Guenther
clearly wants to avoid giving to the term the Western philosophical
connotations that hang about the term will. In a footnote to the main
text he says that it 'refers to the total psychic energy'.[90] So whereas
volition or will refers to the sum of psychic energy available to the
conscious subject, *cetanā* is the whole mind, both conscious and unconscious, seen as a stream of psychic energy moving in a certain direction.

The idea that *cetanā* is a 'mental activity that propels the mind
forward' should not be taken too literally. It's not that there is a thing
called mind which is moving in a certain direction by means of a
faculty of volition which it operates. *Cetanā* is the pressure forward of
the whole subject towards its object, or the whole subject experienced
as psychic impetus, one could say. All the time we are moving or
turning towards an object – now this, now that. We are never just
reflecting things or being aware of things. We always have an object
in view. This is why *cetanā* is translated as 'directionality of mind'. It is
the dynamic aspect of the mind. There is a flow of energy towards
something all the time.

Of course, some of the 'objects' of our attention are people – and as
far as *they* are concerned they are not objects, but subjects. Only when
one becomes aware that other people are subjects as well as objects,
and that from their point of view one is oneself an object rather than
a subject, can true communication take place. It is all too easy to

experience *cetanā* just flowing out to people as objects, but if one is going to recognize other people as subjects, one has to realize that one is oneself the object of someone else's *cetanā*. To refuse to be an 'object' in this way (and one should be careful not to misunderstand the usage of this term) is to refuse to be in communication.

Of course, the ideal here is to transcend all questions of subject and object altogether, entering into a mysterious process of empathy in which the duality between subject and object is abrogated. Upon the attainment of Enlightenment there is no question of directionality of mind towards anything, because – in the absence of the distinction between subject and object – there is nothing there for one's mind to go towards. This is the state called the *apranihita*, the 'unbiased', one of the three liberations or three doors to Enlightenment. The point is that one has no *egoistic* motive for doing anything, so that one is utterly free to respond, out of compassion, to whatever arises. One is left with just energy – both fully conscious and spontaneous.[91] We may say, therefore, that the natural tendency of *cetanā* is to go in quite the opposite direction from Enlightenment.

Being an omnipresent mental event, *cetanā* does not come into operation solely on the initiative of the conscious mind, like volition or will. It is much broader and in a way more fundamental than volition in the ordinary sense – because even when one is not consciously moving towards an object, the mind always has an unconscious tendency to settle on this or that. *Cetanā* is a little like the idea of a life-force, except that the latter refers to a biological as well as a psychological drive.

It's possible to work out a kind of hierarchy here. If one thinks of matter in terms of energy, one can think of living beings in terms of consciousness as well as energy, and of self-conscious beings in terms of volition as well as consciousness and energy. In this sense, the whole universe can be considered as consisting of life or energy that coagulates into more or less separate forms of conscious life. It is as if the whole of life is a stream within which more concentrated currents flow.

So in building up a mental picture of the nature of the universe we should think neither in terms of mutually exclusive interlocking parts, nor of a sort of undifferentiated mass; the reality is somewhere in between. We are separate from each other and from the world, but there isn't a hard and fast division between us. What I think of as me and what you think of as you is in each case the centre of a particular coagulation of the common stream of life. It is difficult to tell where 'I' come to an end and 'you' begin. We shade into each other. It is because of this that we can have a sense – a real sense as opposed to an idea – of other forms of life.

However, in speaking of ourselves in this way, we also have to accept that our own personal coagulation can liquefy again, or disperse into a number of lumps. What one thinks of as oneself is just a tiny fraction of the limitlessly multi-dimensional nature of consciousness. It is apparently possible for one's personality to be so fragmented that when one dies the different streams of one's volitions drift off to form more than one rebirth. At the other end of the scale, it is also said to be possible for someone to be so integrated as to be able consciously to find rebirth in a number of different forms. For example, one of my own teachers, Jamyang Khyentse, was said to be one of five products of such a multiple reincarnation.

For most people, the stream connecting the different bits and pieces is sufficiently strong to keep them all together. But we need to be aware that the form we find ourselves in is a function of our volitional energies, and it is absurd to identify rigidly with that form. We are much more fluid than we appear to ourselves to be. It is therefore important to make the effort to identify imaginatively with others – for example, if one is young and one finds oneself getting impatient with an older person who can't keep up (whether physically or mentally); or if one thinks of oneself too rigidly as being British or Irish or Black or whatever.

Another idea that may help to distinguish the essential features of *cetanā* is the purely Theravādin concept of *bhavanga-sota* or 'life-stream'. This is the basic stream of existence, or becoming, underlying consciousness. It is an unconscious stream of past impressions which emerges on to a subconscious level or into full consciousness only when an external stimulus impinges upon it. According to a traditional analogy, *bhavanga* is represented by a man sound asleep under a mango tree, who wakes up only when a mango drops on his head. The external stimulus is by way of being a disturbance; *bhavanga-sota* essentially flows on independently of the conscious mind and of external stimuli.[92]

Cetanā, by contrast, is a flowing out towards external objects, and it can be both unconscious (or subconscious) and conscious. Like *bhavanga-sota*, *cetanā* goes on regardless, whether we like it or not; but whereas *bhavanga* is *karma-vipāka*, *cetanā* is karma. So we are back again to the crucial distinction between 'things that happen to us' and 'things we do'. And whereas we cannot be aware of *bhavanga*, we can be aware of the directionality of the mind, introduce some conscious guidance, and channel the mind towards skilful rather than unskilful objects.

It is popularly said that we create or produce karma by our actions, but karma actually consists in our volitional actions themselves; what we produce or create is the *result* of karma i.e. *karma-vipāka*. So it is a mistake to think that everything we are is the result of karma. The importance of *cetanā* lies in the fact that it represents that aspect of mind which is not the *result* of karma, but karma itself. We experience *karma-vipāka* in terms of feeling, but the directionality of mind, though it may be reinforced by past karma, is not itself *vipāka*, but fresh karma.

Karma is going on all the time. One might be forgiven for imagining that karma and *vipāka* alternate in some way, so that we are either creating *vipāka* or experiencing it, but in fact karma is going on even while we are experiencing its fruits. It's easy to get the idea that when we do certain things – give to a beggar, say, or steal something – that is karma, but that when we are not doing those things, karma is not going on. In fact, our whole life is karma. *We* are karma.

Of course, like *cetanā*, karma is not always conscious. Sometimes it is said that karma is what we do deliberately, but this mustn't be taken in too narrow a sense. Karmas develop their own momentum over lifetimes so that we don't always notice the general flow. Actions that start off as deliberate choices actually develop more karmic weight if they become our natural, even unconsidered, way of going on. What we usually think of as karmas are only the more noticeable ripples on the surface of the general flow of karma.

In that what makes something volitional is some degree of aware-ness, one could say that in a sense unmindfulness does not have karmic consequences. However, being unmindful confines one to a lower level of consciousness, making unmindfulness part of the gen-eral drift of unconscious tendencies which is part of volition and which *does* have karmic consequences.

Discussion of karma and its consequences of course leads to the consideration of rebirth. As we have already seen, it is quite possible to take the notion of karmic consequences seriously while retaining an agnostic stance on the subject of rebirth. But if one thinks in terms of future lives, in general terms one could say that an overall direction-ality of mind towards characteristically human acts ensures future life as an ordinary human being, while our more consciously determined actions represent more specific, more concentrated karmas which will result in certain specific situations and experiences within the general human context. We cannot stand back from karma as if we were separate from it. We are not things – we are drives. We *are* karma. And if this drive keeps up without serious modifications, we will be reborn more or less as we are now.

This is why in Buddhism so much importance is attached to the constant repetition of positive actions. If one constantly recites mantras and sūtras, if one constantly practises meditation, if one regularly performs pujas and practises generosity and kindness, if one's speech is consistently truthful, helpful, and harmonious, and if one's livelihood supports these practices, then all the time one is modifying the overall karmic flow that is one's directionality of mind or *cetanā*.

If one's directionality of mind is shifted profoundly enough, then one's future life will not necessarily be a human one. One may conceivably be reborn as a god in a 'heaven realm' – one corresponding to the level of *dhyāna* that one has habitually sustained in this life. On the other hand, if one's *cetanā* has habitually gone towards eating, drinking, and sex, and nothing but these activities, there is a chance that one will be reborn as an animal – though it would be difficult to shift one's directionality of mind as profoundly as that without dedicated effort. No doubt a few people succeed occasionally. The same must go for rebirth in any other realm apart from the human. An attitude of neurotic craving or hatred would have to be sustained constantly and intensely for years on end to ensure rebirth in the corresponding hell realm.

This question of the relative intensity of *cetanā* means that actions that are ostensibly more or less the same may have different consequences for different people. Two people may seem to be leading more or less the same kind of life, doing the same sort of things, but although the actions are the same, the *cetanā* and thus the karma may be much stronger for one of them than for the other. If what they are doing is ethically unskilful, one of them may have inherited from past positive karma a degree of pleasant *vipāka* which might reduce the intensity of the craving or hatred he or she brings to that action. On the other hand, if the same two people were performing ethically skilful actions, the one with good *vipākas* would perhaps be more prone to lose mindfulness and become over-elated, careless, or foolish, while the one with bad *vipāka* might find that adversity helped to concentrate the mind.

In short, one cannot tell from people's experience and actions precisely what is going on karmically. For example, in certain kinds of illness, especially fevers, it can happen that the mind seems to separate itself from the body, so that one becomes able to enter into quite profound reflections, and even into a state of awareness that virtually amounts to a higher state of consciousness, quite undisturbed by what is happening to the body. At the very least, a setback in life or a bout of physical suffering, if it is taken as a positive purgation or catharsis, cannot be looked upon simply as a bad thing.

So *vipāka* does not determine karma. But if one performs certain karmas this will tend to enhance one's tendency to perform them. It is as if karma can gather momentum. Hence the insistence within Tibetan Buddhism on performing various practices as many times as possible – the traditional number is 100,000 prostrations, 100,000 mantras, and so on. And hence also the importance of going on retreat: through performing only positive actions over a continuous period, and at the same time greatly reducing the opportunities for unskilful mental action, one gets into the habit of it.

Ideally, of course, one wants to sustain the weighty positive karma of *dhyāna* or meditative absorption. (This expression 'weighty' karma refers to karma, whether positive or negative, that will have a decisive effect when it comes to one's rebirth.) Mantra recitation doesn't usually constitute weighty karma inasmuch as one tends not to want to keep the mantra going as one becomes more deeply concentrated. This is not to suggest that mantra recitation is merely a concentration technique – it is a devotional practice – but as one dwells ever more deeply on the meditation deity symbolized by the mantra, the repetition of the mantra drops away. But even at the level of recitation, if one can maintain it as a regular practice it becomes habitual; and it is generally this habitual karma, the overall karmic trend of one's being, which determines one's future life. In reciting mantras, to stay with that example, one is at the very least passing one's time in a highly skilful manner.

If by the time of death one has – as is quite usual – performed no weighty karma, whether positive, like meditation, or negative, like murder, one's rebirth will be consequent upon the overall directionality of mind, upon one's habitual karma in this life. From the Abhidharma point of view, therefore, what one does habitually is regarded as of extreme importance. If one calculated how much time one spent doing one's various activities, and the intensity of one's involvement in them, one could probably work out the sort of future life one could look forward to. (Just how objective one could be about such a calculation is, of course, open to question!)

In meditation, it is volition that produces *dhyāna*, but what one actually experiences in *dhyāna* is the fruit of that volition. The weighty positive karma of *dhyāna* is not the experience, but the volition. So while *dhyāna* may correspond – as *vipāka* – to the experience of the god realms, it differs inasmuch as the gods are unable to generate fresh karma. They are in a passive state of enjoyment, reaping the rewards of what they have done in the past but accumulating no fresh karma, whether good or bad. When the karma that caused them to be reborn as gods is exhausted, they slip down to a lower level or realm, depending on what residual karma they have to their credit. It is as though they are in such a state of bliss that they are stupefied by it, unable to exert themselves even so as to prolong that state of bliss. The gods are therefore not so much in a dhyanic state as in a world to which those in the *kāmaloka* have access through *dhyāna*. As a result of their experience of higher states of consciousness in past lives they have a very fine material body, which means that all their experience is correspondingly subtle and delicate, and in this sense enjoyable, but it is not truly dhyanic.

It is a little like what happens when one takes a psychedelic drug: certain areas of the mind are temporarily paralysed or inhibited, with the result that one experiences – depending on whether one's past karma has been skilful or unskilful – a 'good trip' or a 'bad trip'. In other words, one's capacity for volition, or karma, is swamped by one's experience of *vipāka*. It is as if – without stretching this illustration beyond the level of analogy – one's capacity for creating fresh karma is suspended, thus making way for the experience of whatever *vipāka* is there to be experienced at that time. The intensity of such experience, whether good or bad, naturally provides a fertile basis for the subsequent arising of fresh karma in the form of craving or aversion once the effect of the drug wears off.

One may say that the meditational experience has in technical terms a *saṃskāra* (volitional) aspect and a *vedanā* aspect. As one enters the *dhyānas* one experiences first the one and then the other. Once one is in *dhyāna*, though, one experiences only the *vedanā* aspect. Well, one can continue to put in volitional action even while one experiences *vedanā*, and thus deepen the experience, but a point may come when one ceases to generate further positive karma. The intensity of bliss tends to submerge the other positive mental events, though they must all be there in some form or other. This is why the Buddha says of his own experience of *dhyāna* that 'pleasure did not lay hold of my mind'; he did not allow himself to be side-tracked or swamped by the pleasure of meditation.

The mind moves towards an object through sense perception (which in the case of a mental object would, of course, be thought). Like *saṁjñā*, therefore, *cetanā* may be classified according to which of the six senses is involved.

> From a broad viewpoint,
> The paths of action are said to be ten
> According to their being wholesome and unwholesome.[93]
>
> *Abhidharmakośa*

What this means is that *cetanā* is also classified in terms of the ten ethical precepts. These are to abstain from harming living beings, from taking what is not freely offered, and from sexual wrongdoing; to abstain from false, harsh, useless, and slanderous speech; and to abstain from covetousness, from animosity, and from false views.[94] Strictly speaking, there is no limit to the different operations of *cetanā*, but the ten precepts may be said to adumbrate the most significant ways in which it functions. *Cetanā* being a purely mental operation, this makes it clear that the precepts are all actions of the mind, although the first three pertain to actions of body as well as mind, and the next four pertain to actions of speech as well as mind, so that just the last three of them pertain to the mind alone.

As far as the classification of *cetanā* is concerned there are, as the above quotation from the *Abhidharmakośa* makes clear, two different sets of ways of action: wholesome and unwholesome. The quotation is also a reminder that what we more usually call vows or precepts are in fact pathways of skilful action, the ten avenues by which skilful karmas come out. Actions in the sense of karmas are movements in a certain direction, intentionalities, so the precepts could be called the ten skilful intentionalities, or even the ten creativities. They are not so much rules to observe as specific channels by which skilful karmas flow out. This is actually the sort of model put forward by the *Dhammapada*:

> Those who make channels for waters control the waters;
> Makers of arrows make the arrows straight;

Carpenters control their timber;
And the wise control their own minds.[95]

The idea is that water can either be used to irrigate and therefore nourish the crops, or it can be allowed to flood over the land and destroy everything. Similarly, the *daśakuśalakarmapathas*, the ten paths of wholesome action, represent so many channels which one opens up for the waters of one's *cetanā* to flow into. *Cetanā*, after all, is always there; one can't block it without opening another channel for it to flow through. Having said this, the analogy is not to be pressed as far as to suggest that *cetanā* works according to the laws of mechanics; it is just an analogy. But the suggestion that ethics consist in giving a certain direction to energy is a revealing one.

4. CONTACT (SPĀRŚA)

It is a determination, a transformation in the controlling power, which is in accordance with the three factors coming together. Its function is to provide a basis for feeling.[96]
Abhidharmasamuccaya

This is *spārśa*, the fourth omnipresent mental event. 'It is a determination' is a rather unhelpful choice of expression on Guenther's part. He is using the term determination in its philosophical sense of specific mode – so a determination of something is that thing existing in a certain mode. The 'controlling power' translates the term *indriya*, which literally means the ruler but is more usually rendered as sense faculty, and here refers to the six sense faculties. (*Indriya* is also often rendered as 'sense-power', which preserves the connection with 'ruler'.)

So contact is a specific mode, a particular transformation, *in* the sense faculty. This takes place in the coming together of three factors: the object, the sense faculty, and the consciousness that arises when the two come together. It is of course possible for object and sense faculty to come together without being joined by consciousness, if consciousness happens to be completely withdrawn from the sense organ in question. For example, if one is totally caught up in one's thoughts, one's eyes can be wide open without one's actually seeing anything. In this case, although the sense organ and the object have come together, contact in the sense of *spārśa* has not taken place.

So the sense faculty connects with an object, and then at least some degree of consciousness needs to be present for sense contact to take place. And when it does take place, then feeling (*vedanā*) arises. So contact provides a basis for feeling. Or – in terms of the *nidāna* chain – in dependence upon contact arises feeling. Put in the simplest terms, contact is a change that takes place in the sense faculty when that sense faculty connects with the appropriate sense object and gives rise to a certain kind of consciousness. This then makes possible the arising of feeling. There are of course six types of rapport or contact, depending on which sense faculty is involved in its operation.

To put it another way, when the sense faculty connects with an object, contact 'captures' the object; this is the modification of the sense faculty. Saying this, we must bear in mind that when we speak of all these various elements that go together to make contact happen, we are speaking not of things or entities but of relations – and not even relations between things, but simply the different terms in a relation.

With the modification of the sense faculty arises feeling, which is pleasant, unpleasant, or neutral. Then, if in place of just feeling pleasure we *take* pleasure, if we delight in the pleasant feeling, craving arises. Whether or not we allow feeling to develop into craving depends on the way we channel our *cetanā*. In terms of the *nidāna* chain, in dependence upon contact arises feeling, and in dependence upon feeling arises craving. Where feeling ends and craving begins is a question of where one ceases to be able to detach oneself quite easily from the object of the pleasant feeling. If it proves next to impossible to give up that object, craving is well established and karma has been set in vigorous motion.

Here we see a fundamental difference between the four omnipresent mental events we have discussed so far. Both contact and feeling are mental events that simply happen. The senses can come into contact with their appropriate objects without any particular movement on the part of the mind. On the *nidāna* chain they are part of the effect process of the present life. Directionality and perception, on the other hand, belong to the cause process which takes us on to the next life; and so does the fifth omnipresent mental event, egocentric demanding.

5. EGOCENTRIC DEMANDING (MANASKĀRA)

It is a continuity having the function of holding the mind to what has become its reference.

Abhidharmasamuccaya

The difference between directionality and egocentric demanding is that directionality brings the mind towards the object in a general move, while egocentric demanding makes the mind jump on this particular objective reference.[97]

Yeshe Gyaltsen

'Egocentric demanding' is Guenther's translation of *manaskāra*, which literally means 'mind-making'. It is a continuity in the sense that its nature is to go on, almost as if it becomes habitual – within a relatively short timescale, anyway. By 'its reference' is meant whatever object the mind has made contact with. The *Vijñaptimātratāsiddhi-śāstra* (in the translation of which *manaskāra* appears as 'attention') deals with a couple of misleading explanations quite constructively:

> According to Sanghabhadra, attention causes the mind to turn towards another object; according to the Abhidharmasamuccaya, it holds the mind fixed on an object. Both explanations are contrary to reason, because, in accepting the first, attention would not be 'universal', and the second explanation confuses attention and Samādhi.[98]

Quite obviously, the mind does not always turn at once to another object; nor does it always remain fixed on the object. In his Buddhist dictionary, Nyanatiloka, quoting from Buddhaghosa's *Visuddhimagga*, gives us a clearer definition of *manaskāra* (Pāli *manasikāra*): it is the mind's first 'confrontation with an object' and 'binds the associated mental factors to the object'.[99] One might still object, though, that rather than an omnipresent mental event something rather like *samādhi* – *samādhi* meaning 'meditative concentration' – seems to be referred to in the second part of the definition.

It is difficult to establish an absolutely clear distinction between the different mental events. But perhaps we can say that if directionality or intentionality is like creeping up on the object, *manaskāra* is like the final spring. Of course, being an omnipresent mental event, it is not just the occasional pounce; it is something one does again and again (hence 'demanding'). So 'egocentric demanding' is quite good as an interpretative translation.

6

A STEADY FOCUS

IN THIS CHAPTER we are going to start getting a much more specific idea of how the Abhidharma's classifications of mental events are of practical use, especially in the practice of meditation. Here we are concerned with another group of five, the 'object-determining' mental events. The Sanskrit term is *viniyata*, which means 'restrained, checked, regulated, limited', but in this context it is taken to mean 'specific' or 'determining'. The object-determining mental events are those in which one applies oneself more particularly to the object of one's attention. They are object-determining in the sense that one determines that it shall be this object and not that object. One comes, as it were, much closer up to the object; these mental events are concerned with it in a much more vital and even dynamic manner than are the omnipresent mental events. The object-determining mental events are therefore brought into operation above all in the context of meditation, which is a process of applying oneself to a particular object with an increasing intensity of involvement.

1. INTEREST *(CHANDA)*

Again, Yeshe Gyaltsen starts his exposition with a quotation, this time from the *Abhidharmasamuccaya*:

> What is interest? It is the desire to endow a desired thing with this or that particular attribute, and has the function of laying the foundation for making a start on assiduous striving.[100]

So this is *chanda*. Guenther translates it as 'interest'; one could also render it as 'eagerness'. Before you fix the mind on an object, you are, as it were, saying 'Let that be the object of my attention,' which implies making a definite effort with regard to that particular object. Obviously this is especially important within the context of meditation. And on the basis of interest the other object-determining mental events gradually come into play.

It is important to note about this, the first of the object-determining mental events (also the first of the *ṛddhipādas*, the four bases of psychic power – see page 27), that it is *not* an omnipresent mental event. Of course, this is not going to be news as far as most of us are concerned; we know very well that eagerness or *chanda* is not part of our experience all the time. Indeed, it is unfortunately possible to go through life without evincing much eagerness for anything whatsoever. This seems to be what being 'cool' or 'laid back' is about. Eagerness is something that has to be established and maintained; and it is established in conjunction with other qualities. First one has to see the value of the meditative state. This is what stimulates interest or eagerness, which is the basis for endeavour or striving, which in turn leads to *praśrabdhi*, or 'integrated exhilaration'.

Eagerness, one could say, is the opposite of laziness, so that the overcoming of laziness and the development of eagerness are closely related. On the subject of laziness, Yeshe Gyaltsen quotes the Tibetan master Tsongkhapa:

> If one is unable to suppress laziness which delights in the non-inclination towards the practice of meditation and which delights in the factors not conducive to the practice, then one quickly loses all interest.... When one has attained a state of alertness which is satiated with happiness and pleasure both on the physical and mental level, and when one is not weary to apply himself day or night to what is positive, then laziness is overcome. In order to generate this alertness, it is important that one has the concentration which is the sustaining

cause of the aforesaid state of alertness and that one makes this a
continuous process. In order to have the power of concentration, one
must have a strong and continuous involvement in concentration. In
order that concentration be a sustaining cause factor, one must
repeatedly invoke a firm conviction which enraptures one's whole
mind because one has seen the virtues and value of concentration. To
understand these qualities and processes in this order must be taken as
the most essential point because they become clear and certain in
seeing them in one's own experience.'
(*Lam-rim chen-mo*)[101]

To summarize what Tsongkhapa is saying here:

a. Laziness must be overcome, because it prevents not only concentration, but continuity of concentration, in meditation.

b. Laziness can only be said to have been overcome when one experiences no resistance in meditation to applying oneself, day and night,
to the positive, and continually feels both mental and physical bliss.

c. To generate this, one needs continuous concentration – that is, one
needs to be involved constantly in the practice.

d. In order actually to achieve this level of involvement, one has
repeatedly to invoke, in the course of practice, a firm conviction of its
value – especially, presumably, when concentration is flagging.

So laziness is to devote oneself to and delight in something in a way
that prevents one from devoting oneself to and delighting in something of greater value. We tend to think of laziness as being about lack
of exertion, but the Buddhist idea of laziness is quite different – and
quite revealing. For Gampopa, for example, the most extreme form of
laziness is devoting oneself day and night to defeating enemies and
making money.[102]

Being lazy really means being busy doing something that is not
conducive to skilful mental states: one's busyness actually prevents
one from being aware of what one might otherwise be engaging in. In
fact, Tsongkhapa goes further than that: laziness, he is saying, is taking
delight in the fact that one is *not* occupying yourself with something
of higher value. It involves a sort of complacency and satisfaction in
the fact that one is occupying oneself with lower things. To overcome
laziness we need to be able to distinguish that which is worthwhile
from that which is less so. This means that we need to think deeply

about the implications of attaining concentrated mental states (*dhyāna*): what it will mean to attain *dhyāna* and what it will mean *not* to attain it. Eagerness (*chanda*) is based on this, and it is established to counteract laziness.

Tsongkhapa's remarks on laziness are especially important, according to Yeshe Gyaltsen, for those who are tempted to immerse themselves so deeply in various discussions and arguments about the teachings of Buddhism that they miss the whole point of them. However conscientiously one occupies oneself with the teachings, if one doesn't put them into practice, such occupation is no more than a form of laziness. This is not at all to say that Dharma study and Dharma practice are necessarily two different things. Study can be a method of practice just as meditation is. Study is, after all, an aspect of the first of the three wisdoms (listening, reflecting, and meditating).[103] Laziness sets in when one does not go on to reflect and meditate on the teachings one has studied.

2. INTENSIFIED INTEREST WHICH STAYS WITH ITS OBJECT (*ADHIMOKṢA*)

It is to stick to the determined thing just as it has been determined, and the function of intensified interest is that it cannot be taken away.[104]
Abhidharmasamuccaya

Here Guenther chooses to translate *adhimokṣa*, sometimes translated as 'resolve' or 'determination', as 'intensified interest which stays with its object'. In this context it refers to an object of meditation, but in fact this resolve may be applied to anything. If the object is the Three Jewels of Buddhism – the Buddha, representing the ideal of Enlightenment, the Dharma, representing the Buddha's teaching, and the Sangha, the spiritual community of those who have realized the higher stages of the transcendental path – then the determination amounts to faith (*śraddhā*). Whereas *chanda*, as a firm conviction regarding the quality and value of higher mental states, will appear in some form at an elementary level of spiritual development, *adhimokṣa* is experienced only by a person who is really committed to the spiritual life.

3. INSPECTION (OR MINDFULNESS OR RECOLLECTION) (*SMṚTI*)

It is not to let what one knows slip away from one's mind. Its function is not to be distracted.[105]
Abhidharmasamuccaya

Guenther gives us 'inspection', and *smṛti* is usually translated as 'mindfulness' or 'awareness', but in fact, as this quotation from the *Abhidharmasamuccaya* suggests, the primary meaning of the word is 'recollection' or even 'memory'. Sometimes *smṛti* quite clearly means recollection or memory, while in other contexts it obviously refers to being aware of something here and now, and sometimes its meaning is a synthesis of the two, which one could term 'mindfulness'. The common characteristic is 'not to let what one knows slip out of the mind'. Whether the object is there in the present or whether it is remembered from the past, the practice of *smṛti* is about holding the object in the mind. This is mindfulness.

We have already briefly encountered the 'four foundations of mindfulness' – mindfulness of body, of feelings, of thoughts, and of reality – as an aspect of the path of accumulation. One can go further, to cultivate what I would call four dimensions of mindfulness or awareness: awareness of things, awareness of self, awareness of others, and awareness of reality.

By awareness of things I mean awareness of the world around us, awareness of our material environment – awareness of nature, if you like. Of course, if we want to be aware of the world, we have to look at it and listen to it, but this is what very few of us ever manage to do. Most people, if challenged, would say that they have no time to stop and look at things. But if we really want to be aware of the world, we need to learn to look at it. We need to learn to look at the sky, at mountains (when we get the opportunity), at flowers, at rocks, at water, at fire – at the familiar things that are all around us, that are there all the time, but that we never really see. We need to look not just at 'poetic' things, but at everything we encounter in our everyday life, even brick walls and unemptied dustbins, if they happen to be what is around.

It is not only a question of looking. We need to learn to hear, to taste, to smell, to touch. No doubt the highest degree of perceptual awareness is possible through the sense of sight, but that does not mean that the other senses should be neglected. We should learn really to look not only at natural objects and familiar household things but, for example, at paintings, sculptures, and so on – things that we often take for granted as part of our cultural heritage. We can also learn to listen – to music, for example. (Many people have music on as a sort of background noise; whether it's Bach or the latest pop song they wouldn't be able to say – it's just a river of sound flowing through the background.) In so many ways we can increase our awareness of the world, both natural and cultural.

Secondly, we need to develop awareness of self. By this I don't mean anything very metaphysical; I mean simply awareness of the changing empirical self, which is in any case all that we usually experience. In Buddhism awareness of self is traditionally said to be of three kinds, of increasing degrees of subtlety. First there is awareness of the body and its movements, including the breathing process, on which, of course, a whole concentration technique is based. According to tradition, as one moves about one should be aware of just how one is moving. If you are standing, be aware that you are standing. If you are sitting, be aware that you are sitting; experience yourself sitting. If you move your hand, be aware that you are moving your hand. If you close the door, be aware that you are closing the door. If you are holding a book, be aware that you are holding it.

If we practise in this way, even for a little while, we very speedily become aware that we have lapses of mindfulness. There are whole periods of time when we literally don't know what we're doing. Although being aware of the physical body is the simplest form of self-awareness, it is still very difficult. But it is very important, because it is the foundation of all the other aspects of awareness of self.

From there we can go on to practising awareness of feeling, noticing whether our feeling-tone is pleasurable, painful, or a sort of neutral grey. Then we can become aware of our emotions, of whether we are experiencing love or hatred or fear or anxiety or desire or hope or jealousy or delight or expectation or disgust – or whatever. The important thing, whatever the emotional state we are in, is to know that we are experiencing it. If we can become aware of our whole emotional life in this way, we will find that this has a twofold effect: our negative emotions will tend to be dissolved – or at least brought very much under control – and our positive emotions will tend to be refined still further.

Then there is awareness of thoughts. It has to be said that very few people really think at all. Usually thoughts just drift through our minds; they take possession of us, as it were. We don't know why they have come and very often we don't know where they have come from; they just come, and there seems to be very little we can do about it. We just have to tolerate them. Even in meditation we just have to watch the thoughts playing – rioting, even – in the playground of our mind, powerless to chase them away. They are not our own thoughts, really;

we are not masters of them. All that is happening is that we are subject to a very loose association of ideas which is easily interrupted or redirected. But if we become aware of what is happening, if we cultivate awareness of our thoughts, our thinking becomes more purposeful. In a sense it becomes our own; it becomes an active rather than a passive process. Wandering thoughts are gradually eliminated, and we experience an altogether more peaceful and harmonious state of mind.

This is the traditional classification of awareness of self: awareness of the body and its movements, of feelings and emotional states, and of thoughts. But other classifications are also possible. We can speak, for example, in terms of various kinds of psychological conditioning – by which I mean the tendency for our actions to be determined, without our realizing it, by previous patterns of existence, often patterns laid down very early in life. This conditioning is of various kinds. We are conditioned by the fact that we are human beings and not animals, or rather that we are humanoid mammals as distinct from non-humanoid mammals. We are conditioned by the fact of being either male or female. We are conditioned by the place where we were born, by our race, by our nationality. We are conditioned by the social group to which we belong – by caste, by class, by profession, by party, even by religion. Such conditioning is also resolved by means of awareness of self, in that to the extent that we become aware that we are psychologically conditioned in these various ways, to that extent we become free from that conditioning.

The third dimension of awareness is awareness of people. Strange to say, this is a comparatively rare thing. Usually, as already discussed, we are aware of people not as people but as things, as objects, as bodies 'out there'. The extreme case, of course, is that of the infant, to whom 'mother' is just an object that gives warmth and nourishment. We like to think that we grow out of this sort of attitude to people, and to an extent we do, but not altogether. All too often in our personal lives we treat other people not as persons but as things. The way to start to change this is simply to learn to look at people. Only if we look at people can we be aware of them. And only if we are aware of them can we love them.

Fourthly, there's awareness of reality, which is of course the highest kind of awareness. Not that this dimension of awareness and the other dimensions are mutually exclusive. One can have glimpses of reality through awareness of nature, of the self, or of other people. But in this fourth dimension, one's awareness of reality is, as it were, direct. In what it actually consists it is very difficult to say, because it is beyond words, but we can perhaps say that it is synonymous with meditation in the highest sense – that is, with meditation as contemplation.

These dimensions of awareness or mindfulness are clearly fundamental to Buddhist practice. Mindfulness was a fundamental aspect of the Buddha's teaching – a whole sutta of the Pāli Canon, the *Satipaṭṭhāna Sutta*, is devoted to an exposition of the four foundations of mindfulness – and clearly it is of great importance to the practice of the Abhidharma. It is a moot point, of course, how far this kind of awareness will take us; as we have seen, some would argue that simply being aware of a mental state is not enough to change it, while one could equally argue that the very act of becoming aware has a transformative power.

In the context of the object-determining mental events, attention is being drawn to *smṛti* as recollection, which reminds us that here we are discussing a mental event. The term recollection in English is ambiguous: it can mean the act of recollecting, in the sense of calling up a mental image pertaining to the past – that is, remembering something – but it can also mean the state of being recollected – being mindful and aware in the present.

As a spiritual practice, recollection may be said to be about remembering what is really important, what life is really about and what one is really supposed to be doing. 'Why am I here? What am I doing this for?' Recollection is often about waking up to the fact that one has strayed away from where one really wants to be. The Sanskrit term reserved for this particular type of recollection is *samprajanya*, sometimes translated as 'mindfulness of purpose' or 'mindfulness with clear comprehension'; we will encounter its opposite, *asamprajanya*, among the list of negative mental events.

When one recollects something one is, as it were, collecting together again what has been lost, even gathering up scattered energies. In recollecting one's purpose, one is recollecting one*self*. In a sense, though, one's ultimate purpose never falls into abeyance. There is no need to be remembering constantly that one is on the spiritual path in a strained and artificial way, but it's always there in the background. It's a bit like an electrified wire. If one does anything that begins to take one away from one's main purpose, one gets a little jolt from that undercurrent of recollection.

Perhaps it is worth adding that, obviously, even *smṛti* in the straight-forward sense of memory has its uses. Memory is quite an odd phenomenon. One has to remember that one has forgotten before one can remember again – that is, one can only recollect one's recollection by means of recollection. Things one wants to remember get submerged by other things, and they have to wait for an opportunity to surface into consciousness; it seems very often just a matter of chance whether one's memory gets jogged or not. The best one can do, perhaps, is set up appropriate conditions in advance for retrieving one's memory. The time-honoured method is to tie a knot in one's handkerchief, but one can set up more elaborate systems of association to stimulate the memory, or write things down, or even employ someone to remember things on one's behalf. Remembering things is so important that quite often we're seized with a feeling that we've forgotten something before we know what it is that we've forgotten – or we get a feeling we've forgotten something when we haven't at all.

There is very often a point to memory loss. When we're stressed, for example, it's sheer self-protection, a way of cutting down on the number of things we have to think about. If there are too many demands being made on us and we don't do anything about it consciously, we reduce the input unconsciously by simply forgetting things.

We also tend to forget things as we get older. When we're young we remember all sorts of details, very often quite trivial ones, because it is not yet clear to us what is going to be important and what is not. What will turn out to be peripheral may at the time look like a matter of great concern. As we get older and the general pattern of our life comes into focus, we want to intensify and deepen that focus, and our memory becomes more selective. As we strive to strengthen the basic pattern, which is presumably what we will carry over into our next life, the things that are irrelevant to the broad brush-strokes of our life cease to make an impression. By the time one gets to the end of one's life one may not be taking in anything that's going on, and one's memory may go altogether. One becomes like a child again, ready for one's next rebirth.

Smṛti is fundamental to spiritual practice; one cannot begin without it. Many devotional practices in particular help to recollect the mind in this general sense, and there is a series of practices that are specifically named the ten *anussatis* or recollections (*sati* being the Pāli version of the Sanskrit *smṛti*).[106] One of these practices is the *ānāpānasati*, the mindfulness of breathing; and another is the *buddhānussati* (Sanskrit *buddhanusmṛti*), which involves calling to mind what one has heard about the Buddha and his qualities.

Mindfulness of one's purpose can be lost just as one loses one's memory, but it involves losing something rather more fundamental than people's names or the day of the week. If you realize the importance of this kind of mindfulness, if you realize that if you lose it you lose, in a sense, everything, then you are going to want to do something a little more radical than tying a knot in your handkerchief to make sure you preserve it. And one very effective way is to develop spiritual friendship. Our friends may literally remind us in conceptual terms of our purpose in life, but we are also frequently reminded of what we are trying to do simply through observing their example.

4. INTENSE CONCENTRATION (*SAMĀDHI*)

The fourth object-determining mental event is *samādhi*, which in this context means one-pointedness of mind that stays with a mental object – that is, an object that is not perceived through the senses.[107] Yeshe Gyaltsen quotes the *Abhidharmasamuccaya*: 'its function is to become the basis for awareness'.[108] But, remembering that most basic formulation of the Buddhist path, the Threefold Way, we can also say that *samādhi* is developed on the basis of ethics, and 'its function is to become the basis for awareness' in the sense of transcendental wisdom or insight. These are the three stages of the path: ethics, *samādhi*, wisdom.

For an important qualification to this definition of *samādhi* we can turn not to Yeshe Gyaltsen's commentary this time, but to the *Ch'eng Wei-Shih Lun*:

> The expression 'concentration of the mind' indicates that the mind is
> fixed where it wishes to be fixed, not that it is fixed on only one object.
> Otherwise, there would be no Samādhi on the 'Path of Insight into
> transcendental Truth' where the ascetic discerns and contemplates
> successively the eternal verities and where, in consequence, the object
> changes from moment to moment.[109]

This can be applied directly to one's meditation practice. Take, for example, the practice of visualizing a particular Buddha or Bodhisattva. One may bring to mind the details of a visualized Bodhisattva, concentrating now on this, now on that element of the visualization, but the idea is that one's concentration (*samādhi*) remains constant even while its object changes in this way. With the *mettā bhāvanā* practice likewise, the aim is to develop a quality of response, *mettā*, that remains constant whoever is the object of one's concentration. *Samādhi* is basically the ability to fix the mind where we wish during meditation.

Yeshe Gyaltsen lists four classes of mental object one may concentrate on.[110] The four are, to paraphrase his list:

a. That which is concerned with the development of *śīla*, morality;

b. That which is concerned with purifying emotions – i.e. by counteracting craving;

c. That which is concerned with developing the four 'abodes of the gods' (*brahma-vihāras*): loving kindness, compassion, sympathetic joy, and equanimity;

d. That which is concerned with the development of wisdom.

These four categories again cover the Threefold Way. The first refers to the ten precepts, while the second and third have as their aim the development of *samādhi* itself. The second category, reflecting as it does the need to counteract the powerful emotions of craving and lust, involves strong measures: meditation on the ten impurities and the various disgusting aspects of bodily existence, in particular the meditation on the stages of decomposition of a corpse. The third, designed to counter the opposite tendency, towards hatred and aversion, consists in the cultivation of positive emotion. And the fourth has as its aim the development of insight into the nature of reality, which involves reflection on the Dharma, including the teachings of the Abhidharma itself.

In his commentary Yeshe Gyaltsen makes it clear that it is only with reference to the *mental* product of perception – an inwardly perceived object – that concentration in the sense of *samādhi* develops. While it is quite common to focus on some external object (traditionally a coloured disc) in order to develop a preliminary degree of concentration, it would be a mistake to imagine that through doing this one could develop concentration in all its stages. The extreme form of this sort of wrong view is held by people who claim that they meditate 'all the time'. Awareness – being aware of what one perceives through one's external senses – is one thing, but *samādhi* is another. Perception through the five senses, indeed, plays no part in *samādhi*. It is possible to meditate with one's eyes open, but even then, once one is deeply concentrated, one is not concentrating on what is before one's eyes; in fact, one doesn't register any visual perception at all.

Having said that, we should remember that the conceptualizing mind also counts as one of the sense faculties, and that the same controlling faculty of mind (*indriya*) operates whether the eye perceives visual form or the mind perceives mental objects. However, whether one starts off by concentrating on some external object perceived through the five senses, or on an object perceived through the sense faculty of the mind (i.e. by means of what Guenther terms categorical perception) the mind one starts off with is not the same mind with which one ends up. The whole process is formulated by the Buddha as follows: 'The senses find refuge in the mind as a sixth sense, but the sixth sense finds refuge in mindfulness; and mindfulness finds refuge in "release".'[111]

> Whether it is real or not,
> Whatever becomes truly familiar
> When you have become fully conversant with it
> Results in a clear feeling of presence without subject–object
>   dichotomy.[112]
> *Pramāṇavarttika*

With this quotation from Dharmakīrti Yeshe Gyaltsen takes us further into the heart of meditation practice, and more specifically visualization practice. You may take as your object of concentration something that can be said actually to exist outside your imagination (like a visualized Bodhisattva) or an invented object (like a unicorn). Either way it is, as the object of your meditation, your own creation: you have produced it yourself. Although you perceive it as an object, your connection with it is actually subjective. When you become fully absorbed you become, as it were, one with the object, and it becomes one with you. If you focus on the object without thinking about it, you get a direct experience of it, not mediated by concepts. And as you 'change' the object, you change yourself, and so gradually the two become one.

Even if the object of one's meditation is a visualized Bodhisattva, even if one merges with that object in *samādhi*, it is still the product of one's mundane mind. It is not the Bodhisattva himself or herself. In terms of Tantric meditation practice, a clear distinction is made between the *samayasattva* and the *jñānasattva*. The *samayasattva*, sometimes translated as the 'convention being', is the Bodhisattva visualized according to tradition but produced by one's own mind. The *jñānasattva* literally means the 'knowledge being' and – in a manner of speaking – it actually exists; that is, it is *not* a product of one's own mind.

By developing the *samayasattva*, one is preparing a counterpart of the *jñānasattva*, a sort of mundane simulacrum into which the transcendental original, so to speak, can descend, or through which it can manifest. One is tuning in to the *jñānasattva*, the actual Enlightened mind of the Bodhisattva, through the mundane meditative experience of the *samayasattva*. When the one descends into the other then one is in contact with the Bodhisattva, and that becomes a transcendental experience.

Of course, you don't necessarily have to know anything about the foregoing technicalities for a Bodhisattva to appear to you. It may just happen by the sheer impetus of your spiritual practice; you may have a vision. But until it does happen, however it happens, though you may be so absorbed that you can no longer distinguish between yourself and the visualized image, the visualization still remains no more than an image, your own mental creation.

5. APPRECIATIVE DISCRIMINATION (PRAJÑĀ)

Its function is to avoid any confusion or doubt.[113]
Abhidharmasamuccaya

Prajñā, which Guenther sometimes translates as 'analytical appreciative discrimination', but which is often translated simply as 'wisdom' or 'knowledge', is the culmination and purpose of meditation. With *prajñā*, one is able to sort out the qualities of the compounded from those of the Uncompounded, distinguishing clearly between that which is impermanent, insubstantial, painful, and unlovely, and that which is permanent, real, blissful, and beautiful. (This distinction is one which, without *prajñā*, one is simply unable to make. Subject to what the Buddhist tradition calls the four *viparyāsas*, the four 'topsy-turvy views', we are prey to the delusion that what is impermanent is permanent, what is insubstantial is substantial, and so on.)[114] With *prajñā* one sees the positive as positive (*kuśala* or skilful), the negative as negative (*akuśala* or unskilful), and the neutral – that which is neither positive or negative – as neutral (*avyākṛta*). *Prajñā* is also characterized as 'appreciative' because it is not just intellectual but value-toned, as Guenther would say.

According to Yeshe Gyaltsen's commentary, there are four kinds of knowledge to be cultivated for the attainment of appreciative discrimination:

a. Awareness of what must be done: Knowledge of activity that is spiritually fitting.

b. Awareness of relationship: Knowledge of the kind of relationships that follow from the principle of dependent origination; that is, the relationship between actions and their consequences, karma and *vipāka* – and, indeed, the whole network of relationships elucidated in the Abhidharma.

c. Awareness of attaining proper validity: Knowledge of that which is ultimately valid and irrefutable, and of how it is to be obtained.

d. Awareness of the absolute real: Knowledge of the Uncompounded itself.[115]

We will discuss further characteristics of this supreme mental event under 'Non-deludedness' – which is the same thing viewed as a positive mental event rather than an object-determining mental event – and under 'Lack of intrinsic awareness'.

With the concept of *prajñā* we come to the main locus of contention between the Hīnayāna and the Mahāyāna. According to the Hīnayāna, *prajñā* consists essentially in seeing what we usually think of as the self in terms of its constituent *dharmas*. The Abhidharma is the systematic study of these *dharmas* so as to preclude the possibility that one might think of the psycho-physical organism as a self.

The Mahāyāna, on the other hand, sees *prajñā* in terms of the intuition of *śūnyatā*. It regards the Abhidharma's classification of *dharmas* as purely provisional and pertaining to relative or conventional truth, holding that the *dharmas* into which the Abhidharma breaks down the psycho-physical organism can themselves be broken down indefinitely. *Dharmas* are not entities, as far as the Mahāyāna is concerned; they are only concepts, and all concepts must be transcended if *prajñā* is to be attained – *prajñā* consisting, as the Mahāyāna maintains, in the intuition or realization of *śūnyatā*, or the emptiness of all concepts. So this – according to some opinions at least – is the Mahāyāna criticism of the Hīnayāna.

The Vajrayāna in its turn would say that the realization of *śūnyatā* in the Mahāyāna is itself limited in that it is purely mental – not that it is merely rational, but that it takes place on just the mental plane. The

Vajrayāna is concerned with the direct experience of *śūnyatā*, and maintains that this must involve not only the mind but also speech and even the body. The Tantra therefore speaks not just in terms of Enlightenment, but in terms of attaining the *trikāya* – that is, the completely transformed body, speech, and mind – of the Buddha. The idea is that the involvement of all the energies of the psycho-physical organism in the process of actually experiencing *śūnyatā* leads to a much more thoroughgoing and complete realization.

In the end, of course, each *yāna* sees the previous one from its own special point of view; whether a real point of view is being criticized when the Hīnayāna or Mahāyāna position is being assailed is open to question. What we can probably say is that a certain solidifying of concepts or settling down with ideas is being criticized in each case. If one reads some of the earliest Pāli texts, for example, one finds little trace of what the Mahāyāna calls the Hīnayāna. Sometimes in the *Sutta Nipāta* or the *Udāna* one feels as though one is not only in Mahāyāna territory, but even in touch with the Vajrayāna. The three *yānas* constitute a useful framework of reference, but this framework should not be applied too rigidly to the historical material involved.

The object-determining mental events clearly represent a progressive series, leading from interest, which may or may not be applied to meditation, all the way to intense concentration, which leaves the external, sense-based world behind altogether. However, the culmination of the series, *prajñā*, brings us back, in a sense, to where we started, because wisdom operates whether or not one is in a meditative state of consciousness. Once one has it one doesn't ever lose it, even when one is out and about in the world. One may not be absorbed in *dhyāna*, but one's *prajñā* is alive and functioning.

When one is experiencing *prajñā*, whatever one does there is no absolutely real subject doing it, and no absolutely real object to apply oneself to either. So with the arising of *prajñā* one gets as close to an object as one can possibly get: the object is known as it really is. It is known, in other words, not as an object, ultimately speaking, at all, but as a temporary condensation of conditions which our own propensity for identification (*saṁjñā*) has labelled as a specific object.

The experience of *prajñā* or transcendental insight is a paradoxical thing. It seems, at least in the early stages, to come from outside oneself, though this impression may be corrected by subsequent experience. At the same time it clearly arises in the midst of oneself. It negates one completely and finally, but at the same time it represents one's true individuality.

Prajñā is of course different from nirvāṇa, which is described as a *dhātu*, a sphere or realm, not simply a state of mind. At least, this is the Hīnayāna Abhidharma point of view. Nirvāṇa, your Hīnayāna Ābhidharmika would say, is an objective reality, existing above and beyond the mundane, independently of whether anybody experiences it or not. This is what makes it ultimately real. It's not dependent upon our experience in order to be what it is. However, it is the nature of reality that it is not to be spoken of in terms either of subject or of object. This is why it can be described either as if it were an experience or as if it existed altogether independently of one's experience. So there is no right answer; all one can do is be aware of the limitations of either approach.

7

THE CREATIVE MIND AT WORK

HAVING OUTLINED the object-determining mental events, Yeshe Gyaltsen moves on to consider the Abhidharma's next classification: the eleven positive (*kuśala*) mental events. The positive mental events come before the negative ones perhaps because it is considered healthier to examine the negative on the basis of an exploration of the positive. (The Indian tradition generally, however, would seem to favour putting it the opposite way round, at least in such teachings as the famous verse from the *Dhammapada*: 'Cease to do evil, learn to do good, purify the heart.')

These eleven are not intended to enumerate a fixed and limited number of mental states. Still, it is notable that just eleven positive mental events are deemed sufficient to set against twenty-six negative ones. The reason for this is no doubt that, as the saying goes, 'There are many ways of being bad, but only one way of being good.' To put it another way, there's a greater variety of sinners than of saints, which is probably why the wicked are regarded as so much more interesting than the good.

Of course, careful consideration of human nature reveals on the one hand what has been termed the banality of evil, and on the other the strong sense of individuality that is an inescapable characteristic of the highly integrated person. But there is no doubt that one follows the 'primrose way to the everlasting bonfire' (as the porter in Shakespeare's *Macbeth* colourfully describes the downward path) in one's own little way, whereas through becoming more developed one comes to have more and more in common with other more evolved individuals. By their very nature positive mental events tend to cohere, to integrate more and more with each other. A positive action or mental state will partake in some sense of all of the positive mental events, inasmuch as if one of them is definitely absent then one is not in a totally positive mental state. Negative mental events, on the other hand, have the opposite tendency: they represent forces of disintegration, they are more differentiated, and there are therefore more of them.

The eleven positive mental events are simply different aspects of the creative mind. They do not represent a cumulative, graded series like, for example, the seven *bodhyaṅgas*: recollection (*smṛti*), investigation of mental events (*dharma-vicaya*), energy (*vīrya*), rapture (*prīti*), tension release (*praśrabdhi*), concentration (*samādhi*), and tranquillity (*upekṣā*).[116] But there are various connections between the eleven positive mental events and the seven *bodhyaṅgas*; in particular, the second *bodhyaṅga*, *dharma-vicaya*, is specifically concerned with reviewing one's own mental events, analysing and understanding them. It is, one could say, a practical application of Abhidharmic thinking in the context of meditation.

If one were to take up this practice at the most basic level one would begin by analysing one's mental state simply in terms of the three skilful and unskilful roots: 'Is craving present in my mind? Or hatred? Or delusion?' – and so on. One just follows the rise and fall of mental events in this way. If one keeps it up for long enough and gets competent enough at it, one's attention remains constant even as its object changes. In principle, this is what is meant by *vipaśyanā* meditation – though it would seem that very often nowadays people are encouraged to take up the practice with insufficient preparation in terms of *śamatha* meditation, so that they are attempting insight meditation on the basis of an inadequately concentrated and positive state of mind.[117]

1. CONFIDENCE-TRUST (OR FAITH) (ŚRADDHĀ)

Faith (or confidence-trust, as Guenther translates *śraddhā*) has to come first. It is enumerated first in all the different traditions of the Abhidharma, which is perhaps indicative of its importance. It provides the basis for sustained interest, interest in turn supports the application of effort, and effort is what makes the development of other positive mental events possible.

> It is a deep conviction, lucidity, and longing for those things which are real, have value, and are possible. It functions as the basis of sustained interest.[118]

This quotation, which Yeshe Gyaltsen selects from the *Abhidharmasamuccaya*, specifies three aspects of faith. One could read it as saying that faith consists in deep conviction of what is real, lucidity as to what has value, and longing for what is possible. These three aspects may be found enumerated in various places in the Pāli Canon, almost like stock phrases, as if together they made up a formulaic description of faith.

According to Hsüan Tsang the first of these, which he describes as 'the deep understanding of, and the ardent desire for, realities, qualities, and capacities' signifies 'profound faith in, and understanding of, dharmas [that is, in very broad terms, 'things'] really existing, things, or principles (verities)'.[119] Yeshe Gyaltsen identifies the object of this aspect of faith as the law of karma, the fact that if one performs certain actions then certain consequences will inevitably follow.

The second quality of faith is lucidity, a limpidity of mind, a state of serenity, clarity, and a very refined sort of contentment. Yeshe Gyaltsen observes that this comes from an acknowledgement of 'such valuables as' the Three Jewels (the Buddha, Dharma, and Sangha). But we should be clear about what this means. This lucid mind does not arise from a cool, objective recognition of the value of the Three Jewels. It is a response to them, a response which at once introduces a certain order and clarity into one's life and mind. Things are sorted out: there are certain things one is going to do, and certain things one is not going to do. Conflict and indecision give way to a great relief and clarity.

The third aspect of faith is a 'longing for those things which … are possible'. This explanation is enlarged upon in the *Vijñaptimātratāsiddhiśāstra*: 'This signifies the profound faith in one's own power to attain and realize all good mundane and supramundane dharmas, and produce the desire and aspiration for them.'[120] Again, Yeshe Gyaltsen draws out the principle in terms of a specific and fundamental doctrine – in this case, the Four Noble Truths: 'When we know that through our efforts these truths can be realized, we certainly will do so.'[121] Faith is therefore the confidence that one may oneself attain the path and the goal represented by the Dharma.

Faith is further characterized by distinguishing it from the mental event with which it is most easily confused: pleasure. Enjoying something – 'getting something out of it' – is different from putting faith in it. Yet, if we're not careful, we don't just enjoy and appreciate ordinary mundane things, we believe in them, we get into them, we emotionally invest in them. The essential difference between faith and pleasure is that the one is unequivocally positive, whereas the other may be positive or negative.

It is not so much that one should not – to use the example offered by Yeshe Gyaltsen[122] – trust one's wife and children, as that one should not trust *in* them. One cannot repose absolute confidence in them. We know this, of course. The admonition 'Put not your trust in princes' is familiar enough to most of us. But it does not stop us from doing it. We repose our trust where we cannot really expect to find ultimate security or happiness. It starts when we are very young, when we are absolutely dependent on our parents for our security, and full satisfaction seems an achievable goal. Though we may be forced to withdraw this naïve trust in life, we retain a need to commit ourselves emotionally, and we therefore give our commitment to the things we enjoy and the people we love. We think, 'Well, what else is there?' We know how uncertain life is, we know how dangerous it is to rely on that which is uncertain, but we don't see any other way. The test comes when what we like is taken away from us: our distress and disappointment is the measure of the trust we reposed in whatever, or whoever, it was we liked or loved.

Our apparently infinite capacity for disappointment comes from this tendency to lump pleasure and faith together. When we start to distinguish them, however, Yeshe Gyaltsen maintains that we have four alternative ways to experience them. His list of the alternatives is certainly to the point: (1) liking something but not trusting, (2) trusting but not liking, (3) both, (4) neither.

To elaborate on these a little, firstly one may like something which is of the mundane world – whether appropriately (wife and children) or inappropriately (getting intoxicated or gormandizing) – but without trusting in it. One reserves faith or trust for the source of one's highest values. This is where some people have trouble with God. It has been said of Cardinal Newman, for example, that he *believed* in God but he didn't trust him.

Secondly, one may trust without liking. One may understand and have faith in, for example, the law of karma – one understands that one's every action will have results – but one doesn't like it much. One doesn't like to have to think about the results of one's unskilful actions. Or there may be a particular spiritual practice which one trusts, believing in its efficacy, but which one doesn't relish much. When faith arose in Milarepa, for example, he didn't like its implications in terms of his future rebirths, should he fail to realize Enlightenment there and then in that lifetime; nor did he enjoy what his teacher put him through in order to prepare him for spiritual practice.

Thirdly, it is possible to have both liking and trust. There is the possibility of joy in one's faith: one is *happy* to trust in the law of karma. If one has practised the Dharma, one is able to rejoice in the merit arising from skilful actions, both one's own and those of other people. When one sees the positive results of spiritual practice one starts to like it, even if it is difficult, demanding practice. However painful it may be to bring about positive change, when one starts liking that positive change, one's attitude to the practice itself will change from faith without joy to joyful faith. We can perhaps observe this development most clearly in our attitude to others who are following the spiritual life. Faith involves a genuine appreciation of and trust in one's spiritual friends as spiritual friends, while at the same time we may like them just as plain friends.

But in the fourth case, where there is neither liking nor trust, all avenues towards happiness of any kind seem closed, and the result is a state of anger and frustration.

Confidence [or faith] … removes arrogance and becomes the root of devotion.[123]

Ratnolkānāma-dhāraṇi

Devotion is an expression of faith, in thoughts, words, and deeds. And faith expresses itself in a sense of humility, gratitude, and devotion towards one's ideal. It is one thing to respect the Buddha as a great teacher, a great thinker, a great reformer, but it is quite another thing – quite a distinct mental event in fact – to respect him as the Enlightened One. Acknowledging the Buddha as the Buddha inevitably prompts one to act – not with a view to *using* the object of one's faith for one's own ends, but simply in order to devote oneself to it.

Unfortunately, devotion is not always an expression of faith. In fact, it is very rarely this. Devotion in the sense of *bhakti* can be delightful and emotionally fulfilling – decorating shrines can give one a great deal of aesthetic pleasure – but smiles and garlands do not add up to true devotion as an expression of faith. In other words, there are two levels of devotion, one antecedent to faith, the other the outcome of faith. The first level has its own value, because it may lead to a genuine receptivity to the Dharma. But devotion as an expression of faith is quite distinct; it is more calm, more serious.

Faith can be identified in a certain sense of care, responsibility, and respect. The precise word is lacking in English, but the quality of mind we should look out for goes back in a way to the old meaning – perhaps the original meaning – of the word 'religion'. It means observing certain things very carefully and mindfully; one is circumspect and scrupulous, even (in this very positive context) fearful, in the way one goes about devotional practice.

It is a very positive thing to decorate a shrine with a genuine feeling of aesthetic pleasure and a certain sense of devotion. But it's possible to do the same thing without that sense of pleasure, and for that to be even more positive – if, that is, one is doing it simply out of faith. When Tibetan Buddhists undertake to perform 100,000 prostrations, say, they do not expect to be getting something out of it all the time. Part of the point of such a massively extended practice is to be able to keep going with it even when one's inspiration dries up and one feels one is just going through the motions.

Faith is not belief in the sense of the acceptance of a set of doctrines; nor is it feeling, whether pleasant, unpleasant, or neutral. It is a separate kind of mental event, a particular kind of emotion felt for the highest spiritual values, especially as represented by the Three Jewels. The test of faith is whether one is able to act on it in the absence of any kind of gratification whatsoever, any kind of pleasurable feeling or emotion associated with the object of one's faith.

Of course, this is by no means always, or even often, going to be the case. But when there is no pleasure, not even spiritual pleasure, to fall back on – when in the midst of a desert of suffering one stays faithful to one's practice – then one can be sure that it really is faith that sustains one's practice. Again taking the example of Milarepa, when his teacher was making him build towers and knock them down again, he had faith even in the complete absence, at least for a while, of any pleasurable feeling at all.

There is a typical story of St Francis on this topic. He and his Little Brothers were having a discussion as to what was the greatest enjoyment they had ever experienced. One said, 'When I was caught up in contemplative rapture – that was the greatest pleasure.' Another said, 'When I was preaching the Word of God and I was carried away by devotion – that was the greatest pleasure.' Each of them had something to relate in this way – and then it was St Francis's turn. He said, 'It's a cold, dark, windy, rainy night. You've had nothing to eat, you've been walking all day, and you've lost your way. You'd give anything for a good hot dinner beside a roaring fire. But you're lost in a wood and the wolves are howling. Then you see a light through the trees, and there's a cottage, with smoke drifting from the chimney. So you knock at the door and it opens … and a woman shouts at you, "Off with you, you miserable, good-for-nothing friar. There's nothing for you here," and slams the door. *That* is the greatest enjoyment.'

St Francis's inner joy is so great that it can transcend all those experiences. It just burns all the brighter. Standing on nothing, not even an enjoyable religious experience, it comes purely from within. This is the kind of faith which is a positive mental event, a positive emotion. If one has it, even though one may be having immense difficulties in some way, one is quite happy: one has faith and that's all one needs. There is – there has to be – a certain kind of pleasure in faith, but it is quite different from the kind of pleasure that is unrelated to faith.

Faith is the indispensable emotional or volitional element of any experience of insight into the nature of reality. It is not like plunging optimistically into the dark. It is not blind. There are degrees of faith, obviously – sometimes one may have enough faith to commit oneself without enough to feel total conviction – but faith contains at least a degree of certainty, a degree of knowledge. In Buddhism there is no association of faith with uncertainty. Once one has experienced real faith of this kind, one may forget it from time to time but one never actually loses it. And if one hasn't experienced it then it seems that one cannot help confusing it with simply feeling very good about the spiritual life.

It may therefore seem contradictory to go on to observe that faith seems definitely to inhere in a whole culture – were it not for the fact that in some cultures faith is just as evidently almost entirely missing.

When I was living in Kalimpong, almost all the Tibetans I met had some touch of real faith, and many had it to a quite marked degree. I hope I am not lending enchantment to the view of the Tibetan people in the early days of their diaspora, but I think that in general my conclusion does hold good: that Tibetan culture is, or at least was, a culture of faith.

It would surprise many Western people to learn that, for their part, the Tibetans regard the Indian people as deeply irreligious. The fact that we in the West conventionally hold a diametrically opposite view simply highlights the stark materialism and cynicism of our own culture, and the degree to which we have lost touch with any under-standing of what faith really is. It is because we have no sense of the real meaning of faith that we regard devotion as somehow naïve and superstitious – which of course it is when it is not an expression of faith. Faith is nurtured by a climate of faith, and great spiritual teachers arise in a culture that is able to recognize them. Conversely, it is very difficult to develop faith within a materialist culture, because there is no aware-ness that anything is missing.

Quite a high proportion of Western Buddhists seem to be ex-Roman Catholics; perhaps this is because as children they had drummed into them the idea that the worldly life isn't everything. If one is brought up Catholic, even if one loses one's faith in the Church, it seems that one still needs to go on looking for something to replace it. Roman Catholics take their faith very seriously indeed, which is why they tend to avoid any serious attempt at dialogue with other faiths. They understand the nature of faith sufficiently clearly to appreciate that such a dialogue is more well-intentioned than meaningful.

I knew a Japanese monk who experienced a clever, not to say jesui-tical, example of non-dialogue from the Vatican. On his way to England he had stopped over in Rome, and being the head of a Buddhist sect in Japan he had secured an audience with the Pope. He was really delighted with what the Pope said during their interview; the pontiff apparently spoke very appreciatively about Buddhism and sent him off with a letter as a record of their amicable exchange. The monk was so overjoyed at this that I asked to have a look at this letter. Although it was on Vatican notepaper it had not been signed by anyone, nor was it addressed to anyone, and all it said was that Buddhism was a very good human teaching. The monk did not see the implication of this statement, but of course the point being made was that Christianity was, by contrast, divine revelation, the teaching of the son of God. So while Buddhism is no longer, at least on the diplomatic level, regarded by the Catholic church as totally false or evil, it is dismissed as a 'human teaching' on a par, say, with the philosophy of Socrates. It is not recognized as a faith.

Faith is action; it is karma, one could say, very weighty karma, although it is not technically classified as such. One might even say (and it is with technicalities like this that the Abhidharma gets a little tricky, so one must tread carefully) that it isn't just weighty karma. When it is categorized as 'lucidity' and 'longing' (though not 'deep conviction') faith is tinged with the transcendental. When as a Buddhist one has faith, one goes for Refuge to the Three Jewels; and the determination to go for Refuge carries that transcendental trace.

But faith is inherent in any positive mental state; it doesn't have to be faith in the Three Jewels as such. It can manifest as simply a vague but powerful inkling of something higher, a conviction that there is something more. Wordsworth describes this sort of feeling:

> ... *a sense sublime*
> *Of something far more deeply interfused,*
> *Whose dwelling is the light of setting suns,*
> *And the round ocean and the living air,*
> *And the blue sky, and in the mind of man.*[124]

2. SELF-RESPECT (OR SHAME) *(HRĪ)*

> ... if self respect and decorum are not there, one is incapable of restraining any evil action.[125]
> Yeshe Gyaltsen

Yeshe Gyaltsen links this second positive mental event with the third one (which he translates as 'decorum') because they are regarded as a pair throughout the Buddhist tradition. In the Pāli Canon they are jointly referred to as the two *lokapālas*, the two guardians of the world: *hiri* and *ottappa* in Pāli or *hrī* and *apatrāpya* in Sanskrit.[126] They are the guardians of the world because there would be no social order, no civilized existence, without them. The idea that they are the only restraint on our evil actions is perhaps hyperbole, but they are mentioned in all schools of Buddhism and considered very important indeed.

In his very brief remarks on *hrī* (which is translated as 'self-respect'), Yeshe Gyaltsen says, paraphrasing the *Abhidharmasamuccaya*:

Self-respect ... is to refrain from what is objectionable by having made oneself the norm.[127]

Having made oneself 'the norm' one is setting oneself the highest standards of behaviour. This is self-respect. There are certain courses of action that one's self-respect will not allow one to follow. They just would not be proper, not becoming, not worthy. One would be demeaning oneself to do such things. In its highest development – in the Tantric context – this is what is called 'vajra pride' or 'Buddha pride': one wants to act according to the dictates of one's essential Buddha-nature.

An interesting association is suggested by Lama Govinda in his discussion of the archetypal Buddha Amitābha in Foundations of Tibetan Mysticism. Amitābha's colour is red, and his bīja mantra or sacred seed syllable is in fact this word, hrī, which literally means 'to blush', 'to feel shame'. Govinda suggests that the colour represents the blush of shame, that is, one's own self-respect responding to one's wrong-doing: 'What makes us blush is the shame we feel in the presence of our better knowledge, our conscience.'[128]

3. DECORUM (OR RESPECT FOR WISE OPINION) (APATRĀPYA)

Yeshe Gyaltsen goes on to define apatrāpya as:

to refrain from evil action ... 'because others will despise me'. The primary realm of restraint is the fear that one's guru and teacher and other people deserving respect would be annoyed.[129]

This definition should not be misunderstood. Apatrāpya is not really 'to refrain from evil action ... because others will despise me'. 'Others' have all sorts of views of what is objectionable. The implication here is that one's teacher and other people deserving of respect simply stand at the centre of an indeterminate locus of authority made up of 'others', but this is wrong. Apatrāpya is not about slavishly bowing to external pressure, public opinion, and conventional proprieties, which Guenther's translation of it as decorum would suggest. The more usual definition, in both Pāli and Sanskrit texts, is 'not doing something for which one would be blamed by the wise'; this makes things much clearer.

In his Manual of Abhidhamma, a translation of the Pāli Abhi-dhammatthasaṅgaha, Narada Thera describes ottappa (the Pāli equiva-lent of apatrāpya) as fear of consequences that arise from without,[130] but this is no better because it fails to convey the fact that this is a positive mental event. The essence of the term's meaning is not wanting to do something that will disappoint people whom one respects as one's spiritual friends, even as being wiser than one is oneself. 'Respect for wise opinion' seems the best translation.

There is no question of being motivated by a feeling of guilt. Guilt is associated with a fear of the withdrawal of affection – but our spiritual friends are not going to withdraw their affection and care, however badly we behave. So there is nothing to fear in that respect. We need be afraid only of letting them down.

In the interests of peace and quiet one may well want to conform to models of behaviour deemed acceptable by society in general, in so far as these do not hinder one's spiritual development. But one has to know what one is doing, and take care that one is not conforming simply out of fear of arousing the disapproval, execration, scorn, or ridicule of society at large. I have sometimes referred to the distinction between 'society', or the aspects of society with which one is person-ally in contact, and the Sangha, which in the broadest sense means the community of men and women who follow the Buddha's teaching, as the distinction between the 'group' and the 'spiritual community'. One must be able to distinguish between the group and the spiritual community, and between conforming to the expectations of the group and living up to the expectations of other members of the spiritual community. Sometimes, indeed, it may be necessary to incur the disapproval of the group in order not to incur the disapprobation of the spiritual community.

It is a question of what one believes in, where one places one's faith. The first three positive mental events are closely related: self-respect implies faith in oneself, while fear of blame implies faith in others. Obviously these other people one has faith in will be spiritual friends: one will have faith both that they have one's best interests at heart, and that they have the insight to know what one's best interests are, to know what is helpful to do and what isn't. The whole point of *apatrāpya* is not to submit to other people's ideas of what one should be doing – ideas that other people want to impose on one – but to follow the ideal that one has chosen for oneself, with the help of certain people, whom one has also chosen.

Having a true regard for one's spiritual friends, and knowing that they really want one to make progress, one doesn't want to make them unhappy by doing something that is going to get in the way of one's spiritual development. One trusts them to help reinforce one's better self against one's weaker self. One is able to use their expectations of one as a support in moments of weakness, and perhaps as an inspiration in times of strength. One has chosen them to be one's spiritual friends because one shares their view – or at least one's better self shares their view. Of course, it may be that sometimes *they* will need the support of one's own better self: sometimes *apatrāpya* is mutually interchangeable between spiritual friends, so that each fears the blame of the other. It needn't be a one-way thing.

It follows that in order to develop *apatrāpya* one needs to be in good, almost familiar contact with the spiritual community, with one's spiritual friends. It's vital never to isolate oneself from the people one looks up to when one is at one's best. A distant and apparently slightly threatening body of people becomes, in one's mind, a kind of authority; it is this sort of perception which probably gives rise to the inappropriate idea that *apatrāpya* is about fearing that others will be annoyed or despise one. Real *apatrāpya* is more like a concern that one's spiritual friends will be troubled, perhaps grieved or even hurt – there isn't the precise word for the emotion in English – by one's unskilful action. And for this kind of mental event to become operative one needs regular contact with 'the wise'. It is not enough just to fear that they might get to hear about what one is doing.

Nor is it enough to regard the Buddhas and Bodhisattvas as one's spiritual friends in this regard. After all, Christians believe that 'the eyes of the Lord are in every place, beholding the evil and the good'. They 'believe' that God sees literally everything that they do. But do they really behave as though they believed this? How many good Catholics are more afraid of God than they are of the local priest? This is the kind of frailty that draws the withering scorn of Alexander Pope:

> Yes, I am proud; I must be proud to see
> Men not afraid of God, afraid of me.[131]

It is therefore safer not to rely entirely on one's ability to fear the discommendation of the Buddhas and Bodhisattvas. At the same time though, this kind of relationship with the *ārya-saṅgha*, with those who have gained Enlightenment through following the Dharma, can be very beneficial. Of course, there is much that could be said about the nature of this relationship; we have had a hint of it in Yeshe Gyaltsen's verses of praise – but here perhaps we can simply make the connection with the idea of protection. The Buddhas and Bodhisattvas are said to be protectors. They represent the qualities – wisdom, compassion, purity, energy – we ourselves have the potential to develop in their fullness, and in that sense they protect our aspirations to fulfil our potential.

Likewise, *hrī* and *apatrāpya* are called the protectors of the world; but they can also be considered to be protectors of oneself and one's spiritual practice. For example, if one takes a vow in front of a shrine, one is consciously drawing to oneself the protection of *apatrāpya* or fear of blame. One is calling upon the Buddha, the Bodhisattvas, and one's personal friends to witness one's vow, so that they will know the precise standard of behaviour to expect of one with regard to one's practice.

4. NON-ATTACHMENT (ALOBHA)

In its most exalted sense, non-attachment is to be not attached to compounded existence or saṁsāra – that is, not attached to the three *dhātus* or worlds: of sense desire, of archetypal form, and of no-form. Non-attachment is ultimately, therefore, to be free of attachment to the highest heaven realms, even the most refined levels of meditative experience.

According to the *Vijñaptimātratāsiddhi-śāstra*,

> It is the nature of this Caitta to remain detached from, and
> uninfluenced by, the three states of mortal existence in the three
> Dhātus and the causes of this triple existence. Its special activity
> consists in counteracting covetousness and accomplishing good
> deeds.[132]

Non-attachment or *alobha* (literally, non-greed) is not one of the most popular virtues. It can sound like a purely negative state, consisting merely in the absence of attachment. But as a positive mental event in its own right there must be more to it than this. Non-attachment is not a sort of bloodless lack of interest, although the term might seem to suggest it. It provides the basis for positive action – 'accomplishing good deeds'. In fact, one can only become non-attached by being selectively and consciously attached to what is skilful and positive.

Non-attachment is not quite the same as detachment. 'Detachment' suggests that one's attachment is taken away from something: there are previous or potential objects of attachment from which one has de-tached oneself. But non-attachment has no reference to any particular object. The traditional image for the condition of non-attachment is that of thistledown blown on the wind. One is serene, confident, balanced in oneself. One doesn't settle on or stick to things, because one is self-contained. One doesn't feel the need to reach out for something to make one feel better, to make one whole or complete. One doesn't need to be appropriating things or people so as to feel fulfilled. One doesn't insist on keeping certain elements of experience to oneself, or maintaining certain patterns of experience that support a particular idea of oneself. One has the confidence and the wider vision to be free from being neurotically involved with things. As should be clear, generosity is intrinsic to this positive mental event.

Being non-attached does not mean being self-contained in a hard-edged way. It is not quite the same as being self-sufficient, which might imply a certain self-protectiveness, even a certain insecurity. If non-attachment means being self-contained, it is also about being an individual, being self-aware, objective, responsible, and sensitive. It is not about self-assertion. Of course, if circumstances require it one has to know how to stand up for oneself, but it is not intrinsic to being an individual to be asserting oneself all the time.

Self-assertiveness is not an intrinsic part of the definition of the true individual, because there are all sorts of circumstances that don't call for it. Self-assertion may simply be evidence of a dependence on the group, a sense of one's own weakness in relation to a projected authority. It's true that an individual is strong, but one should take care not to throw one's weight around with the mistaken view that one is thereby expressing one's individuality. People who demand to be treated 'as an individual' are often simply demanding attention, or claiming special treatment and indulgence.

Non-attachment is a state of individuality, independence, freedom, and creativity, but these are qualities of mind. You don't require them to be recognized by others, and you don't feel that they are under threat when someone resists letting you have your own way, because these qualities are developed in conjunction with responsibility and concern for others. So non-attachment is a state of equilibrium. You don't have to please everybody all the time; but you don't feel you have to displease them either. And if someone tries to pressure you, you may feel sorry or amused, but you don't feel pressured or threatened in any way.

5. NON-HATRED (*ADVEṢA*)

Yeshe Gyaltsen, again treating the subject very briefly, chooses to illustrate this fifth positive mental event with a quotation from the *Abhidharmasamuccaya*:

> It is the absence of the intention to torment sentient beings, to quarrel with frustrating situations, and to inflict suffering on those who are the cause of frustration.[133]

To this we may add, from the *Vijñaptimātratāsiddhi-śāstra*:

> It is the nature of this Caitta to remain non-irritated by the three kinds of suffering and their causes. The three kinds of suffering are: suffering produced by direct causes, suffering by loss or deprivation, and suffering by the passing away or impermanence of all things.[134]

Adveṣa or non-hatred means, firstly, not wanting to hurt people who have given us no cause to hate them. Hatred is the way we react to suffering; and we don't necessarily feel the need to discriminate clearly between worthy and not so worthy objects of our hatred. We simply feel a need to hate someone. Secondly, *adveṣa* means not getting angry with unsatisfactory situations – which means, ultimately, not even raging against the inevitable decay and passing away of things. Thirdly, it means not feeling any ill will towards people who have hurt us, even if they have done so deliberately. *Adveṣa* is not to react to suffering in any of these ways. Although hatred certainly produces suffering – inasmuch as hatred is, at the very least, an immediately painful experience – suffering does not have to produce hatred. We can cultivate *adveṣa* instead.

Non-hatred as the absence of the intention to inflict harm also means that one is not providing the occasion for hatred in others. Hatred spawns more hatred; it is contagious. Hatred causes both oneself and others to suffer, and that suffering carries both oneself and others on to further hatred and further suffering. This seems quite obvious: one doesn't inflict suffering directly, and one doesn't deprive someone of what they value, because, apart from anything else, to do so would cause hatred to arise in them.

However, there is the implication in the quotation from the *Vijñapti-mātratāsiddhi-śāstra* that one can become an object of hatred simply by being impermanent. You can be totally faithful to someone all your life, but when you die the person left behind can feel real resentment, as though it were your fault. 'Why did this have to happen to me?' they think, 'Why did you have to die just now, when I needed you so much?' It's irrational, but it happens. Resentment *is* irrational. Even if someone has an accident or contracts a disease through no fault of their own, and they need looking after, it seems that as the carer one naturally feels resentful from time to time. This is not to say that we are responsible for other people's hatred of us; even the Buddha was hated by some people.

There is a close relationship between hatred and attachment; perhaps this is most evident in the context of sexual relationships. One could say perhaps that where attachment is present in a sexual relationship, hatred is bound to arise sooner or later. Are they so very surprising, those terrible fights and quarrels that flare up between sexual partners? They are the inevitable fruit of attachment. If there are no flare-ups, if you can go on for a number of years without violent hatred breaking out, and without just getting into a rut, the likelihood is that attachment is not strongly present and that the relationship is relatively healthy. But in a sense a healthy relationship ceases to be a relationship. The very term suggests that you are officially together, that you've got to be together, and woe betide anybody who sees you as separate people or treats you as two distinct individuals.

> When a good mind is born, whatever may be its object of perception, it always manifests itself as non-attachment in regard to existence and non-irritation in regard to suffering. This means that non-covetousness and non-anger are established in relation to 'existence' and 'suffering', but it is not necessary for the mind actually to consider existence and suffering in order to manifest these two Caittas. Similarly, the sense of shame and that of integrity are established in relation to good and evil, but it is not necessary for the mind actually to experience good and evil in order to manifest these two Caittas. It follows from this that non-covetousness and non-anger accompany all good minds.[135]
> *Vijñaptimātratāsiddhi-śāstra*

All these terms – shame, fear of blame by the wise, non-attachment, and non-hatred – represent positive mental events, not just negative mental events that have somehow failed to materialize. In order to experience or manifest them, one doesn't have to be tempted to do something shameful or blameworthy, or feel on the brink of attachment or aversion. It may seem misleading that grammatically negative expressions are used for positive qualities, but this is a general characteristic of Pāli and Sanskrit; the addition of *a-* as a prefix produces the negative counterpart of a word, rather as adding the prefix 'non-' does in English (so that here we have *dveṣa* meaning 'hatred' and *adveṣa* meaning non-hatred).

It is not usual in English, though, to refer to positive qualities in this 'double negative' sort of way. But there is one obvious example of an English word which is constructed in this way: the word immortal. It literally means 'absence of mortality', but of course it has a very positive connotation of its own. Terms like non-hatred need to be recognized as carrying a similarly positive connotation.

But if 'non-hatred' is not merely the absence of hatred, if it is a positive quality in itself, why is that quality not just termed, say, love or *maitrī* (*mettā* in Pāli)? Actually, there is a real point to expressing certain qualities in terms of their opposites, because they acquire thereby an elusiveness that is essential to their meaning. Yes, these qualities are hard to get at through this negative terminology, but that may not be such a bad thing. Faced with these 'negative' terms, we have to ask ourselves, 'What is actually meant here?' The word itself does not allow us to imagine that we know all about it just because we know what the word means. We begin to realize that we have to get a sense of the thing itself – *alobha* or *adveṣa* – as an experience in order to understand what it is about; it isn't enough just to be able to make clear sense of the label. And in fact there is a distinction between these 'negative' expressions and their positive counterparts. For example, loving kindness goes beyond non-hatred. If you are in a situation where someone is making things very difficult or unpleasant for you, you can experience non-hatred without necessarily experiencing loving kindness, which suggests that the two are distinct mental events.

In the *Bodhicaryāvatāra*, Śāntideva – apparently following Mahāyāna tradition – regards *kṣānti* (patience) as the positive counterpart of hatred or anger. *Kṣānti* is a form of awareness, an awareness of suffering in which one does not react with anger. It is even a form of transcendental insight in that it arises together with the next positive mental event, non-deludedness. The way Śāntideva puts it, here are all these people effectively helping you to practise *kṣānti* by giving you a hard time – and what do you do? You get angry with them, you poor deluded fool![136]

While non-hatred and non-attachment support each other – inasmuch as there can be no hatred without attachment, and no attachment without hatred – both are brought into being only through 'non-deludedness', the mental event which follows. Together, these three fundamental positive mental events form the three wholesome roots of all positive action.

6. NON-DELUDEDNESS (AMOHA)

It is a thorough comprehension of (practical) knowledge that comes from maturation, instructions, thinking and understanding,...[137]

This is part of the quotation from the *Abhidharmasamuccaya* with which Yeshe Gyaltsen begins his commentary on the positive mental event non-deludedness. He goes on to remark:

It is a distinct discriminatory awareness to counteract the deludedness that has its cause in either what one has been born into or what one has acquired.[138]

So non-deludedness or *amoha* is a thorough knowledge that comes in four different ways. It arises firstly from maturation, by which is meant the natural intelligence one is born with, as a result (*vipāka*) of having developed one's moral and intellectual understanding in the past. The other three ways consist in the active cultivation of non-deludedness through the three knowledges: *śruta-mayī-prajñā, cintā-mayī-prajñā, bhāvanā-mayī-prajñā*: literally 'the wisdom arising from hearing, the wisdom arising from thinking/reflecting, and the wisdom arising from meditation'.

The first of these is the understanding one gets from instruction – that is, Dharma study, ideally with one's teacher. The second is the result of consideration: thinking, reflecting, turning the teachings over in one's own mind, and relating them to one's own experience. And the third knowledge comes from understanding or intuition, which refers to meditation: focusing on the teaching while in a state of meditative concentration, and thereby gaining insight into it, making a real experience of it, actually being changed by it. So learning provides the raw material for thinking which in turn provides the raw material for meditation.

We get another angle on this from the *Vijñaptimātratāsiddhi-śāstra*:

According to one opinion, non-delusion is of the same nature as discernment [i.e. *prajñā*], because the Abhidharma says that 'non-delusion has as its essential nature the certitude which arises from retribution, instruction, demonstration, and intuition'.... Although non-delusion is discernment by nature and is essentially a special Caitta, still, in order to indicate that the good aspect of discernment possesses a superior power for the accomplishment of good acts, it is separately regarded as a 'good Caitta' ...

According to another opinion (Dharmapāla), non-delusion is not discernment; it has a separate self-nature. For it is directly opposed to ignorance and, like non-covetousness and non-anger, it is comprised among the roots of good ...

It is true that the Abhidharmasamuccaya says that non-delusion is discernment by nature; but this text explains the nature of non-delusion in terms of its cause and fruit.... The cause of non-delusion is discernment.[139]

The point of controversy here is whether or not non-deludedness is the same as 'discernment' (by which is meant *prajñā* or wisdom). If they are the same, why is *prajñā* a 'special *caitta*' (what Guenther calls an object-determining mental event) while non-deludedness is a 'good *caitta*' (i.e. a positive mental event). But if they are different, why is non-delusion defined by the Abhidharma in such terms as to suggest that it is *prajñā*?

It was above all the teaching of Dharmapāla, who was the abbot of the great monastery of Nālandā in northern India, that inspired the author of the *Vijñaptimātratāsiddhi-śāstra*, Hsüan Tsang, to found the Fa-hsiang School on his return to his native China. Not that Dharmapāla was Hsüan Tsang's personal teacher – in fact the abbot had been dead for many years by the time of Hsüan Tsang's arrival in India – but the legacy of Dharmapāla's interpretation of the Dharma was the Chinese pilgrim's inspiration. Generally, therefore, Hsüan Tsang favours Dharmapāla's interpretation over those of the other nine commentators he consults. But on this occasion he does not offer an overt opinion of his own, which might suggest that he actually disagrees with Dharmapāla, but doesn't want to say so out of respect.

As to whether *prajñā* and *amoha* are the same or different, the controversy is more apparent than real. We have to remember that we are concerned not with things, but with relations. Object-determining mental events have the function of getting to ever closer grips with the object, and wisdom does this by dispelling doubt. Non-deludedness, on the other hand, is a positive mental event in its own right. It is not that it confronts or gets to grips with the object but that it provides the basis 'for the accomplishment of good acts', 'for not becoming involved in evil behaviour'.

It is tempting to try to simplify things by seeing non-delusion as *prajñā* manifesting on a different level, so to speak. However, the Abhidharma is very careful to avoid using this kind of language. Yeshe Gyaltsen describes non-deludedness as a *'distinct* discriminatory awareness' – in other words, a special form of wisdom that counteracts delusion or ignorance as to what is skilful and what is unskilful. This is why Guenther adds the word 'practical': 'It is a thorough comprehension of (practical) knowledge'. In brief, therefore, *amoha* is a positive mental event that is *prajñā* (primarily an object-determining mental event) in its aspect of distinguishing in practical terms between what is skilful and what is unskilful.

Appreciative discrimination (*prajñā*) is, if you like, concerned with knowing what *is*, while non-deludedness is concerned with knowing what to do. It seems that most people tend, perhaps by temperament, to be more interested in one than the other, but it is generally metaphysics that holds the greater appeal; questions of ethics tend to be dismissed as being dry or boring. Certainly when I was young – in my late teens and even my early twenties – I was much more interested in knowing 'what is' than 'what to do'. It was as though what one did more or less took care of itself, leaving the mind free to think about 'what is'.

For example, I remember that when as a young soldier in the last war I was stationed in Singapore, some friends asked me why I was not a vegetarian. As it happened I had simply never thought about it before. I'd never thought 'Is it skilful or unskilful to eat meat? Would it not be more skilful to become a vegetarian?' In several years of reading books about Buddhism it had never crossed my mind to question my own behaviour in this way. But when it was questioned *for* me I realized at once that a Buddhist had to try to be a vegetarian, which is what I did. But it was not the sort of thing I was interested in. I was interested in knowing about *śūnyatā*, the One Mind, and so on, not in knowing which actions were skilful and which were not. That came very much later on.

Very generally, one could say that the sort of people who want to know 'what is' attend lectures and read books on Buddhism, while those who want to know 'what to do' go along to meditation classes and join in other Buddhist activities. Perhaps it is a question of age, responsibility, and experience. If one has had some involvement with the world, one will have had to live with the choices one has made, perhaps for a long time, which will make one realize the importance of knowing how to behave skilfully. When one is young, on the other hand, one is less likely to have this sort of perspective; one's focus is more likely to be on wanting to know things as they are in reality.

This distinction is not, of course, between knowing and doing, theory and practice, but between two kinds of theory. Having developed an understanding of what is skilful and what isn't, one still has to put that theory into practice. As well as maintaining a balance between these two aspects of knowledge one needs also to maintain a balance between knowing why one practises and actually practising. However, the practical aspect of *prajñā*, non-deludedness, is the vital link between the ultimate metaphysical questions and our own existential situation, and the Abhidharma tradition considers it so important that it enumerates it as an independent skilful mental event.

This emphasis reflects what it's actually like to become involved with Buddhism. In a sense one has already determined 'what is' by the very fact of having taken up the practice of Buddhism. One has accepted that Enlightenment is the ultimate goal, that the transcendental is there beyond one's mundane experience of the world, and that one is trying to work towards that. One acknowledges that it is a long way off, and that in the meantime one just has to get on with whatever lies to hand. One presses on with one's meditation, gets on with one's work, cultivates one's spiritual friendships, goes on retreat, and all the rest of it. Whether in the end one is going to experience the Void, or the One Mind, one can probably quite safely wait and see.

This is the attitude of many practising Buddhists, including monks in the East, particularly if they have no great aptitude for metaphysics. They don't think too often or too deeply about the whys and wherefores of their practice. It has to be said that some Theravādins take this attitude too far and completely ignore ultimate questions of metaphysics, even claiming that the Buddha told his followers not to think about such matters. This is, of course, a mistake. What could be more practical and down to earth than exploring the true nature of reality?

However, there is a great deal of sense in making up one's mind once and for all about the general spiritual pattern within which one needs to work and then fully involving oneself in it. This doesn't mean becoming mechanical and superficial and getting in a rut. After all, one's regular practice includes meditation, mindfulness, reflection, and study. As Candrakīrti robustly puts it, 'Those who go through the day without wondering about the existence or non-existence of things are not fit to be called human.' But wondering about the existence or non-existence of things does not mean questioning the very basis of one's practice. It does not mean constantly wondering whether perhaps the Sufis or the Vedantins have a more profound conception of 'what is' than is to be found in Buddhism.

The aspect of one's practice which does need consideration from time to time is the question of what is truly and deeply skilful and what isn't. From time to time one may need to review one's practice and see if any modification is required – but not all the time. One can't stop every minute of the day to work everything out all over again. Once, as a result of some thought and investigation, one has made the decision to accept a particular pattern of spiritual practice – because it seems to be a positive, helpful one – one has to commit oneself to it, otherwise one will never be able to test its validity for oneself. If one is always questioning it one cannot very well commit oneself to it, and then one will never know anything much about it anyway. One is likely to arrive at some kind of Perfect Vision – actually seeing 'what is' and indeed also 'what to do' – not by working out 'what is', or even 'what to do', but by getting on with regular practice.

Non-deludedness is cultivated through studying the Buddha's teachings in one form or another. Yeshe Gyaltsen lists twelve different classes of teaching (collectively known as *dharmapravacana*, 'Exposition of the Doctrine') identified by the Sarvāstivādins (though the Theravādins recognize only the first nine). The first five are: *sūtras* (discourses in prose), *geyas* (mixed prose and verse), *vyākaraṇas* (predictions to Enlightenment), *gāthās* (verses), and *udānas* (inspired utterances). The sixth class of scripture is the *nidāna*. *Nidāna* means 'connection', and the connection is usually between the past and the present via, say, a *jātaka* story. Whereas a *jātaka* is simply the story of one of the Buddha's past lives, a *nidāna* makes the connection with the present, with one character in the story being identified as the Buddha's companion Ānanda, another as the Buddha, and so on. *Nidāna* also means a continuous narrative – for instance, a connected account of certain events in the life of the Buddha.

The other classes of scripture are *avadānas* (heroic deeds of disciples of the Buddha in their previous lives), *ittivṛttakas* ('Thus it was said' – sayings of the Buddha), *jātakas* (birth stories), *vaipulyas* (extended discourses), *adbhutadharmas* (miraculous happenings), and *upadeśas* (instructions).[140]

Yeshe Gyaltsen goes on to point out that the teachings may also be classified according to the three *piṭakas* or baskets: the Sūtra Piṭaka, the Vinaya Piṭaka, and the Abhidharma Piṭaka. We can get an idea of the balance of the content of these three collections by considering to what extent they cover the stages of the path: *śīla*, *samādhi*, and *prajñā*. One could estimate that the sūtras – or rather the suttas – of the Pāli Canon deal more or less equally with all three; by and large, the *vinaya* is concerned with *śīla* and *samādhi*; while the Abhidharma is devoted entirely to the development of *prajñā* through a review of the *dharmas*. (According to the Hīnayāna, especially as developed in the Abhidharma, *prajñā* consists in an understanding of the content of the Abhidharma itself.)

The Vinaya Piṭaka is conventionally regarded as consisting in a specifically monastic code of rules, but this is not really so. The original separation of *sūtra* from *vinaya* occurred as part of the oral tradition, before these teachings were written down – and before the first compilation of the Abhidharma – and it was meant simply to distinguish the teachings as a whole from an account of their practical application in terms of 'discipline', particularly as exemplified in the everyday activity of the Buddha himself.

The Vinaya is, therefore, the product of non-deludedness or *amoha*; it is the product of practical wisdom. It is not simply a matter of observing rules. In fact, thinking exclusively in terms of observing rules can have a deleterious effect, spiritually speaking, in that you get depressed when you break a rule and elated when you keep one. One also inevitably seems to attach too much importance to certain rules, and this unbalanced view of one's practice leads one to veer from one emotional extreme to another. It is fair enough to standardize skilful mental attitudes in the form of rules, though this term is perhaps not ideal; but the point of them is to help one do what is skilful in a regular and constant manner.

This is perhaps clearer if we think in terms of precepts rather than rules. Of course, the rules of the Vinaya were originally laid down as specific applications of the ethical precepts; many of them had reference to the specific cultural situation of the time, and make little sense today. But in general, rules – appropriate rules – give stability to one's whole life, and thus in fact remove elation and despondency. So it is less a matter of observing rules than of having a firm basis to fall back on, a disciplined way of life that protects one against ups and downs.

The cultivation of non-delusion is not, therefore, a matter of learning rules any more than it is a matter of amassing facts. This said, study of some kind is probably essential:

> Knowing little, the blind men do not know how to bring contemplation
> to life.
> Because they lack that, they cannot think of anything.[141]
>
> Aśvaghoṣa

Of course, one has to be careful in criticizing the way other people go about their practice. One has to make due allowance for differences of temperament: there are doctrine followers (*dharmānusārins*), who are particularly stimulated and inspired by study; and there are faith followers (*śraddhānusārins*), who are much more concerned with actual practice: meditation, maintaining close contact with their teacher, and so on.[142]

However, taken to extremes, either of these approaches can leave us high and dry. If we don't develop *śruta-mayī-prajñā* (the wisdom arising from studying the Dharma) and *cintā-mayī-prajñā* (the wisdom arising from reflecting on what we have studied), we will not be able to develop *bhāvanā-mayī-prajñā*, the transcendental insight that arises from meditating upon what we have studied and reflected on. In short, we will have nothing to meditate on.

On the other hand, some of the more learned *geshes*, particularly of the Gelukpa tradition, get so deeply into study that they make no time, even towards the end of their lives, for meditation. I have met one or two Tibetan geshes who say that meditation isn't necessary, although this is not the orthodox Gelukpa view. Some even openly scoff at the tantras: 'What is the point of all this ringing of bells and banging of drums?' they say. 'Buddhism is really all about metaphysics and logic!' What we all need, of course, is a balance; the lives of Buddhism's most eminent practitioners exemplify a balanced approach. Padmasambhava, for example, was a great scholar as well as a great yogi, and even Milarepa had a comprehensive knowledge of the tantras.

Taking the three wholesome roots of non-attachment, non-hatred, and non-deludedness together, we find they can be experienced at three different levels. On the first level, the three poisons (that is, their negative counterparts, attachment, hatred, and delusion) are overcome as regards this life, but they have been displaced on to a future life, perhaps in heaven. At this level, while one has no attachment to this life – one knows it is impermanent – one is attached to the idea of a permanent heaven, and woe betide anyone who gainsays that. The second level represents the Arhant ideal of the Hīnayāna – at least according to the Mahāyāna. According to this, while there may be no attachment to any form of satisfaction whatsoever, whether now or in future lives, there is still a very refined attachment to the attainment of nirvāṇa itself. This allows for a third level to be posited by the followers of the Mahāyāna, who look forward not to a nirvāṇa that can be localized or particularized in straightforward contradistinction to saṃsāra, but to the *apratiṣṭhita* nirvāṇa, that is, a non-localized or, more literally, non-established or non-abiding nirvāṇa.[143] Even in the attainment of nirvāṇa, it seems, there is to be no settling down.

7. DILIGENCE (OR ENERGY IN PURSUIT OF THE GOOD) (*VĪRYA*)

Vīrya is another of those terms for which there is no adequate English translation. In fact, even the Sanskrit word did not originally carry the full meaning that it bears as a specifically Buddhist term. It means 'strength' or 'energy', but in the Buddhist context it means more than this. For a start it has a purely positive connotation. The important corollary is that energy as such is not necessarily *vīrya*, or even necessarily positive. It is commonly assumed that 'freeing up one's energy' is somehow positive in a spiritual sense, but in fact it is positive only when the energy freed up is directed towards the positive.

We get a truer feeling for the idea of *vīrya* if we take the emphasis away from the notion of energy altogether, and translate it as intentness on, or a powerful inclination towards – in the literal sense of bending towards – the skilful. This also helps to emphasize the fact that we are talking about a mental event here – not simply busying oneself doing good. That is, *vīrya* is a mental event that expresses itself in action; it is not the activity itself.

Yeshe Gyaltsen has quite a lot to say about *vīrya* (which Guenther translates as 'diligence'). Here we will focus on one of the quotations given from the *Abhidharmasamuccaya*, a list of five kinds or stages of *vīrya*:

a. Diligence which is ever ready
Gyaltsen elaborates on this with the help of a quotation from the *Pāramitāsamanāma*:

When the mind, having been released from the frustrations of
One's round of *saṃsāra*, becomes ever active,

Immovable and infinite, that (mind) becomes possessed of
The capacity towards the wholesome which is a brave mode of action,
And is said to be the first of the pure things to be grasped.[144]

This is the pure capacity for *vīrya*, before it has been manifested in action. It is the readiness to apply oneself. Yeshe Gyaltsen characterizes this stage as 'to put on the heavy armour', which is quite a common idiom in Buddhist texts – as it is in the Christian tradition: St Paul talks of putting on the full armour of Christ, for example. The spirit of the image is clearly voiced in the words of William Blake:

Bring me my bow of burning gold:
Bring me my arrows of desire:
Bring me my spear: O clouds, unfold,
Bring me my chariot of fire.

I will not cease from mental fight,
Nor shall my sword sleep in my hand,
Till we have built Jerusalem
In England's green and pleasant land.[145]

Putting on armour simply means getting ready for battle. We should be careful not to take from the phrase the impression of a hard, rigid, resistant attitude being adopted. *Vīrya* is not about sealing oneself off. We should also be careful not to take the idea that *vīrya* is 'the first of the pure things to be grasped' too simplistically. We have already been told that *śraddhā*, for example, is the spiritual quality upon which all others depend; from which we can only conclude that these positive qualities are not to be found as separate entities. They tend to arise together; in a sense they are aspects of each other. Where there is energy in pursuit of the good, there one will find some measure of faith, and vice versa.

b. Diligence which is applied work
When one actually gets down to applying oneself, one exhibits *vīrya* in two quite different ways. One can steadily plod along the path one knows one needs to follow even though it may currently be a rather joyless exercise; or one can follow the same path enthusiastically. These two modes of *vīrya* may seem different, but the first will eventually lead to the second. Directing one's energies towards what one knows to be wholesome in a steady, systematic, persistent way – albeit

without a lot of joy – will have positive effects, and enthusiasm will naturally tend to arise more and more as one keeps going.

The second can unfortunately give way to the first from time to time as well – one's enthusiasm can sometimes melt away – and then *vīrya* consists in carrying on without it. The crucial point is that enthusiasm is not necessary in order to keep up a steady practice. To say 'I don't really feel inspired about doing this (whatever it is), so it would be better if I didn't get involved,' is a rationalization, a specious excuse for laziness. Motivation, enthusiasm, and inspiration will arise as long as we just get on with the job.

c. Diligence which does not lose heart
This is *vīrya* as stout-heartedness, applying oneself with courage and confidence, not losing heart in moments of personal frailty. It calls for a measure of *śraddhā* in the sense of confidence in one's own potential.

d. Diligence which does not turn back
One may take it upon oneself to achieve a certain goal and, having foreseen quite clearly all the obstacles that are likely to arise, one may estimate that one has the resources to fulfil the task one has set oneself. But what happens when one runs up against an obstacle that one had not anticipated? One may quite reasonably feel like saying, 'This was not in the bargain. What has arisen is outside the range of conditions under which I was prepared to make an effort. Sorry.' But one needs to realize that in fact this almost always happens. Some unforeseen difficulty or other almost always crops up, whatever one is trying to do. If what one is trying to do is skilful, this is where *vīrya* – in the sense of applying oneself with complete thoroughness, not turning back – comes in. One doesn't abandon one's original intention just because the going has become more difficult than one had expected.

e. Diligence which is never satisfied
Whatever one has achieved, however exalted it may be, one never rests on one's laurels. The very nature of *vīrya* is that it goes on and on, as long as there is something higher to be achieved – and of course there always is. When, in the *White Lotus Sūtra*, the Buddha announces this fact to an enormous gathering of Bodhisattvas, Arhants, Stream Entrants, laymen, laywomen, *rākṣasas*, *gandharvas*, and many other beings, it is altogether too much for some of them. Five thousand 'persons of overbearing arrogance' simply walk out. The revelation

that they cannot rest satisfied with their attainment is just too much.[146] One could say that *vīrya* in this sense involves a perception and understanding of the full extent of development, represented by the path.

8. ALERTNESS (OR TRANQUILLITY) (*PRAŚRABDHI*)

Guenther's translation of *praśrabdhi*, 'alertness', will not do at all. Many of his translations are exceptionally precise and helpful, but sometimes it seems that he translates the word but not the meaning. He is at pains to call upon contemporary, philosophical, linguistic, and analytical terminology in constructing his translations but he doesn't always relate the result back to actual spiritual experience, even though he always made much of the Tantric emphasis on 'actual experience'. Like Mrs Rhys Davids' notorious translation of *jhāna* (the Pāli equivalent of *dhyāna*) as 'musing', Guenther's translation of the Tibetan word for *praśrabdhi*, however correct from a philological point of view, does not help us to understand what is actually being talked about.

Literally, *praśrabdhi* is tranquillity, relaxation, calming down. What, though, is being calmed down? We can get an idea of this from considering *praśrabdhi* as the fifth of the twelve positive *nidānas* or links comprising the spiral path that leads us from the endless wheel of compounded existence to Enlightenment.[147] It comes between *prīti* (ecstasy or rapture) and *sukha* (bliss), and it signifies the whole process of calming down and releasing unresolved energy in *dhyāna* (higher meditative states).

As we have already seen (page 86), all five factors of meditation are present in the first level of *dhyāna*: *vitarka* and *vicāra* (initial thought and sustained thought), *ekāgratā* (concentration), *prīti* (rapture), and *sukha* (bliss). As absorption deepens, thought dies away and one experiences a clear, conceptless concentration together with ecstasy and bliss. Then, as absorption deepens still further, the element of physical ecstasy – *prīti* – is increasingly contained by or assimilated into a growing experience of purely mental bliss – *sukha*. This process of containment or assimilation is *praśrabdhi*; it is by means of *praśrabdhi* that absorption deepens.

Yeshe Gyaltsen asserts that *praśrabdhi* is twofold:

Physical alertness means that when through the power of concentration the sluggishness of the body, which does not allow one to do anything, has been overcome, one feels light like cotton floating in the air and the body can be made to work towards any positive value one wishes. Mental alertness means that when through the power of concentration, mental sluggishness has been removed, the mind moves on towards its object without friction and can operate smoothly.[148]

Thus there are two aspects of *praśrabdhi*. It is physical, though not in the sense of the physical body but in the sense of the mental factors of feeling (*vedanā*), perception (*saṃjñā*) and motivation (*saṃskāras*), which subside as the attention is withdrawn from the body and its concerns. And it is also mental, in that the unconscious energy which arises in the form of physical ecstasy is absorbed into the experience of purely mental bliss.

It would seem as though in the state of *prīti* deeper sources of energy are tapped, blocked energy is released, and the upward rush of that energy is experienced as intensely pleasurable in a bubbly sort of way. But it isn't completely integrated and it may even bubble over – as one is sitting in meditation, one may start laughing or twitching or shaking. All this is unintegrated energy breaking out in various ways. It is possible to find oneself completely taken by surprise and thrown off balance.

As *praśrabdhi* begins to develop, the effervescence subsides, but one doesn't return to a comparatively emotionless state: one is left with a feeling of exhilaration which is no longer out of control. The rapture does not disappear, or even lessen. It simply contributes to the intensification of the blissful feeling, giving it a light, floating quality, while at the same time it becomes quieter, so to speak, more pure and stable.

This is in no way a passive state – in fact it makes it very easy to do anything, either mentally or physically. Everything becomes very pleasant, flowing, smooth, spontaneous. *Praśrabdhi*, sometimes translated as 'pliancy', makes the mind pliable, adaptable, easily worked with. Obviously, a very useful quality.

9. CONCERN (OR NON-HEEDLESSNESS) (*APRAMĀDA*)

From taking its stand on non-attachment, non-hatred, and non-deludedness coupled with diligence, it considers whatever is positive and protects the mind against things which cannot satisfy.[149]
Abhidharmasamuccaya

This is *apramāda*. The very last words the Buddha spoke before he died were apparently (in Pāli) *appamādena sampādetha*, usually translated 'With mindfulness, strive on.'[150] But *apramāda*, which is sometimes translated 'conscientiousness', means mindfulness in a special active sense: it is to keep up mindful attention in order to guard against unskilful action. A very full account of this quality appears in a beautiful little memoir of Surendranath Dasgupta by his wife Surama. Dasgupta was possibly the greatest Indian scholar of modern times and also a distinguished Bengali poet. His wife's account of his life includes a large number of letters he wrote to her, from one of which are extracted the following reflections on *apramāda*:

> The word *pramāda* means inadvertence. In simple Bengali it means lack of attention. Therefore the term *'a-pramāda'* will mean absence of inattention.... But ... why should the scriptures use the word in a negative form, i.e. instead of emphasizing attention ... why should they speak of 'lack of inattention'?

> The word *'pramatta'* ([he] who is under *pramāda*) means a drunkard or a lunatic.... So we see the word *'pramāda'* means error, ignorance, drunkenness, inadvertence or carelessness and laxity.... The negative particle [prefix] *a-* stands here in the sense of the 'least amount' of *pramāda*. Therefore *apramāda* does not mean that we have been able to eliminate *pramāda* completely, but that we have been able to reduce it.... All the time, inattention and errors are trying to get hold of us, but our mind, keeping alert all the time, is trying to drive them away.

> [*Apramāda*] is not one of those functions of the mind which we call accomplished or stabilised. In *apramāda* we get the idea of a movement or a process. The brightness of intellect, tenacity and firmness are steady characters of the mind. But *apramāda* is of the nature of movement. Our mind is always drawn towards small achievements in the outside world. We have, therefore, to withdraw our mind from those small interests, keep it alert so that we are not dragged into a current to other goals, and we have to be very careful that we are moving towards the achievement which we value and which we desire.

> [*Apramāda*] is not the same as the presence of attention, because the attention that we require for study is punctuated with gaps; we try to collect knowledge and move on from one object to another. Therefore our attention also shifts from object to object. It is not like the continuous flow of the River Ganges,... Therefore, we should

distinguish between *apramāda* ... and the presence of attention, by accepting the former as an attribute of the spirit.[151]

So according to Dasgupta *apramāda* is expressed in this negative form because it is not a quality that is achieved, but a process, an activity, that one engages in. Because things are always happening we have to be continually on our guard, continually taking precautions against the ever-present possibility of being taken unawares. If *vīrya* is like arming oneself, then *apramāda* is the battle itself – in other words, one needs *vīrya* to apply *apramāda*. But though energy in pursuit of the good provides one with the spiritual fuel to advance along the whole front of one's spiritual practice – developing the positive as well as warding off the negative – the main thrust of one's practice at the outset of one's spiritual life is generally to engage this quality of non-heedlessness.

Clearly, non-heedlessness is supported by mindfulness, especially by mindfulness of purpose (*samprajanya*). But it should not be confused with mindfulness as such – as it is in the common translation of the Buddha's famous last words. As we have seen, *smṛti* is firstly 'recollection' in the sense of calling up something of the past, and secondly 'mindfulness' in the sense of being aware in the present, whether that awareness is of one's body, one's thoughts, one's feelings, or the Dharma itself. When, as a result of directing one's awareness towards the Dharma, one gains insight into the truth, that awareness becomes knowledge in the sense of *prajñā*.

Non-heedlessness, however, is mindfulness in an essentially defensive posture – the quality of being on the alert for interruptions, temptations, and unskilful states. It is of crucial importance; indeed, as the *Dhammapada* suggests, it is the difference between life and death:

Non-heedlessness is the basis of immortality. Negligence is the state of death.[152]

10. EQUANIMITY (UPEKṢĀ)

It is a mind which abides in the state of non-attachment, non-hatred, and non-deludedness coupled with assiduousness [*vīrya*].... It is a state where mind remains what it is – a state of being calm and a spontaneous presence of mind. Its function is not to provide occasions for emotional instability.[153]

Abhidharmasamuccaya

As we have already seen, there are three levels or types of equanimity or *upekṣā*. The first is hedonic indifference, a state of indifference with regard to feelings coming in through the senses (discussed under the omnipresent mental event *vedanā* – see page 77). We are all familiar with this basic level of *upekṣā* – which is in no way a positive mental event – and we need to be careful not to confuse it with the others.

The third form of *upekṣā* is synonymous with nirvāṇa, and it is in this sense that it occurs as the seventh and last of the *bodhyaṅgas* or factors of Enlightenment. As we have seen, it is a state of equilibrium with regard to all mundane things whatsoever. From the Mahāyāna point of view it is a state of equilibrium between saṁsāra and nirvāṇa. One might also describe it as a state of metaphysical axiality: that is, one becomes – in a manner of speaking – the axis upon which the universe turns. Again, this third level of *upekṣā* should not be confused with the second level, which is the positive mental event under discussion here.

This second level – *upekṣā* as a positive mental event – is equanimity as a factor of the fourth *dhyāna*. We have seen that the higher one's consciousness progresses through the four *dhyānas*, the fewer the mental factors: not that mental factors are eliminated, but they become more and more fully integrated with one another. This gradual process of consolidation, integration, and refinement leads towards a state of greater and greater stability.

In the third *dhyāna* the factor of physical ecstasy is absorbed into the factor of bliss through the process of *praśrabdhi*, so that one is left with just the factors of bliss and one-pointedness or concentration (not that one-pointedness is a separate mental factor as such – it is a way of describing the integration itself). And in the fourth *dhyāna* the process continues. The bliss becomes transformed into *upekṣā* or equanimity, while one-pointedness becomes unshakeable. So equanimity in this sense is the strength that comes from complete emotional integration and stability.

11. NON-VIOLENCE (AVIHIṀSĀ)

To quote from Yeshe Gyaltsen's own commentary:

> Non-violence is patient acceptance [*kṣānti*] which expresses itself in the sentiment of how wonderful it would be if suffering sentient beings could be released from all their frustrations ...

To fulfil the *vinaya*, it is necessary to carry about a water strainer in order to avoid harming life in water. Since a person who does not carry a water strainer is one who goes against loving kindness taught by the Buddha, he must be uprooted from his foundation of harming another and be earnestly advised of the need to actualize the four attitudes by which one becomes an ascetic, namely,

1. Even if one is reviled, he should not revile in return.
2. Even if one is angered, he should not retaliate with anger.
3. Even if one is struck, he should not strike back.
4. Even if someone pries into one's affair, he should not pry into someone else's affair.

   … the renunciation of violence is the quintessence of the teaching.[154]

Avihiṁsā or abstention from harming is the first and most fundamental of the precepts; in a sense, any breach of the precepts is an act of violence. At the same time, inasmuch as it is about not having even the slightest idea of harming any living being – that is, in that it is a positive mental event – it is very closely akin to loving kindness (*mettā*) and even compassion (*karuṇā*).

Of course, the principle of non-violence is virtually synonymous with Buddhism in many people's minds, but it still seems that Buddhists themselves rather take it for granted. There's much more to it than one might think; it means an entirely different mode of operating. Sometimes I have characterized it as operating according to the 'love mode' rather than the 'power mode'. But if one thinks about it, a great deal of life in society is based on force, on the power mode. Exercising power isn't just about literal violence; it includes emotional blackmail, and all sorts of subtle methods of coercion.

But if one wants to follow a spiritual life one has more or less to abandon the power mode and operate in accordance with the love mode. Sometimes one may be in a situation in which the use of power is necessary; for example, if you run a business and someone owes you money, it may be necessary eventually to take him to court, which is in a sense invoking force. If you know that he has money, that may be the best thing to do; but if, on the other hand, you are aware that he is in real financial difficulties, you may decide not to pursue the matter.

Within the spiritual community power should never be used, because that would be to negate everything the spiritual community stands for. If you use violence towards someone, whether overtly or covertly, you are not treating him as an individual. To the extent that one does act violently, even to the extent of speaking harshly, one no longer belongs to the spiritual community.

The principle of non-violence is to be practised not just with regard to other people, but also with regard to animals, and to our environment. The water strainer Yeshe Gyaltsen refers to is one of the eight requisites, the eight things with which monks are provided when they are ordained, together with the three robes, the needle and thread, the bowl, the razor blade, and the girdle.[155] Presumably without a water strainer it would have been all too easy, when drinking from pools and rivers, inadvertently to swallow all sorts of minute living things.

This is just one indication of how seriously the first Buddhists took their practice of non-violence. But how far do we need to carry this principle of *avihiṁsā*? The Buddha made a clear distinction between what is intentional and what is unintentional – so that if you accidentally swallow a fly, say, this does not constitute bad karma. (This is implicit in the doctrine that karma equals *cetanā*.) However, for Mahāvīra, the founder of Jainism, even the unintentional taking of life was bad karma. Therefore, whereas the followers of the Buddha were enjoined simply to take reasonable precautions, the Jains went to extreme lengths – wearing masks over their faces and sweeping the ground before them – so as to avoid the remotest possibility of swallowing or stepping on any insects. Of course, with the discovery of microscopic living organisms, the Jain position is very difficult to sustain.

How far one takes one's practice of *avihiṁsā* in this respect will depend upon one's sensitivity; perhaps the best thing is to take it just a little bit further than one's sensitivity to the issue demands. One very basic aspect of practising *avihiṁsā* is being vegetarian. Perhaps you still eat cheese, drink cow's milk, or wear leather shoes, but you draw a firm line at actually eating meat. If one is not a vegetarian, there must be a question mark over whether one is really a Buddhist at all.

For me one of the saddest experiences of living in the East was that so many people calling themselves Buddhists – particularly Buddhist monks – were so unwilling to consider becoming vegetarian. Chinese, Vietnamese, Korean, and Indian monks were almost invariably vegetarian, as were some Sinhalese bhikkhus, but the Japanese and Thais were not, and amongst the Burmese there was a real prejudice against vegetarians, amounting in some cases almost to hatred. Their attitude was that vegetarians were trying to go one better than the Buddha himself. They used to say that the Buddha ate meat, that he didn't insist on vegetarianism. And this is quite true; he made no hard and fast rule about it.

At least, this is true for the Pāli Canon. The rule that the Buddha did make, according to the Pāli texts, was that 'meat is not to be accepted (as alms-food) in three cases: if one has seen, heard, or suspects that the animal was specially killed for the monk'.[156] In a later, Mahāyāna scripture, the *Laṅkāvatāra Sūtra*, the Buddha is quoted as saying, in the chapter 'On Meat-eating': 'It is not true, Mahāmati, that meat is proper food and permissible for the Sravaka when [the victim] was not killed by himself, when he did not order others to kill it, when it was not specifically meant for him.'[157] So here is a hard and fast rule supposedly made by the Buddha *insisting* on vegetarianism.

But in the Buddha's day, if you were a wandering monk, as the Buddha himself was, your practice was to take what you were given; and living in a carnivorous society, you would be given meat. Under those conditions the Buddhist attitude would be that inasmuch as you were leading an ascetic life, living on alms, and practising indifference towards food, these factors would counterbalance the unskilfulness inherent in actually eating meat. Illustrative of this attitude is the story of a famous ascetic who ate somebody's thumb which, as a result of a nasty accident in the preparation of some food, had ended up in his bowl. Because he made a point of not picking and choosing, he ate the thumb along with everything else. If you are practising extreme asceticism of this kind, vegetarianism doesn't come into it. But if you have a choice about what you eat, you also have a responsibility, particularly if you can influence the society you live in by choosing to be vegetarian.

I used to make this point to some of my Thai bhikkhu friends and they would say, 'But what can we do? The lay people always give us meat, and we don't want to hurt their feelings by refusing what we are offered.' And it is true that whereas in some cultures the meat is served separately from the vegetables, every Thai dish has meat in it – sometimes pork, chicken, and fish all in the same meal. But the fact is that the lay people were their disciples. The monks were scrupulously insistent on the correct etiquette being observed in the matter of *how* food was offered to them – what to say, how to bow, and so forth – so it should have been possible over a period of several hundred years to persuade the lay people to offer vegetarian food. The Vietnamese had managed it amongst a laity with the same appetite for meat. It is not as if there was any shortage of vegetables.

In this respect Tibet is a special case. The land yields practically nothing in the way of fruit and vegetables so Tibetan Buddhists have been traditionally obliged to eat meat – which is fair enough: if the alternative to eating meat is starvation, one must eat what is available. The Tibetans never tried to pretend that what they did was skilful – but when vegetables did become available to them, they generally continued to eat meat. I used to be told that, coming as they did from a meat-eating country, their constitution required meat.

The Thais used this argument too. If one pointed out that Westerners like myself also came from meat-eating countries and still managed to make the transition to a vegetarian diet, they would laugh and say 'Well, your mind is very strong.' No doubt there are a few vegetarians among the Thais and the Burmese as well, but they have to keep quiet about it unless they are very eminent indeed, as otherwise they are looked upon as 'holy Joes' who want to show everyone else up. The whole subject is fraught with embarrassment and guilt for them and therefore arouses quite irrational reactions at times.

Non-violence is not, of course, just about being vegetarian. It might even be said that in many parts of India an exaggerated importance is attached to this particular expression of the principle. One can extort money from the poor, one can be a usurer, one can let one's cow die of starvation, but as long as one is a vegetarian one has nothing to worry about, spiritually speaking, while if one is not strictly vegetarian, any attempt one makes to lead any kind of spiritual life is dismissed out of hand. Of course, this is just an illustration of the way we exaggerate the importance of whatever we ourselves are able to achieve and minimize the significance of whatever we are disinclined to attempt.

The *vinaya* itself, it has to be said, provides any number of convenient issues upon which one may appear to take a moral stand. I remember a friend telling me that a German monk in the Thai tradition once told him off for offering him a cup of tea while he was standing up. 'Don't you know the *vinaya*?' he said. In fact, there is no *vinaya* rule about what is really just a matter of Indian etiquette, but a lot of monks like to stand on ceremony in this way.

However, just as a clever lawyer can probably find that everyone is breaking the law in some way, likewise one can fault even the strictest monk over some point of *vinaya*. For example, one is not supposed to shave one's face without shaving one's head, but virtually all monks ignore this rule, as they shave every day but get their heads shaved only once a fortnight.

If Theravādin monks are open to the charge of losing sight of fundamental spiritual principles in favour of the minutiae of the *vinaya*, it should be said in mitigation that – in Sri Lanka anyway – they do tend to be in thrall to the laity, who of course can hardly be expected to make such distinctions. The laity in Sri Lanka are vicarious Buddhists: they have no spiritual ambitions themselves; the monks are expected to earn merit on behalf of the whole community in return for their support. If they contribute a son to the Order a couple can certainly look forward to going to heaven when they die, so a lot of monks have been pushed into ordination.

Not that it isn't a pleasant enough existence being a monk: there's plenty to do – teaching, building temples, engaging in various cultural activities. The bhikkhus constitute a set of kind, generous, and good-natured bachelors, but generally not much more than that. And they tend to be nagged and bullied, even terrorized by the laity. For example, if it's getting on for twelve o'clock, the lay people, especially the women, will say 'Come along, come along – it's time you were eating your lunch....' They keep a close eye on what 'their' monks are up to so that they can say, 'Oh, *our* monks are pure, very pure, not like all those Japanese monks, you know!'

THE POSITIVE MENTAL EVENTS CONSIDERED GENERALLY

Yeshe Gyaltsen ends his chapter on the eleven positive mental events with remarks on the general characteristics of positive mental events and the categories of circumstances under which they arise. His enumerations of these are clearly not exhaustive, but they do provide a starting point for one's own personal reflections.

To begin with, he lists five characteristics of positive mental events that are wholesome by their very nature.[158] To elaborate a little on what he has to say:

a. Wholesome by their very nature: They are positive in themselves, without reference to other factors; that is, they need no qualification. So they may be termed the eleven *primary* positive mental events.

b. Wholesome by being related: They involve an association of mind and mental events by means of the five functional co-relations (see page 64). That is, where there is a positive mental event, mind and mental events are, as it were, permeated by the same feeling, they refer to the same object, and so on.

c. Wholesome by being related to that which follows: Although they are positive in themselves, they are the basis for further production of the positive.

d. Wholesome by inspiring: They are positive on account of the fact that they have been inspired by faith; or by virtue of the inspiring quality of faith.

e. Wholesome in the ultimate sense: They are positive in the ultimate sense; that is, they are not positive as opposed to negative – they have no negative mirror image. They are positive with a capital P, as it were – like Plato's concept of the Good.

In considering these characteristics, we need to bear in mind that positive mental events are not actual entities. This should in any case be clear from the fact that there is a certain amount of overlap between them, and that each one obviously arises in some kind of relation with other positive mental events.

Yeshe Gyaltsen goes on to enumerate eight occasions for the arising of the positive mental events.[159]

Firstly, they may be innate; that is, we may carry over a predilection for or inclination towards the positive from a previous existence. The implication is that our mental states, and indeed our qualities in general, are determined, at least to some extent, by a general attitude that would seem to have been there from birth. Handel, for instance, had a quite unmusical background and ancestry, and yet displayed an outstanding interest in and aptitude for music from a very early age.

Secondly, they may be developed through being involved in the setting up of the essential conditions for the attainment of Enlightenment in one's own life: spiritual friendship, Dharma study, attention, mindfulness, watchfulness, and realization of what leads to the attainment of Enlightenment – i.e. Going for Refuge to the Three Jewels.

Thirdly, positive mental events may arise in association with some kind of skilful action. They produce skilful actions and they also arise as a result of skilful actions. There are, of course, very few actions, apart from involuntary ones, that are wholly unaccompanied by intentional – and therefore positive or negative – mental activity, so it's really a question of the degree of volition or intentionality brought to an action. An act of giving, for example, might be accompanied by warm, generous feelings, or by a sort of half-conscious contempt. It might even be stimulated by quite mixed motives, and might also give rise to quite mixed emotions. On the other hand, we cannot say that a good action is entirely a question of the quality of intention behind it. Good and evil cannot be thought of in terms of just actions or just intentions; they involve a combination of both.

Fourthly, they may arise through the four means of conversion (*saṅgraha-vastus*) exercised by a Bodhisattva: *dāna* or generosity, *priya-vāditā* or kindly speech, *arthacaryā* or exhortation and encouragement, and *samānārthatā* or exemplification.[160]

Fifthly, positive mental events may arise by way of a thoroughly integrated attitude behind one's action, ensuring, from a mundane point of view, the best possible return in terms of *puṇya* or merit. Yeshe Gyaltsen cites as an example 'special bright pure actions that make one attain heaven or the good things in life'.[161] By this is meant actions producing what in Chinese Buddhism is described as 'red merit' – that is, mundane merit, as opposed to 'white merit' or merit leading to Enlightenment. The only necessary distinction between an action to which accrues white merit and one that produces red merit is in the intention behind the action. Apart from that the action may be equally 'special, bright, and pure'.

Sixthly, they may arise with the overcoming of negative mental states. Seventhly, they may arise with the cessation of craving and thus the end of suffering. And eighthly, once Enlightenment has been attained, positive mental events arise simply in dependence upon positive mental events.

8

FORCES OF DISINTEGRATION

YESHE GYALTSEN has taken us to the pinnacle of life's potential, the most positive experience possible: Enlightenment. Now, scarcely pausing for breath, he plunges us into the subject with which the rest of his – and our – commentary is concerned: negative mental events. It's a shock, but a salutary one; it is simply a fact of spiritual life that as well as understanding how to recognize and cultivate positive mental states, we need to know how to spot and deal with negative ones.

According to the Abhidharma there are six basic negative emotions and twenty proximate negative emotions. Yeshe Gyaltsen's enumeration of the characteristics of negative mental events – which he offers as a counterpart to his general remarks about positive mental events – makes a good starting point. First he lists five characteristics of 'negative mental events that are unwholesome by their very nature'. Here they are, together with a few explanatory comments of my own:

a. Unwholesome by its very nature: The six basic negative emotions and the twenty proximate negative emotions are negative in themselves, under all circumstances. They can't become wholesome, or be interpreted as wholesome, under any circumstances, even by being related to something else that is wholesome.

b. Unwholesome by being related: A negative mental event is associated with a simultaneously and similarly negative mind.

c. Unwholesome by being related to that which follows: Negative mental events provide the basis for the development of further negative mental events.

d. Unwholesome by inspiring: Negative mental events inspire all sorts of unskilful activities of body and speech.

e. Unwholesome in the ultimate sense.

We must be clear about this final characteristic. In fact, of course, everything within saṁsāra is ultimately negative, inasmuch as it is not nirvāṇa. It may be true that from the perspective of nirvāṇa one no longer stands upon the distinction between the positive and the negative, but this perspective takes us beyond the Abhidharma altogether, and one should be very cautious indeed about deciding that one has gone beyond the perspective of the Abhidharma. If one does go beyond it, all well and good, but one cannot invoke, as it were, the Perfection of Wisdom hypothetically.

But although in a sense everything within saṁsāra is ultimately unsatisfactory, we should not derive from this the notion that saṁsāra is completely negative. Quite the contrary. We have, after all, already seen that positive mental events may arise that have a purely mundane result, but they remain positive for all that. The experience of *dhyāna*, for example, may bring about no more than happiness in this world and the next, but this cannot be said to be an unsatisfactory result in anything but an ultimate sense.

From an absolute, metaphysical perspective, even pleasant, positive experiences constitute *duḥkha*, in so far as they do not constitute Enlightenment, but as experiences they remain positive and pleasant. There should be no mistake about this: a jaundiced, cynical, pessimistic, negative attitude towards the world is no basis for any kind of spiritual realization. To dismiss the relatively skilful, the relatively wholesome, and the relatively positive as being unskilful, unwholesome, and negative is itself simply unskilful, unwholesome, and negative. As long as one is in saṁsāra, one can't afford to take up negative attitudes towards it. It is possible to have a positive experience of disillusionment, but this is quite different from disgruntlement; in fact, one can be disillusioned with things in the sense of seeing their limitations even while one is thoroughly enjoying them.

We in the West are particularly prone to miss the point that there is that which is relatively positive as distinct from the absolutely positive. We tend not to see this on account of the ethical absolutism we have inherited from the Judaeo-Christian tradition, which gives us the idea that there are things which are absolutely right and things which are absolutely wrong. To take just one example, from the Judaeo-Christian viewpoint it cannot under any circumstances be right to bow down to a graven image: that is absolutely wrong. The Muslims have much the same feeling with regard to what they call 'joining others with God' – any deviation from strict monotheism is absolutely wrong. One could not, as a Muslim or a Christian, say that polytheistic worship, mistaken though it may be, is better than no worship at all.

The Buddhist position may be summarized as comprising a distinction between doctrine and method. In doctrinal terms, all compounded existence – according to the first of the four 'Noble Truths' – is ultimately *duḥkha*; it is unwholesome in that it is not nirvāṇa. But methodologically speaking, one cannot make any progress towards nirvāṇa – via the fourth Noble Truth – unless one distinguishes, within saṁsāra, between the relatively unwholesome and the relatively wholesome, so that one may move from the one to the other. Thus one needs to be able to perceive that a good retreat is more wholesome and positive – and even more enjoyable – than a good party, say, even while recognizing that both are ultimately unsatisfactory inasmuch as one remains unenlightened.

Yeshe Gyaltsen goes on to list seven occasions for the arising of negative mental events. Again, to elaborate a little on his list:

a. One may be innately predisposed to unskilful mental states as a result of volitions carried over from a previous life.

b. One may develop unskilful mental states by involving oneself with unskilful influences.

c. One may develop unskilful mental states through performing unskilful actions.

d. One may develop unskilful mental states by harming sentient beings. (Logically speaking this category is supererogatory; it is enumerated separately presumably to emphasize the fact that non-violence or non-harm is the central point of the Buddha's teaching.)

e. One may pursue the unskilful with such thoroughness as to ensure rebirth in the hell realms.

f. One may harbour views that obstruct the path towards Enlightenment.

g. One may harbour views that actually destroy all possibility of spiritual development.

It is evident from this list of Yeshe Gyaltsen's[162] that clear thinking is going to be of crucial importance when it comes to avoiding the arising of negative mental events. The various categories of wrong views will be discussed more fully and systematically later in this chapter, under the heading of the sixth of the *mūlakleśas.* But here one might observe that there are two 'pernicious views' of a general nature that are traditionally mentioned: the view that actions do not have consequences; and the view that no beings exist in the world who have realized higher stages of spiritual development.[163]

There are also some pseudo-Zen views that are dangerous in this way – like the idea that we are all in some sense Enlightened already, or that it is useless to make any effort to attain Enlightenment, or that we have Buddhahood within us if we could only wake up to the fact. To these one may add the idea that any attempt at spiritual development is spiritual materialism, and the misunderstanding that occasionally finds currency in the West to the effect that there is no place for emotion in the spiritual life, that all emotion is to be overcome. This last one fits in nicely with the idea that everything in saṁsāra is negative, and appeals particularly to people who are most comfortable cultivating aversion or hatred. It is quite easy for plain hatred of the mundane to disguise itself as disillusionment with the mundane.

We cannot simply accept the truth of everything that comes out of the East. Sometimes the problem is one of translation from one language or culture to another, but occasionally, unfortunately, there is a real degeneration of the teaching. We have already taken account of the dangers of an attachment to study for its own sake. At the other end of the spectrum, one can meet with supposed Tantric practitioners who can only be described as charlatans.

The Tantra can seem to be an easier path as well as a higher path – and what could be more attractive than that? It seems to condone certain things that other paths do not condone; and it also seems that with the Tantra one doesn't have to give anything up. In a certain sense that is true, but it is true in a profound sense which is simply not accessible to the person who enters upon it without proper preparation. The Tantra looks like a very relaxed way of going about things, but actually it is a knife-edge path.

It is a similar note of caution that Yeshe Gyaltsen sounds in a few verses which, he says, 'are meant to summarize what has been said so far' – and which also serve as a good introduction to the commentary on the six basic emotions that follows:

> The eye of intelligence which distinguishes the path from that which is not
> Is blinded by the foul waters of the fools and idiots.
> To claim that one can walk the path and scale the spiritual levels by
>   using an artificial staff
> That resembles the *dharma* is too ridiculous for words.
>
> Oh friends with intelligence and sustained interest,
> If you want to search for the jewel that elevates your mind to the two
>   positive qualities,
> Then follow Tsong-kha-pa, the supreme Bodhisattva, and
> Dive deep into the ocean of the Buddha's words which is like a Wish-
>   fulfilling Gem.[164]

THE SIX BASIC EMOTIONS (MŪLAKLEŚAS)

The Sanskrit term being translated as basic (or negative) emotion here is *kleśa*, which means both 'that which torments' and 'that which defiles'. Thus one could translate it as 'defiling passion' – except that modern usage fails to connect the term passion with its original meaning of 'suffering'. We tend to think of passion as meaning uncontrolled emotion of any kind, but with the *kleśas* we are dealing with unequivocally negative emotions. These first six are the *mūlakleśas*, the negative roots from which all other negative mental events grow.

While the positive emotions are characterized essentially by an underlying quality of calm and serenity, the defiling passions have a quality of ego-centred restlessness. It is true that positive emotion may sometimes contain a certain amount of effervescence or rapture (*prīti*), but this is a transitional phase in the process of developing the calm and stable condition of bliss (*sukha*). *Prīti* – the experience of submerged energy, as it were, rushing to the surface – is certainly not ego-centred restlessness.

The six basic emotions are, as translated by Guenther, cupidity-attachment, anger, arrogance, lack of intrinsic awareness, indecision, and opinionatedness. So here we have variants of the three poisons –

usually referred to as greed, hatred, and delusion – together with arrogance, indecision, and 'opinionatedness', often referred to as 'wrong views'.

1. CUPIDITY-ATTACHMENT (*RĀGA*)

Cupidity-attachment is a hankering after any pleasurable external or internal object by taking it as pleasing to oneself.[165]

Tsongkhapa

This is *rāga*. The term is often used interchangeably with *lobha*, but there is a difference of connotation, *lobha* generally being translated as 'craving' while *rāga* is more powerful, more like 'passionate attachment'. In the Tantric context *rāga* sometimes carries a positive connotation, but in the context of the Abhidharma it refers to a purely negative emotion. Neither *lobha* nor *rāga* may therefore be translated simply by the word 'desire' – because, of course, desire is not necessarily negative. For example, the Bodhisattva's desire that all beings may attain Enlightenment is utterly positive.

What makes cupidity or craving or passionate attachment negative is that it involves desiring pleasure from the object one is attached to. This can get quite complicated. For example, there's the do-gooder. Do-gooders don't actually want to make others happy; they want to make themselves happy, using others as the means. This is not to say, of course, that doing others good for the sake of what one gets out of it personally, whether in terms of personal development or in any other way, is at all a bad thing, as long as one is aware of what one is doing. The trouble is that one is not always aware of one's motivations. The harm sometimes caused by do-gooders arises from the difficulty of detecting in oneself the subtler manifestations of craving or attachment.

Craving may be experienced in relation to an object in the present, the past, or the future; and it may be experienced in relation to the *kāmaloka*, the realm of sense desire, or, at a more subtle level, in relation to the *rūpaloka* or the *arūpaloka*, the realms corresponding to the experience of *dhyāna*. Craving does not arise when one is actually experiencing *dhyāna*, because *dhyāna* by its very nature does not include negative mental states. But in the absence of *prajñā* craving can arise in anticipation or recollection of the experience of *dhyāna*.

Indeed, craving of a very subtle kind is still present even in a Non-returner, that is, in one whose transcendental insight has broken through the first five fetters of mundane existence: belief in a separate and unchanging self, sceptical doubt with respect to the Buddha's teaching, dependence upon morality and observances, sexual desire, and ill will. With all this accomplished there is still desire for existence in the world of form and desire for existence in the formless world (the sixth and seventh fetters) to be overcome.

In *dhyāna*, *lobha*, *dveṣa*, and *moha* are just suspended, not destroyed. Only *prajñā* can remove them permanently. In *dhyāna* they are simply held in abeyance. But they cannot be held in abeyance indefinitely. Sooner or later they will reassert themselves and one will then come out of *dhyāna*. One may even say (though the Abhidharma does not go this far in its discussion) that throughout the *dhyāna* experience there is a potentiality of negative mental states present, a substratum of unmanifested *kleśas* waiting to come to fruition.

Craving is obviously very difficult to eradicate, but a useful approach to changing this, and indeed any other negative state of mind, is to use the imagination. Dr Johnson once defined imagination as the capacity to emancipate oneself from one's present experience and project oneself into the past or the future. He was thinking of the term in a rather negative sense, but in this context his simple definition highlights a capacity we all have and use when it suits us. It doesn't always suit us to use it, of course. When we indulge ourselves without considering the fact that our actions will have consequences, when we do not consider how others will be affected by what we do, all this can, in a way, be put down to a basic failure of imagination.

Through the imagination we can emancipate ourselves from our own experience and project ourselves into the experience of someone else, or foresee the possible consequences of our present actions. Imagination is really a matter of clarity. When we are in the grip of craving we are blinded by our present experience. When we're carried away by, say, sexual passion, present experience sweeps away our ability to imagine someone else's needs and feelings, or what might happen as a result of our passion. All thoughts of past, present, and future, this world and the next, disappear. It is only after one has had what one wanted that one's imagination slips into gear again and one thinks, 'Oh my God, how will her husband feel?' It is as if one has been in a dream.

This is why the poet Shelley speaks of morals in terms of imagination.[166] Ethics are about going out of oneself, not being limited by one's present mode of being. Giving, for example, is simply a matter of feeling the needs of another person as vividly as one feels one's own needs. It is a matter of imagination. Seen in this way, ethics are not about keeping a tight rein on oneself, but about freeing one's imagination, being less bound by one's present situation.

2. ANGER (PRATIGHA)

> It is a vindictive attitude towards sentient beings, towards frustration, and towards that which gives rise to one's frustrations. Its function is to serve as a basis for fault-finding and for never finding even a moment of happiness.[167]
>
> *Abhidharmasamuccaya*

Pratigha is generally a kind of blind rage or fury, but its description here as a 'vindictive attitude' implies that it also has an element of hatred. Hatred, though, translates another Sanskrit word, *dveṣa*. And, of course, hatred and anger are different things. Hatred involves a definite intention to do someone harm, but anger is more like an explosive release of energy with a view to breaking through an obstacle. One can get angry with someone without wishing to do them any harm; someone obstructs one's energy and this frustrated energy just accumulates until one cannot contain it any longer.

Of course, anger cannot be said to be a skilful mental state, because it does burst out in a violent manner; yet it can be deployed quite skilfully in that it is quite possible to get really angry and be careful at the same time not to do any real harm or actual damage. Anger, one could say, is not entirely incompatible with *mettā*, at least in the long run. The average person experiences anger much more often than hatred; and this anger, paradoxically, is directed mostly towards one's nearest and dearest – that is, those who are going to be treading on one's corns on a regular basis.

For some people, experiencing anger can be a step forward. If a strong feeling like desire or anger gets repressed, perhaps because one is afraid to face one's own disapproval by fully experiencing it, one can be angry or full of craving, say, without knowing it. Indeed, failing to acknowledge what one is feeling enables it to develop into an ever more powerful negative emotion. In this way, by not allowing oneself to feel anger or desire, one becomes repressed or alienated.

Being alienated from one's most powerful emotions also means being alienated from one's energy. It is then very important to re-contact one's emotions in almost any way one can. All of which is not to say that someone who is placid and easily contented must be in some way alienated or repressed; they might just be gentle and innocent by nature. Nor would one want to suggest that becoming angry is a necessary element in one's relations with others. It can often be the case that one begins to seethe with anger as a result of not having been firm and direct about something in the first place. This said, one should not necessarily be afraid of getting angry – as long as one is very careful that one's anger does not develop into hatred.

There can never be any justification for hatred. As a 'vindictive attitude' – he's done you down and you want to get even by doing him down – hatred has a lot to do with egotism; it involves a subtle sense of one's having been diminished in the eyes of others. Suppose someone abuses you. You can think 'Well, he just lost his temper. He said some foolish things, but in the end it's his problem, not mine.' If you take that attitude, you won't feel put down, and you won't need to get even – because you feel 'even' anyway. Your evenness has not been disturbed. Alternatively, you may think 'Oh, he has called me a fool – who is he to call me a fool? He has made me look a fool in the eyes of others.' If you think like this – that other people's opinion of you matters so much – you are going to get very angry indeed, because you have been hurt in this crucially sensitive place.

If *maitrī* is the opposite of hatred, tea and sympathy generally is not. There is very often something false about sympathy. People who are not genuinely pleased when one is in a very positive mood are going to be delighted when one is feeling low because they can then start to be sympathetic, relishing their own superior position in the guise of being warm and kind. This satisfaction in someone else's weakness, as well as being corrupting for the perpetrator, reinforces the weakness of the recipient. It is all the more damaging for both parties because its true nature as a very subtle form of hatred or malice goes unrecognized.

Ironically enough, instead of detaching oneself from the source of one's suffering one seems to want to get closer to it – perhaps in order to get even. *Pratigha* cannot, therefore, be translated as 'aversion', which simply means 'turning away'. One becomes as attached to one's enemies as one does to one's friends – and this negative attachment is of a particularly unhealthy and neurotic kind. It may even appear in the context of a sexual relationship, where a couple have no truly positive feelings for each other. It is possible, as I have suggested, to express anger towards one's nearest and dearest, but it is also possible for a couple to stay together in order to satisfy their hatred of each other, rather than quietly going their separate ways.

There is no limit to the range of possible objects of hatred. One can feel hatred towards oneself, towards friends, towards animals, towards inanimate objects, towards people one has known in the past, even towards future or prospective situations. It arises from paranoia – the feeling that others have it in for us – and from an insistence on finding a source for our suffering. It is the rage of the victim for redress; it is the way we avoid taking ultimate responsibility for the state we find ourselves in.

The Mahāyāna regards hatred as the worst of negative mental states – certainly as worse than craving, because craving at least shows some affinity for life, for people, and holds out at least the possibility of experiencing some pleasure, however transient. But hatred does not allow us to enjoy those ordinary pleasures that are available. This is why it is sometimes said that hatred is ridiculous. In a hateful mental state we don't want something pleasant; we actually want something painful.

In a hateful mood, if we can find something unpleasant, some fault or weakness, we are pleased. If someone tries to cheer us up, or placate us, or show us that we don't need to feel hatred, we're displeased because our hatred is precious to us – we don't want it taken away from us, and we will hate anyone who tries to take it away. We even find ourselves saying 'I've every right to be angry!' as if claiming the privilege of enjoying some rare pleasure.

What we are trying to claim, of course, is that our anger is righteous indignation. However, whether indignation or anger can really ever be counted as righteous is open to question. There may be moments of crisis when some kind of high-energy vociferation or action is called for. If, for instance, one saw someone beating a child, one might experience a sudden hot anger which would lead one to say or do something drastic to stop that person engaging in that unskilful action. Or if someone appeared to be about to do something stupidly dangerous to themselves or to others, then again some sort of high-energy response would be in order. But righteous indignation in any sense other than this is generally going to be unskilful. An outburst may make one feel better oneself, but it is not going to do anything to enhance one's relations with the people against whom it is directed. In any situation where one might be inclined to get impatient or angry, one will find that the exercise of patience and persistence is the more skilful and effective option.

Even when it comes to discussing the ideals that one holds most dear, there is no justification for getting angry. One may be able to browbeat someone into submission by getting hot under the collar, but one will not convince them thereby. Wrong views with regard to the spiritual life generally have deep roots and they need to be dug out with patient persistence. It is no use just hacking away wildly at them. Outbursts of righteous indignation are only going to reinforce those wrong views.

Hatred is unskilful not only with regard to its effect on others; it has grievously deleterious effects on the person doing the hating. It alienates our friends. It makes us act recklessly. It takes away our capacity to judge what is skilful and what is unskilful. We are unable to take pleasure in anything. It is traditionally said to make one ugly – it certainly makes one unattractive. It even takes away one's sleep (conversely, one of the benefits of *maitrī* is said to be that it gives one sound sleep). Ultimately, one falls into subhuman, demonic states: that is, one becomes something worse than just a bad human being – one becomes a demon, a being dedicated purely to negative and destructive ends.

Hatred is linked with greed (cupidity-attachment) and ignorance (lack of intrinsic awareness) in a familiar trio – the three poisons or poisonous roots. They are all present in the unenlightened mind, in varying degrees. In the *Visuddhimagga*, Buddhaghosa identifies three different psychological types or temperaments (*caritas*) based upon them: the greed type, the hate type, and the delusion type.[168]

The greed type basically finds life more pleasant than painful. That is the starting point for the formation of that particular kind of temperament. Presumably as a result of having performed skilful actions in the past, the greed type experiences pleasant *vipākas* rather more than unpleasant ones, and therefore tends to experience craving more than hatred. Buddhaghosa describes the behaviour of each type in terms of the monastic life – because that was the usual context within which his work would be studied – and he says that the greed type would favour brightly-coloured robes: everybody's robes would of course be yellow, but those of the greed type would be *bright* yellow. The greed type would also eat nicely, making his rice and curry into neat balls and popping them gracefully into his mouth. When he sweeps the floor he does so smoothly and thoroughly, including the corners; when he walks he goes elegantly, wearing his robe neatly and correctly (with the upper robe exactly four inches shorter than the lower robe) and when he speaks his voice is mellifluous and gentle.

The hate type is just the opposite. He is a person for whom existence is definitely more painful than pleasant, putting him in a general mood of irritation and resentment. Everything he does will be performed impatiently, carelessly, or harshly, reflecting his darker and more disagreeable view of the world.

Finally, the deluded type is one whose experience of pleasure and pain is fairly equally mixed. Sometimes he finds life pleasant, but then circumstances change and life seems altogether unpleasant. So he would not be able to make up his mind on the matter once and for all. He couldn't really say whether life was pleasant or not, and it probably wouldn't occur to him to try.

There are three refined versions of these three types. The greed type tends to becomes the devotee, the faith type. The hate type on the other hand becomes the wisdom type; that is, in the same way that the hate type sees the faults of the hated object, wisdom sees the faults of compounded existence. As for the deluded type, he or she becomes what is usually called the intelligence type. Whereas wisdom is the faculty that sees through things, that penetrates through the compounded to the Uncompounded, intelligence is a more versatile, creative, faculty. A standard definition of intelligence is 'an ability to use concepts creatively'; while wisdom brushes aside concepts in order to penetrate to the reality behind them, intelligence is the ability to express what wisdom sees, to communicate what that reality is and how it is realized. So to begin with one needs faith, which is replaced by *karuṇā* (compassion) when wisdom is attained – and finally one needs intelligence to communicate the content of that realization. There is even a Bodhisattva of intelligence, Akṣayamati, whose name means 'indestructible intelligence'.

3. ARROGANCE (MĀNA)

It is an inflated mind as to what is perishable and its function is to serve as the basis for disrespect and frustrations.[169]
Abhidharmasamuccaya

Māna is arrogance as distinct from pride. There is a healthy pride that guards one from doing things of which one should be ashamed; and one can have a healthy confidence that one is capable of achieving worthy ends. But arrogance is different; it is an inflated idea of oneself in comparison with others. Of course, one cannot help making comparisons, and although making any sort of comparison is very subtly unskilful, there is probably little harm in objectively recognizing that one is in various respects superior, equal, or inferior to others. Practically speaking, one may certainly need to be able to make a judgement as to who is best qualified to do a particular task. But if one wants to make something of this state of affairs – whether or not it really is the case – if one insists on some kind of recognition, or relishes the fact that one is better at something than other people are, this is arrogance. Yeshe Gyaltsen distinguishes seven different varieties of arrogance:

a. You overvalue yourself in comparison with others who are less gifted, less wealthy, less successful, and so on, than you are. You look down on them in an overbearing way, like Lord Curzon in the anonymous verse:

> My name is George Nathaniel Curzon,
> I am a most superior person.[170]

Though Lord Curzon was indeed very able, his arrogance was such that he was said to have died of disappointment at not becoming Prime Minister.

b. You imagine that you are superior to your peers, to those who are, in fact, your equals.

c. You fancy yourself superior to those who are, in fact, your superiors.

d. You are unable to identify with anything other than your own five skandhas – that is, other than your body, feelings, perception, volitional impulses, and consciousness. You firmly identify yourself with the five skandhas, which in effect is to see oneself as the centre of the universe. This is obviously quite a subtle form of arrogance.

e. You boast of your achievements or your position, whether or not they represent any real attainment. This includes arrogance with regard to social class, physique, age, and education, and it is well expressed in the celebrated couplet about Benjamin Jowett, the Master of Balliol College in Oxford:

> I am Master of this College:
> What I don't know isn't knowledge.[171]

f. You take an inordinate pride in your humility; that is, your arrogance comes in disguise. This can be illustrated by a little story concerning a meeting between representatives of the different orders of the Catholic church. The Dominican says 'Of course we Dominicans are the most learned order,' and the Jesuit says 'Yes, but we are certainly foremost in the educational sphere.' Then the Franciscan pipes up, a little diffidently, and says: 'Well, that's all perfectly true, but I rather think that when it comes to humility, we're the tops.'

In fact, one cannot actually cultivate humility. There is a well-known story about Mahatma Gandhi, who was quite keen on inculcating humility in his followers. He drew up a list of rules for those who were involved with his ashram, and right at the top he put 'Practise humility.' But someone pointed out to him that real humility can never be self-consciously cultivated, so he crossed it out and wrote at the bottom of the list 'All these to be practised in the spirit of humility.'

Humility is necessarily unselfconscious. Other people may see it in you, but the moment you see it yourself it's no longer there. Indeed, when it is a deliberate attitude, humility seems to be entirely negative, a sort of grovelling posture. (One thinks of the odious Uriah Heep in Dickens' *David Copperfield*.) However, if arrogance serves as the basis for disrespect then non-arrogance should serve as the basis for respect. If one cultivates respect, or even reverence, which of course can readily be cultivated in a very positive manner, one can more or less forget about the need for humility, because humility naturally comes with reverence.

g. The seventh variety of arrogance is 'inverted arrogance'. You are proud of, say, having got drunk and made a fool of yourself; or having come bottom of the class at school. Instead of feeling sorry or ashamed you feel, perhaps, that such failings or weaknesses make you more interesting as a person; or you may simply want to get attention, and think that the way to get it is by playing the fool. You belittle yourself, you pretend to be more stupid than you really are. People are sometimes even proud of having made a mess of their life. It is possible to be proud of being ignorant, of having no education, of being blunt or rude or brutal, of being hard and cynical.

These are the traditional seven forms of arrogance; but we don't have to stop there. For example, there is a kind of vicarious arrogance whereby you attach yourself to someone you admire and, while having no personal ambition to emulate their achievements, bask in their reflected glory: 'My teacher is better than your teacher.' There is also the arrogance of egalitarianism: you refuse to recognize that anyone can be truly superior to anyone else. Some people take this to the extreme of saying – to use the current expression – that a Buddha, for example, is not 'more developed' than other people so much as 'differently developed'.

The karmic consequence of arrogance, from the traditional point of view, is that one is reborn in particularly humble circumstances. More immediately, one makes it very difficult for oneself to learn anything, because one fails to recognize one's own limitations and thus one's need to learn. One also fails to recognize those from whom one might learn, because one is unable to acknowledge their superiority to oneself.

This could perhaps be said to be a particular problem in the West, where we have recently developed a social climate in which teachers are not greatly respected. The respect is not there basically because the values that the teachers are supposed to stand for and pass on, including the cultural heritage of the community, are not valued by the society they serve. A further problem derives from the way some of us have been brought up to regard religion as something that cannot be taught. In the traditional religion of the West, Christianity, the emphasis is not generally on methods. One can learn its history, one can study the Bible, but on the whole most people are not taught how to practise religion in the way that one can be taught how to practise carpentry or law or architecture. Certainly there is nothing in the West really equivalent to the passing on of knowledge from teacher to disciple which is so much part of Eastern religious tradition.

Integral to arrogance is the negative mental event which follows it here, lack of intrinsic awareness. We are arrogant on the basis of failing to see the true nature of things, and thus failing to see that we really have nothing to be arrogant about. The way to overcome a tendency to arrogance is therefore to reflect on the Dharma – on impermanence, the Four Noble Truths, and so on.

4. LACK OF INTRINSIC AWARENESS (AVIDYĀ)

It is a lack of being aware to one's fullest capacity and it covers the three realms of life. Its function is to serve as a basis for mistaken stubbornness, doubt and emotionality about the entities of reality.[172]
Abhidharmasamuccaya

The existence of *avidyā* as a negative mental event suggests that one can't be unaware of reality in a purely privative sense. Ignorance of reality has consequences: it automatically plunges one into confusion and bewilderment, which lead to a course of misguided thought and action. It's not just that one doesn't know something; one doesn't know that one doesn't know. Lack of intrinsic awareness (*avidyā*) represents a stubborn refusal to accept anything that might threaten one's ego-identity. The more one lacks intrinsic awareness, the more one digs one's heels in against developing that awareness. *Avidyā* is a resistance, a rigidity, a lack of receptivity. This underlines the fact that theory and practice are not separate. Ideas cannot be kept separate from action; if one is confused in thought, one will blunder in what one does.

Lack of intrinsic awareness is of two kinds. Firstly there is lack of practical wisdom; that is, not being able to distinguish clearly between what is skilful and what is unskilful, and thus not perceiving the consequences of one's actions, not appreciating the law of karma. The result is suffering and rebirths in painful realms.

Secondly, lack of intrinsic awareness consists in lack of *prajñā*, in the sense of not knowing 'mind as such'. Even though one may have realized practical wisdom to the extent of ensuring good future re-births, one is still short of attaining to ultimate wisdom and thus one's happiness is still subject to impermanence. Even in the formless *dhyānas*, if one has not broken the first fetter – *satkāyadṛṣṭi*, or self-view – one will still have a subtle but very strong experience of the self or ego.

There is a Pāli term, *mahaggata*, meaning 'grown great', which refers to what is generally called expanded consciousness. It is possible to dwell in very refined states of expanded consciousness while still lacking intrinsic awareness. Simply to expand one's consciousness is not enough – unless one expands it beyond all limits whatsoever, in which case one is no longer the starting point of the expansion and there is no longer a centre from which one expands. The five *jhānas* are called *mahaggatacitta* in that unlimited sense.

Avidyā is usually rendered simply as 'ignorance', but Guenther's interpretive translation – 'lack of intrinsic awareness' – is very helpful. Of course, the word awareness carries quite a broad range of meanings in English; what precisely should we understand by it here? I would suggest that if we take Guenther's rendering of *prajñā* as 'analytical appreciative understanding', we should be able to take the step of interpreting his rendering of the related term *vidyā* as awareness to mean 'aesthetic appreciative understanding'. For Guenther, wisdom has this appreciative, even aesthetic character. It can be described in aesthetic terms because it represents an essentially non-utilitarian vision of things. Inasmuch as one is not looking for what one can get out of the world for oneself, one's vision is appreciative – one appreciates things for their own sake. One is satisfied purely to contemplate things, to appreciate them, even to become absorbed in them. Schopenhauer draws the same sort of parallel between aesthetic and mystical experience.[173] According to him there is in both a suspension of what he terms Wille, which as he interprets it is the selfish and blind urge of life that is the source of our suffering.

There is then the question of how one functions in the world with this aesthetic appreciative awareness. But in practice, no such question arises. One has to make use of things; the only difference is that one's overall orientation is not a selfish, egoistic one. Making use of things in this way – to meet one's own objective needs and to help other people – does not conflict or interfere with one's intrinsic awareness at all. The nature of intrinsic awareness is that it produces spontaneous activity without any such conflict or problem.

Taking the aesthetic analogy again, there is on the one hand the aesthetic vision of the finished work of art, and on the other the concrete work of art in the making. The artist makes use of certain materials and tools within the overall context of his or her vision of the finished work of art, with the intention of making something – a painting, a poem, a piece of music – that conforms to his or her imaginative vision of what it should be. It is said of Mozart, for instance, that before writing a symphony, he heard the whole composition simultaneously, in a single moment, in his mind. This sort of vivid pre-apprehension of the work to be produced seems to be characteristic of the very greatest artists. The work of creation is done before they even start. It is all there already, like a great spool waiting to be unrolled; they have just to translate the work from eternity into time.

Likewise, if one has an experience of intrinsic awareness, one could say that while this experience takes place on the plane of the absolute, one is at the same time working to make life on the relative plane of existence conform to or manifest that vision. All one's energies, all one's activities on the relative plane, are directed towards that end, and therefore take place within the overall context of one's aesthetic perception. Everything one does is geared towards the transformation of the everyday world, through the manifestation of that experience of intrinsic awareness.

The realm of goal-oriented activity, inasmuch as it is not ego-related, takes place within what I have elsewhere called the greater mandala of essentially useless, appreciative awareness.[174] One may have realized the greater mandala for oneself, but as far as the world in the midst of which one is working is concerned – and as far as one is concerned oneself as well, inasmuch as one is identifying oneself with that world – it is still an ideal to be realized. This is the dual nature of the Bodhisattva: he or she is in nirvāṇa and at the same time in saṃsāra, working along with other beings towards nirvāṇa.

When one loses that aesthetic appreciation, when one loses that awareness, one falls into bewilderment and confusion, and then one wants to make use of things, to manipulate them for one's own satisfaction. That is *avidyā*, the first of the twelve *nidānas* or links on the Wheel of Life, in dependence upon which arise the *saṃskāras*, the second *nidāna*. As we have seen, the relation between the first two *nidānas* is traditionally likened to the relation between the state of drunkenness and the actions of body, speech, and mind inspired by that drunkenness. Hence *avidyā* is not just ignorance, but an emotional darkness, on the basis of which all other *kleśas* arise. *Avidyā* is therefore the root of saṃsāra. Once intrinsic awareness has been lost, there can only follow an uninterrupted sequence of confused actions. This said, *avidyā* is not all bad, in so far as these essentially confused actions will include skilful as well as unskilful ones. They will all spring from a lack of intrinsic awareness, but some at least may help to 'restore' it.

The three terms *vidyā*, *prajñā*, and *jñāna* are very closely related, and between them they cover the characteristics of what we may call awareness of reality. They are not used altogether consistently throughout the Buddhist canon, but it is certainly possible to work out a standard usage based on the way they are generally used.

Guenther's translation of *avidyā* in this context as 'lack of intrinsic awareness' suggests – whether or not Guenther consciously intends this – that *vidyā* is the basic, original awareness which 'subsequently' becomes overlaid or obscured. As for *jñāna*, this term is usually translated by Guenther as just 'awareness' – presumably the same awareness of which *avidyā* is the lack. Perhaps one could say that the difference between *vidyā* and *jñāna* is that whereas *vidyā* is the awareness that has been lost, *jñāna* is the awareness that has been regained.

And where does *prajñā* come in? In terms of the six perfections or *pāramitās* practised by the Bodhisattva, *prajñā* is the sixth *pāramitā*, while in the context of the ten *pāramitās* it is explicitly distinguished from *jñāna*, which appears as the culmination of the series.[175] Taking this perspective, one might say that *prajñā* could mean awareness in the process of emergence, or it could mean *jñāna* in action. When one applies one's *jñāna*, one's awareness, to something so as to know it as it actually is, that application of awareness could be called *prajñā*.

As the dynamic function of awareness – as *jñāna* in action – *prajñā* is thus the main counter-agent to *avidyā*. One could go as far as to say that to develop *prajñā* is to follow the path. First one studies the teachings – that is, one practises *śruta-mayī-prajñā*; then one reflects on those teachings – *cintā-mayī-prajñā*; finally one meditates on them – *bhāvanā-mayī-prajñā*. The first two kinds of *prajñā* support the third, which is transcendental *prajñā* proper. One could also say that the first two are the foundations of the meditation – *samādhi* – that is required to transform the first two kinds of *prajñā*, study and reflection, into wisdom in its fullness.

At the same time, *prajñā* is the support of *samādhi*; meditators commonly alternate between *śamatha* (calming) meditation practices and *vipaśyanā* (insight) practices. If you develop a certain level of *samādhi* you may use that concentrated energy to penetrate into reality – that is, to develop *prajñā*. But the depth of that penetration will be limited by the level of concentrated energy behind it; so to deepen your experience of *prajñā* you have to channel your effort into deepening your experience of *samādhi*. Or, to take another approach, you can make the *samādhi* you have previously experienced the basis for the development of *prajñā* – by, for instance, reflecting on the impermanence, and hence the unsatisfactoriness, of the *samādhi* experience. As one gets further and further along the path, the two reinforce each other until they become indistinguishable: *samādhi-prajñā*. *Samādhi* becomes the internal dimension of *prajñā*, *prajñā* the external dimension of *samādhi*.

To put the matter simply, we can refer to *prajñā* as awareness in the making, *vidyā* as intrinsic awareness that has been lost, and *jñāna* as recovered awareness. But this is to speak in terms of time. It would be more accurate to speak of a falling away from eternity and a gradual return to the realization of being in eternity, beyond the vicissitudes of temporal existence. However, this is still misleading, because it suggests a certain point when we bite the apple and fall from grace, fall away from eternity, and another point when we are restored to eternity. In reality, it is not that we fell from grace at some point in the past; each of us is falling from eternity now, at every instant. And – to look at it more positively – intrinsic awareness really is intrinsic; it is there within us, within our reach, all the time.

5. INDECISION (*VICIKITSĀ*)

> It is to be in two minds about the truth.[176]
>
> *Abhidharmasamuccaya*

Vicikitsā is not doubt of a purely intellectual, abstract kind. It is not just being unsure about what is the case, or questioning things, or thinking things through for oneself. Quite the contrary. It is an emotional inability to make up one's mind one way or the other. It is, in short, the kind of doubt that manifests as indecisiveness, a cognitive event that carries a reaction in its wake in the same way that, say, *avidyā* comes with the *saṃskāras* in its wake. Doubt and indecision are in a way two sides – the cognitive and the reactive – of the same negative mental event. Just as a fundamental unclarity leads to unskilful action, so the function of doubt is to lead to indecisiveness. If one is in two minds about what is good or right, that will inhibit one from acting. Unless one knows for sure what one should be doing one cannot act decisively, thoroughly, vigorously. As the Zen saying goes, 'Whatever you do, don't wobble.'

Vicikitsā is doubt and indecision with regard to the Dharma, with regard to what we know at some level to be the truth. It concerns the conflict between what I have sometimes called the gravitational pull of the conditioned or compounded and the gravitational pull of the Unconditioned or Uncompounded.[177] (By 'conditioned' I mean everything that is within the Wheel of Life, everything that is within saṃsāra, everything that is marked by impermanence, unsatisfactoriness, and insubstantiality, while the Uncompounded – nirvāṇa – is free of these constraints.) We know that if we do make up our mind, then *ipso facto* we commit ourselves to a certain line of action which, even if we recognize it as being positive, may also be uncomfortable, even painful. We are going to have to let go of our attachments, we are going to have to give. There is also the consideration that resolving this conflict in favour of nirvāṇa is going to be ultimately and essentially irreversible. By contrast, a decision in favour of the compounded cannot stand for ever and is therefore not really a decision at all. Such a 'decision' is characterized by doubt and indecision.

That is to look at the nature of this mental event on a grand scale. But this inability, this unwillingness to make a decision, needs first of all to be addressed at quite an ordinary, basic level. Sometimes we are faced with an important, perhaps complex, issue about which it is genuinely difficult to come to a decision, perhaps because of insufficient information. But very often we are indecisive about trivial things, about which we are simply unwilling to commit ourselves through timidity or laziness or obstinacy.

Being indecisive can give weak people a sense of power, if in doing so they can keep others waiting. Children try to get attention in this way: you offer them a box of chocolates, and the longer they can draw out the business of choosing which one they're going to take, the longer they have your attention. It may be appropriate sometimes to indulge children in this way, but not adults. On the other hand, dithering can mean surrendering power in that a ditherer is often waiting for circumstances – which usually means other people's decisions – to make the decision for them. In the meantime, their indecision tends to have the effect of making others anxious.

Doubt as a negative mental event is essentially a response to the truth, so doubt in this sense is not present where one has not yet perceived what the truth actually is. One can be so confused as to be unaware that there are any alternatives to choose from. One may think, for example, that 'it's all one', that all religions have the same truth as their goal, or that there is literally no difference between saṁsāra and nirvāṇa, and that one need not therefore distinguish between skilful and unskilful actions. In this way one may avoid doubt and indecision, by remaining in a dark cloud of unawareness. If, on the other hand, one experiences some kind of doubt while in the process of trying to perceive or understand more clearly, this is obviously not doubt as a negative mental event.

The counter-agent to doubt in the negative sense is clarity of thought. But how do we clarify our thinking? To begin with, we need to appreciate that clear thinking is not developed on its own. The whole of our spiritual life – at least indirectly – contributes to clarity of mind in some way. One starts off, therefore, by adopting skilful modes of action even though they do not necessarily spring naturally and spontaneously from one's mental state. This is going to be easier for some people than others. If one is a faith follower one may tend to get caught up in other people's skilful modes of action and work out the reason for it afterwards – which is fair enough. This sort of enthusiastic mentality certainly helps to get one's spiritual life off the ground in the early stages – as long as one's enthusiasm has lighted upon the right object, i.e. the Dharma. However, the answer to doubt and indecision is not indiscriminate enthusiasm, but clarity. If one is a faith follower one may not appear to experience much doubt and indecision, but one will still need to develop clarity.

If one is a doctrine follower, on the other hand, one will want to make sure exactly what one is letting oneself in for. One will see perhaps quite early on the implications of becoming a Buddhist in terms of one's whole way of life. One doesn't want to make big, perhaps painful decisions for the sake of something that is not going to stand up to rational scrutiny, or that is not going to produce happiness and joy, in the long term if not in the short term. This sort of careful examination of the Dharma is not doubt and indecision but clear thinking.

One's doubt and indecision is one's own, and one has to make one's own decisions. However, others can help one clarify the issues involved. Some people go to a divination system of one kind or another for help. If one consults, say, the I-Ching, one is saying, in effect, 'Let's leave it to the wise old man: see what he says.' But what he generally says is 'Well, if you do this, perhaps something like that will follow.' One still has to make up one's own mind; the exercise has simply concentrated one's mind more clearly and coolly on the situation.

A more straightforward way of objectifying one's situation is to talk with an actual person – a spiritual friend – who will help one to clarify the issues. For instance, one may want to follow a certain line of action, but feel afraid or guilty about doing so. There may be a conflict between a desire to do what one wants to do, and a desire to meet other people's expectations: if one's desire to please other people is very strong one may well want to sacrifice one's own wishes in order to retain their approval. Alternatively, there may be a conflict between the needs of an objective situation and what seem to be one's own personal needs; again, it is a matter of delicate judgement to decide how to balance the one against the other. Unless one can become aware of these conflicts, which are often quite unconscious, one will remain more or less in their power. What one needs is for someone to encourage one to admit that 'Yes, I'd like to do that – but …' and help one sort out what the 'but' amounts to and whether or not it is valid. They may even venture an opinion – but without pressurizing one into accepting it.

If one is the person being approached for clarification one needs to bear in mind that some people are going to be inclined to take one's opinion as an implicit directive; they will not just hear what one says, but do as one says. In that case one has to be careful to refrain from giving one's opinion at all. It can also happen that one's clarity can make someone who is naturally confused even more confused because it brings them up against all sorts of unconscious impulses and assumptions which they are unable to rationalize. They may say 'Yes, I understand' but that understanding is perhaps just on a superficial rational level, while deep down they're saying 'No, no!'

Real clarity is not about offering someone some sort of straightforward, common-sense solution and then telling them to pull their socks up and get on with it. It involves understanding their underlying confusion, taking into account their deeply rooted difficulties and objections, while at the same time being uncompromisingly clear with oneself. If someone comes to you for help, are you going to be sufficiently concerned for them that you are prepared to ask them some hard questions or point out that there are some difficult choices to be made?

Sometimes when one is being soft with others one is really being soft with oneself. One doesn't want to appear to be making life more difficult for someone, one doesn't want to be involved in someone else's suffering – not because of their pain but because their pain hurts oneself. Perhaps one feels guilty; or one may be emotionally dependent on being a popular, easy-going person. So it is not as simple as it seems. One needs to be clear about one's own problems as well as those of the other person; otherwise one won't be of much use in helping them solve anything.

Doubt and indecision lie at the root of our difficulties with the spiritual life, and that is where we have to bring clear thinking to bear. If one doesn't really believe that it is possible to develop as an individual, one won't be able to put into that development the energy that will enable one to develop. If one is unsure about the value or effectiveness of meditation, so that one does it with an attitude of just seeing how it will turn out, hoping something will come of practising it, one probably won't get very far. One can't start off with no doubts whatsoever, but there must be at least some sort of willing suspension of disbelief; one must have a degree of conviction sufficient to fuel one's practice with the requisite energy and decisiveness and thus produce a result tangible enough to confirm the rightness of the original decision. In this way there is a possibility of something tentative and provisional being proven on the anvil of experience.

For example, perhaps one believes that psychological development is possible but one is not sure about the whole idea of spiritual development – or vice versa. Either way, one has to be clear about what these notions actually amount to before one decides to commit oneself to them. The reason we so often fail to put in the commitment required to realize our ideals is that we have not addressed our underlying doubt and indecision about them.

Does one, for instance, really believe in the non-reality of the self? What *is* the self? In what sense is it unreal? And has one thought out one's position as regards oriental Buddhism and Buddhism in the West? As regards the three *yānas* – the Hīnayāna, the Mahāyāna, the Vajrayāna? As regards the Arhant ideal and the Bodhisattva ideal? Is one trying to be an Arhant, or a Bodhisattva? Or has one vaguely kept the two ideas (which are supposed to be ideals) in different compartments of one's mind, unsure how they might hang together – except that one day one somehow feels that it's time to get down to being an Arhant, while the next it's the Bodhisattva spirit that seems the thing.

One probably feels it's hardly worth thinking about, but inasmuch as one cares about these ideals at all, one hopes that in the long run they'll turn out to be more or less the same thing. Perhaps one likes to be pragmatic: perhaps one thinks that abstract theorizing and metaphysics are all right if you like that sort of thing, but they butter no parsnips. One has perhaps picked up the idea that the truth of things is not to be approached through the rational mind at all, but that it will suddenly vouchsafe itself while one is muddling along, and then everything will become clear.

But it is not going to be like this. One penetrates beyond the rational by way of exhausting the resources of the rational mind. The thing is not going to be achieved except through the tension of the rational mind stretching itself to its limit. Even more immediately practical matters require more clear thinking than we generally like to afford them. Why exactly should one be a vegetarian, for instance – what are the principles involved? Or why does one meditate – what actually is the point? You can't just say 'If you're a Buddhist, these are the things you do.' Well, you can, but you won't thereby make much of an impression on a sceptical non-Buddhist.

It may be true that not everything one does as a Buddhist is fully susceptible to rational analysis. The Dharma does point towards something beyond the grasp of the rational mind. But there are rational considerations that certainly do arise, and which may be communicated in response to enquiries about why you do what you do. There can be a false humility in admitting that you have no clear idea about what you are doing.

Fortunately, if one has the idea at the back of one's mind that it is rather unspiritual to be too clear about things, the Abhidharma is there to put one right. As should be quite clear by now, the Abhidharma hammers home at every point the crucial importance of distinguishing very precisely and accurately between what is skilful and what is unskilful.

6. OPINIONATEDNESS (DṚṢṬI)

Opinionatedness is Guenther's translation of *dṛṣṭi*, which literally means a sight, a view, a vision, a perspective. It means seeing things in a particular way, from a particular point of view – the implication being that this view or perspective, whatever it may be, is a limited, narrow one. It is, in fact, *mithyādṛṣṭi* (*micchādiṭṭhi* in Pāli) or 'wrong view', that view which is under the influence of *kleśa* – as opposed to *samyagdṛṣṭi*, right or perfect view.

In some of the earliest Pāli texts the Buddha is reported to have said that 'the Tathāgata is free from all views'[178] – including even right view. The term 'right view' is a contradiction in terms, from that absolute – so to speak – point of view. But from our own point of view, we need right view in order to displace wrong view. Only then will we be able to go beyond views altogether.

So *samyagdṛṣṭi* is not a closed system of ideas to which one permanently adheres, but a skilful attitude provisionally adopted in order to get rid of unskilful states of mind. It is a wrong view, therefore, to believe that one must give up all views in order to attain to right or perfect view. One cannot realize absolute truth without taking one's stand upon relative truth. To be paradoxical, one could say that all views are wrong views, and one of them is that one should give up all views.

One does encounter people with this kind of wrong view from time to time, people who profess a sort of intellectual and even spiritual hospitality or open-mindedness. They don't want to confine themselves to any particular philosophy or religion. They aspire to a universal vision – which is, practically speaking, beyond them. Without right views, there is no basis for right action, no basis for ethics. And without right action there is no possibility of attaining to universal vision. Only a Tathāgata has no views; while this should certainly be one's aim, one can realize it only by taking one's stand upon right views and practising on that basis.

According to Yeshe Gyaltsen's commentary there are five kinds of *dṛṣṭi*: they are – and here I am giving my own translations rather than Guenther's – fixed self-view, extreme views, attachment to ideologies, attachment to moral codes and religious observances, and wrong views regarding actions and their consequences.

a. Self-view

> It is any acceptance, claim, opinion as dogma, fiction and opinion about the five psycho-physical constituents as a (eternal) self or as belonging to a self, and its function is to serve as a basis for all other views.[179]

This is the text Yeshe Gyaltsen quotes from the *Abhidharmasamuccaya*. He goes on to give his own interpretation of what it means:

> *Acceptance* insofar as one is not afraid of what is contrary to every evidence;
> *Claim* insofar as one is involved with objects which are contrary to all evidence;
> *Opinion as dogma* insofar as one has rationalized it;
> *Fiction* insofar as one is enamored with it;
> *Opinion* insofar as one makes it the content of one's thinking.[180]

Self-view is the fundamental wrong view underlying all the others. It is the view that the five *skandhas* add up to, or contain, or form an aspect of, or can be identified with, the idea of a self or ego. The wrong view arises because one posits an absolutely substantial self on the basis of one's psycho-physical experience.

We fondly embrace the assumption that we are absolutely real: that the self we experience has some ultimate validity. This misunderstanding constitutes the frame of reference within which all our other views are held. It is not just the content of our thinking; it is, as it were, the 'continent' of our thinking. It is as if as human beings we are entranced or mesmerized by this misunderstanding, even sometimes proceeding to rationalize it into the basis of a philosophy or religion.

All this is despite the evidence of the Buddha's experience and teaching, and in fact the evidence of our own reason and observation. It doesn't appear to us to be evidence, of course, because we have adopted an interpretation of our experience which is not in accord with the experience of Enlightenment, and which does not allow us to appreciate the evidence available to the Enlightened mind.

We present our views in rational terms even though they are based on an essentially irrational premise – that is, on our emotional need to believe in our own secure and unchanging ego-identity. On an ordinary day-to-day level we rationalize in this way all the time. To justify our viewpoints or actions we provide reasoned explanations which serve to disguise the true reasons for them. We like to dress up our gut reactions as rational responses to make them respectable. Then we amass more and more evidence and argument on top of the original purely personal feeling. It is possible eventually to elaborate a whole philosophy out of certain basic personal human weaknesses. One begins with a certain experience of oneself and refuses to consider any evidence that challenges this experience. On the basis of this false idea of oneself one becomes involved with objects, and this whole position is presented as a philosophy or religion. One then proceeds to become attached to this view, even enamoured of it, and eventually it becomes consolidated into certain assumptions which one never subsequently questions.

Any philosophy that is not the product of an Enlightened mind is inevitably constructed in basically this way. The rationalizations are all too easily observable, even though they may be shot through with profound insights. It is sobering to reflect that all the systematic philosophies we have, and perhaps even all the religions as well, are pseudo-rational presentations, at least on a certain level, of experiences that are essentially limited. One could even go as far as to say that any systematically worked-out view must be suspected of being a rationalization in some sense.

This is why Nietzsche wrote in the form of strings of aphorisms, especially toward the end of his life. Each aphorism represents an intuition, an insight, but he doesn't attempt to string all the insights together and work them into a comprehensive system of thought. It is significant that his *Thus Spake Zarathustra* is presented as poetry rather than philosophy. If one really wants to get to the truth of things, to the heart of the matter, the imagination is arguably a more reliable faculty than the intellect alone, and the poet a more reliable guide than the philosopher.

There are said to be twenty possible forms of self-view.[181] This figure is arrived at by distinguishing four different ways of projecting the idea of a self on to each of the five *skandhas* (form, feeling, perception, volition, consciousness), making twenty in all. If one takes form or body (*rūpa*), for example, one could say:

i. I am my body and nothing beyond that. My body is my self; my self is my body. Body and self are identical.

ii. The body is possessed by the self as something apart from and beyond the body. This is a common idea of the nature of the soul, that there is a psychic element, identified as the self, to which the body belongs.

iii. The self is located within the body.

iv. The body is located within the self – that is, the self is a wider non-material entity within which the body is contained.

One may apply this series of possibilities to each of the *skandhas* individually, or indeed to all five *skandhas* collectively. None of these views is consonant with the reality that whatever we think of as a self is no self. This is an aspect of the insight one gains when one becomes Enlightened. A statement about the Buddha's own experience of himself is to be found among what are called the 'fourteen inexpressibles' (Sanskrit *avyākṛtavastūni*). Well, the 'statement' is really a non-statement. There is nothing to be said about the Buddha's experience; it is literally ineffable.

These fourteen inexpressibles emerge from a conversation between the Buddha and the wanderer Vacchagotta. Vacchagotta asked the Buddha four questions, each presented as four (two in the case of the last question) alternative views, according to the conventions of Indian logic.[182] The first two questions concerned whether or not the universe is eternal and whether or not it is infinite. The third question was whether or not the Buddha – and by extension any other fully Enlightened being – can be said to exist after death; or whether he simultaneously exists in one sense and does not exist in another sense; or whether he neither exists nor does not exist. The Buddha rejected all these alternative views as to his status after death. None of them fits the case, he said, and to hold any one of them would be to hold a wrong view. Even during his lifetime, so the Buddha said, he is inconceivable. How can one even consider the nature of his existence after his death?

Vacchagotta's fourth question – consisting of the last two 'inexpressibles' – is the one we are concerned with here. Can it be said that the *jīvitindriya*, the life principle or life faculty of the Buddha, is identical with this physical body? This is a question of a kind that still exercises thinkers today: whether life, or mind, or whatever you like to call it, is identical with the physical body or not. The Buddha rejects both views.

It's as though he is refusing to accept the assumption that the relation between body and life can be discussed in terms of their being either one thing or two.

In fact, it is impossible to think in terms of absolute dualities of any kind. Once one has a duality one is faced with the problem of reconciling it, which in the case of an absolute duality is impossible. So it's not a question of reducing what we think of as body to what we think of as life, or vice versa. The Buddha is suggesting that we shouldn't think in these terms at all. Perhaps we should follow Blake and say 'The body is that portion of the soul which is perceptible by the senses in this age.'

The Buddhist position would appear to be that one always has a body of some kind; it isn't always a *physical* body. If you encounter a dead body, you don't get the impression that the person himself or herself is actually there in the body. Even though it looks just like them, you don't feel that you are in the presence of that person. But put it the other way round: supposing you have the experience of encountering someone who is dead – by which I mean a purely mental experience of them, not seeing a ghost – do you experience them as a sort of disembodied intelligence or spirit? Well, no – if you've ever had that sort of experience you will know that you experience them as having a body. It isn't a physical body, but they have a body, just as they had during their lifetime.

Or take the case of so-called out-of-the-body experiences: even though one has the experience of withdrawing from the body, one still feels complete – one still has subtle sense-experience. That is, one is in possession of what in the Pāli texts is termed the *manomayakāya* or 'body made of mind'[183] – through which one has supersensory experience: telepathy, clairaudience, and so on. So the body does not necessarily have to have a material medium. 'Body' is more like a principle of configuration, a unitive principle.

In short, whether or not the body one experiences at any one time can be said to be identical with one's 'life principle' is impossible to say. The whole question of the nature of the body is philosophically quite abstruse. It is not essentially the physical body, even though that may be the way one experiences it at the moment, because clearly one can leave the physical body, whether through death or an out-of-the-body experience; but equally clearly, one doesn't get away from having a body completely. In the bardo of death one could say that one has a body, albeit of a different kind from that one had while alive. Furthermore, one is always connected to a physical body, if only potentially, in terms of one's karma generating a future material existence.

But a Buddha is said to have gone beyond birth and death – and yet he still has a body. How is this? Well, one's own physical body, the experience one has in dependence upon the body and its organs, is a *vipāka*; it comes to each of us as a result of our past karma. Our bodies are, in a sense, our past catching up with us. This is true also of the Buddha. One could say – although any statement about this matter is necessarily cryptic – that in realizing the non-duality of saṁsāra and nirvāṇa, one no more ceases to have a body than one continues to have a body. In short, once one is Enlightened, no statement as to the relationship between one's Enlightened being and one's physical body is appropriate.

And, as the entire Abhidharma tradition goes to considerable lengths to show, our own physical existence is more mysterious than we usually think. 'Who am I?' is a question most of us leave behind with our adolescence, but it continues to be relevant. There is no 'me' apart from the flow of physical and mental events, apart from the five *skandhas*, which continually change. Deep down we don't really believe this; and yet, as I say, the evidence is there for us to experience.

The meditation practice called the contemplation of the six elements has as its specific purpose the overcoming of the wrong view that one has a fixed, permanent self. In the course of the practice one reflects that each of the elements of which one's body is composed – earth, water, fire, air, space, and consciousness – is not really one's own. When one dies, one will have to give back these elements to the universe; they have only been 'borrowed' for the duration of one's life. Even one's consciousness, once it is no longer bound up with the body, cannot really be said to be one's own.

b. Extreme view

> It is any acceptance, claim, opinion as dogma, fiction and opinion
> which is completely biased taking the five original elements as eternal
> existence or as non-existence, and its function is to prevent gaining
> certainty through the understanding of reality as it comes through the
> middle way.[184]
> *Abhidharmasamuccaya*

To some extent we have already dealt with extreme views. There are the two extreme views we may hold with regard to views themselves.

On the one hand we may adopt a dogmatic, possessive attitude towards views, clinging to them as though they did fully express ultimate truth. The opposite extreme view is to consider it unnecessary to have any views at all, even skilful views, right views.

The fourteen inexpressibles also represent extreme views, to which the only appropriate reply was for the Buddha to stay silent. His silence was not the silence of ignorance, or of suspension of judgement; nor was it even simply the *āryan* silence, the noble silence of the second *dhyāna*, when the thought processes of *vitarka* and *vicāra* are suspended. All the alternative views he was offered were inapplicable, and he knew no explanation could be articulated in words, so he remained in the silence of the Enlightened mind.

Traditionally, the extreme views which are held to be representative are eternalism and nihilism: the view that the self is eternally existent, and the view that the self is totally non-existent.[185] In ancient India these two views concerned whether or not the self survived death in some form. The eternalist view was that the self persisted unchanged from life to life; this is akin to the Christian view of the soul, that it survives death intact and goes on to heaven, hell, or limbo. The nihilistic view was that the whole psycho-physical organism was totally annihilated at the moment of death – which is of course the common, modern, secular view.

Such is, we may say, the psychological aspect of these two extreme views. They may also be put in a more metaphysical context. This version offers the view that mundane existence, in terms of the five *skandhas*, is ultimately real in some way, and at the other extreme the view that it is completely unreal and illusory at every level.

Thirdly, in ethical terms, eternalism and nihilism may be interpreted as the two extremes of self-indulgence and self-torture. It is possible to see self-indulgence – in the philosophy of 'eat, drink, and be merry, for tomorrow we die' – as a form of nihilism. And it is possible to see self-torture – for the purpose of releasing the eternal soul from its prison – as a form of eternalism. However, this is just from the viewpoint of the traditional idea of the two extremes as representing attitudes to the possibility of life after death. It is probably more true to the psychological reality to say that self-indulgence expresses a belief in the absolute reality of mundane existence, while self-torture expresses self-hatred, and thus a desire for self-destruction and, by extension, for the destruction of mundane existence.

The Buddhist doctrine of *anātman*, no-self, is unfortunately some-times interpreted in such terms as to appeal to this tendency towards self-destruction. If this teaching is interpreted as a total negation of the self, it will be very attractive to people who want to express their own self-hatred. Quite a few people seem to have this sort of attitude, a fascination with the *anātman* doctrine as an essentially life-denying principle. But the idea that the doctrine of no-self declares life to be worthless, meaningless, and in fact non-existent, is simply not Buddhist.

The *anātman* doctrine can also be used as a way of avoiding personal responsibility, or of sitting on one's natural energies. Anything one decides to do, particularly in an energetic or wholehearted way, be-comes an expression of ego and thus doctrinally suspect. Again, this is a wrong view. The goal of Buddhahood is to go beyond the individual self, not to regress from the achievement of individual selfhood.

The ego is no more than the tendency to absolutize one's present state of being. It is not a thing, but a faulty interpretation. One is seeing something that just isn't there. The individual is there in a process of continuous change and therefore of ever-present potential develop-ment; delusion may also be there, in the form of a belief in a fixed, unchanging self or essence or soul. But that fixed, unchanging self or essence or soul or ego is not there; it never was, and it never will be. And because it isn't there, one can't do anything with it – get rid of it, go beyond it, or whatever. The best thing to do as far as the ego is concerned is just to forget about it.

We are not just an absence of self; we are an absence of *fixed* self, a flow of ever-changing components, physical and mental. The Buddha himself was evidently a powerfully distinct individual, with a very clear idea of who or what he was. To have a self-view means to identify oneself with a sort of cross-section of the flow of *skandhas* and imagine that one can arrest the flow at that point. It is just a state of arrested development, like being a child who says, 'When I grow up I'm going to fill my house with toys and eat sweets all day,' unable to imagine the transformation involved in growing up.

The five *skandhas* – the world which we experience as both subject and object – is neither the ultimate reality (because according to the Buddha's Enlightened experience things are not as we perceive them) nor completely illusory (because our experience, unenlightened though it may be, has its own validity on its own level). It is in response to our tendency to embrace one or another of such extreme views –

which are of course reflected in various philosophies and dogmas, both Western and Eastern – that the Middle Way was formulated.

The Middle Way is to see the five *skandhas* as having a conventional or relative existence – that is, to see them as having arisen in dependence upon causes and conditions. If the extreme views are to see conditioned existence as either unconditioned or totally illusory, the Middle Way is to see the conditioned as what it is, simply conditioned. We tend to treat concepts like existence and non-existence, reality and non-reality, as absolutes, whereas so far as conditioned or relative existence is concerned (and conditioned existence is where we are when we make these distinctions) there are no absolutes.

Everything conditioned, everything phenomenal, everything mundane, arises in dependence on conditions and ceases in the absence of those conditions. The world is not completely real, but neither is it absolutely unreal. It is there to be experienced, we are involved in it, but it is not to be mistaken for absolute reality, for something that exists in an ultimate sense. It's as simple as that. It's the Middle Way, the way in which Buddhism sees the world. Really, it is just common-sense.

But, of course, we want absolutes. The Buddhist approach is to get us to think for ourselves, to see into the complexity of the situation we find ourselves in, all the different factors involved, trying to understand it truly and honestly, not sliding off that Middle Way into easy answers. To think about something objectively in this way can be very frustrating. It also takes courage, because it means taking responsibility for one's conclusions.

Most people put their faith and trust in someone who makes a strong impression, someone who is very emphatic and certain and self-confident. If you try to be careful about what you are saying, introducing qualifications where appropriate and suggesting that yours is only a certain way of looking at things, that there are other ways, and that one will have to make up one's own mind, you will make a comparatively feeble impression. On the whole, people want to know what to think, which means something black and white. They want certainty. What they are certain about is less important to them than the certainty itself. They will believe any farrago of nonsense as long as they have permission to believe in it absolutely. It is not clarity but certainty they are looking for. Certainty is security; and being exposed to the difficulties and confusions of having to think seriously is to be thrown into insecurity.

Many people seem to want to rush to take up views where, one may say, angels fear to tread. I have noticed this in, for example, Hindus with a smattering of religious knowledge. I remember on one occasion when I took the public jeep from Kalimpong to Siliguri, I was sitting in the front next to the driver when there was a hold-up of some sort, and the Bihari policeman who was controlling things, seeing there was a sadhu in yellow robes – i.e. myself – waiting there, and having nothing better to do for the moment, strolled up and started asking the usual questions: 'Are you a holy man?' and so on. Then he began to tell me all about how the universe had evolved from Brahman, and how it was all unreal, and how the soul was the same as God. He held forth in this way for about fifteen minutes and then strolled off again. There was a Tibetan Buddhist sitting behind me who had observed all this with mounting horror: 'That man was talking about the Dharma,' he said at last, as if he couldn't believe his ears. That someone with a few undigested religious notions rattling around in his head should shoot his mouth off about them, in public, to a total stranger, had left him almost speechless.

As a Buddhist one finds that one has to resist a tendency in people to look for absolutist views. They might ask about a certain gifted but wayward Buddhist teacher, 'Is so-and-so a Bodhisattva or is he a total fake?' Of course, the fact is that such a person is a complex human being and worthy of more than a snap judgement either way – or even somewhere precisely in between. Or someone might say, 'What's the Buddhist view on such and such: hanging, abortion, astrology, extra-marital sex?' What they want is a definite, simple answer to take away with them.

But there is no 'Buddhist view' as such; there is no hierarchy of authority from which to draw one's views. One can have one's own view as a Buddhist, but it will not have the stamp of authority that Christians have from God or the Bible or the Pope. And people generally want the kind of security one gets from a source of authoritative judgements. As a Buddhist, the best one can do sometimes is to say, 'Here are the Four Noble Truths. Do what you can with these.'

By looking for ready-made 'Buddhist' answers – the party line – people also want to be able to categorize one as a Buddhist. Just as people say 'He's an Aries,' or 'She's a greed type,' or 'He's an account-ant,' and think they've got that person dealt with, classified, docketed, likewise, if they can categorize Buddhism, then they can put one in the Buddhist category. Again, one needs to resist this tendency. It's a way of dismissing you, disposing of you, not being concerned with you as an individual. What to think of you has been settled by the fact that you are a Buddhist. This is not to say that one should be afraid of saying that one is a Buddhist – or an accountant, for that matter – but that one should not imagine (or hope) that being a Buddhist puts one as an individual in a category.

c. Attachment to ideologies

It is any acceptance, claim, opinion as dogma, fiction and opinion to hold the five psycho-physical constituents – as far as they are occasions of an opinion about them – as the supreme, the principle, the particularly sublime, and the absolutely real. Its function is to serve as the basis for becoming even more enmeshed in wrong views.[186]
Abhidharmasamuccaya

We have seen how an ideology is established. First of all one has a *dṛṣṭi*, a view, representing a certain limited and emotionally negative perspective. One rationalizes this into a philosophical position or ideology, and then one proceeds to become attached to that position, to cling to that ideology. To take a simple example, someone who felt very unsure of himself, inadequate, insecure, might perhaps be drawn to some form of, say, fascist ideology. Embracing that ideology would make him feel more sure of himself, so he would then become more and more attached to it, and more and more certain in his adherence to it.

Not all ideologies are as unskilful as this, of course, but an element of wrong view is always going to be there somewhere. Clinging to ideologies means fixing our attitudes so that we won't have to think or feel or see for ourselves. Faced with the fundamental issues of life and finding there are no obvious easy answers to them, we find security in a certain limited perspective, which we formulate into a set of views. Almost all of us do this to some degree: our personal desires, whims, and perhaps neuroses bring all kinds of views or rationalizations in their wake. Some of these we are aware of, others not. But usually our wrong views underpin the emotional basis for the way we look at the world. In a sense we *exude* our wrong views – they aren't just there as a little intellectual tangle we've got into in a little corner of the brain.

We will probably find that even our involvement with the Dharma is at least partly based upon these views, these ideologies. It is almost inevitable that we start off with impure motives. We probably have some cherished notions that we associate with Buddhism, that we feel Buddhism ought to endorse, but into which we do not enquire too deeply, for fear of being disappointed. This is where the trouble starts. If we have embraced Buddhism for the wrong reasons – which is quite common – we need to make sure that we don't cling to it in such a way as to reinforce the original weakness on account of which we embraced it in the first place. Otherwise we will be embracing not Buddhism but our own preconceived views, which we can hold even more tightly because we imagine that they are sanctioned by the Dharma.

Take the example of the person who comes to the Dharma with a mistaken view of the doctrine of *anātman*, interpreting it as a total negation of the self, unconsciously finding it attractive because it seems to reflect their own self-hatred. They might then study this subject that they find so fascinating, research it, even write books on it. Finally they might become a well-known expert on the *anātmavāda*. In this way their whole life would have revolved around their basic neurosis and the rationalization built upon it.

Right view with regard to the self is that in truth or in reality it is a non-self. However, one can hold this view in one of two ways. One can adopt it as a skilful attitude by which one will be able to progress towards eventually transcending all views whatsoever, or else one can adhere to it as a dogma. It is possible to adopt the *anātmavāda* (the doctrine of no-self) in an unskilful, egoistic way.

This is certainly a criticism that might be levelled at some Theravādins, that they have had a tendency to advocate the *anātma-vāda* in an aggressive, even belligerent manner, violently criticizing anyone who professed the opposite view. Not that these Theravādins always understood quite what they were talking about, but they were still very attached to their doctrine as a key element in their cultural and intellectual heritage, something which clearly marked them off from Hindus. One of my own teachers, Jagdish Kashyap, once re-marked in the course of a lecture he was giving in Sri Lanka that one could not understand what *anātman* meant without first under-standing what *ātman* or self meant. He was shouted down by the monks in the audience, who said that they didn't want him 'bringing his Hindu philosophy here'.

Such is clinging to ideology in a Buddhist context. This kind of unskilful attitude towards that which is specifically meant to help one to be skilful is a serious matter. As Candrakīrti says, if the medicine itself becomes poisonous, where will you turn for the treatment you need?[187] It is clear that sometimes what is technically a wrong view may temporarily serve a skilful purpose. For example, on the basis of a belief in an essential self or soul one may perform certain skilful actions; and on the basis of the skilful mental states arising from those actions one may realize that the idea of a self or soul could not be in accordance with reality. Up to this point that wrong view has served a useful purpose. The fact of the matter is that, until such time as we are Enlightened, we need a self; in fact, most of us actually need to strengthen and define our individuality. In the Pāli scriptures the Buddha himself speaks of 'making the self strong'[188] – because a weak self is simply not capable of sustaining the shattering experience of transcendental insight.

The crucial issue is not so much whether the view held is right or wrong, but the manner in which it is held. If one holds it sufficiently lightly, so that one is able eventually to see its limitations and discard it, then at the very least one will be able to move forward. Right view that is treated as dogma is being taken as an end in itself. It is then no longer useful and therefore no longer right view. Right view must always be held as what Guenther calls an operational concept. It is all right to believe that as a Buddhist one's operational concepts are reliable, effective, and long-lasting, but only if one keeps bearing in mind that they are still only operational concepts.

A dogmatic attitude towards right views turns them, practically speaking, into wrong views. If you try to hit someone over the head with Buddhist truth, it effectively ceases to be Buddhist truth. In any case, we have no idea at all at present what the Enlightened state – the state of realized non-ego – is like. Even to describe it as a state of non-selfhood gives us so little idea of it as to be conceivably quite misleading.

The followers of an ancient Hīnayāna school called the Pudgalavāda provide an interesting slant on this issue. They posited the existence of a *pudgala* or person which is distinct from the concept of *ātman* or self, supporting this view by referring to texts such as the *Ti Ratana Vandana* which speak of the eight noble *pudgalas* (*aṭṭha-āriya-puggalās* in Pāli), and pointing out that the Buddha refers to himself as a *pudgala*: 'There is a *pudgala* who has arisen for the benefit of the world.'[189] So they advanced the idea of a *pudgalavāda* which is not an *atmavāda* – a position which can be defended rationally. Their opponents, of course, interpreted the key texts which the Pudgalavādins cited in support of their views differently, holding that the *pudgalavāda* was in fact a form of *atmavāda*. However, the other Hīnayāna schools admitted that Pudgalavādins could gain Enlightenment.

So the view advanced by Edward Conze in his important account of Buddhist philosophy, *Buddhist Thought in India*, that the Pudgalavādins were not really Buddhists, does not ring true.[190] This view – that early converts to Buddhism, unable to give up their Brahminical belief in the ultimate reality of the *ātman*, tried to smuggle in their heresy in the guise of *pudgala* or *ālaya* or *bhavanga* – rather misses the point. In India at this time the discussion was not conducted in terms of whether or not the Pudgalavādins were really Buddhists. The term 'Buddhist' itself hardly existed. The important point, which all parties recognized, was that they were all trying to gain Enlightenment.

The more fruitful line of inquiry is to ask: why did they introduce this doctrine? If we reflect that the Buddha himself continued, even after his Enlightenment, to experience himself as himself, the answer seems clear enough. If the Theravādins reject the *pudgala* doctrine out of hand, this is perhaps because it is a purely metaphysical position, and they are sometimes quite unsophisticated, even naïve, when it comes to metaphysics.

The fact is that although the Pudgalavāda School and its own recension of the scriptures have not survived it was one of the most important schools of early Buddhism. As it happens, one of the most respected Pāli scholars of modern times, A.P. Buddhadatta, came to the conclusion that they were right. Nobody bothered him about it; it was just considered a mild eccentricity on his part to be a Pudgalavādin.[191]

In the end we should have the attitude of the true Mādhyamika – the follower of the Middle Way – which is to find the truth and be receptive to it, whatever it might turn out to be, even if it threatens everything that up till now we have based our life upon. To some extent, it is bound to do this – if it is really the truth – and we should be prepared for that.

d. Attachment to moral codes and religious observances

Its function is to serve as the basis for uselessness.[192]

Abhidharmasamuccaya

It is said that there are 'ten fetters' which hold us back from the ultimate freedom which is Enlightenment, and the breaking of the first three, according to tradition, is synonymous with the dawning of transcendental insight. The first two fetters are 'fixed self view' and 'doubt with regard to the Three Jewels'. *Śīlavrataparāmarśa* is the third. *Śīla* means 'ethics', and in this context it refers to a formulation of rules or precepts, while *vrata*, which literally means 'vow', is a pre-Buddhist, Vedic term for a certain kind of brahminical observance. And *parāmarśa* means 'being attached to, hanging on, being under the influence of'. A good interpretive translation of this term would therefore be 'clinging to ethical formalism and conventional religion as ends in themselves'. To be bound by this fetter is to think that observing the outward forms of religious observance purely mechanically or compulsively will suffice to bring about deliverance from compounded existence. It is a superstitious belief in the inherent spiritual or salvific efficacy of, say, bathing in the River Ganges, going on pilgrimage to Mecca, receiving absolution from a priest, and so on.

It being so crucial to one's spiritual progress that one should break these three fetters, it is a good idea to approach them from every angle. I have sometimes described them in psychological terms as habit, vagueness, and superficiality,[193] while in social terms they could be described as attachment to psychology, philosophy, and religion. So here we are concerned with an essentially superficial approach to spiritual practice – that is, religion.

Saṁsāra is essentially an expression of compulsiveness. The fixed sense of self, the ego, is essentially compulsive, inasmuch as it has continually to reinforce its fixation by going over the same ground again and again. Such practices as bathing in the Ganges and so on are inherently egoistic acts, inasmuch as their rationale is based on the idea of a separate, unchanging self to be liberated or admitted to heaven or paradise. Such attachment to conventional religious or ethical observances simply binds us more securely to saṁsāra.

Buddhism itself, of course, has its own tendency towards this form of attachment. In Theravāda Buddhism, for example, many people are strongly convinced that things like shaving one's head, wearing yellow robes, and not eating after twelve o'clock make one a monk – and that these things are the most fundamental prerequisites to being a monk. But this is simply ethical formalism in the guise of Buddhism. In fact it is worse than that, because although the Theravāda itself recognizes that these observances are matters of conventional rather than natural morality, if you try flouting these conventions in a Theravādin country, you will find you have committed a major offence.

There was an Indian bhikkhu I knew who spent a number of years in Sri Lanka, and it happened once that he picked up a severe cold in the head. He was staying up in the hills where it can get quite cold and – being an Indian – he put on a small woollen cap. This provoked a tremendous hullaballoo: there were pictures of him in the paper under such headlines as 'the shameless monk who wears a woollen cap' and people hooted after him in the street. For years afterwards he was nicknamed 'the cap-wearing bhikkhu'. Of course, this happened over forty years ago; no doubt the Theravāda is more relaxed about adherence to its conventional observances than it used to be.

When I returned to England after spending many years living as a bhikkhu in India, I myself provoked an astonishing reaction when I started letting my hair grow – this was while I was still wearing robes. This caused disquiet not just in Theravādin circles; Mahāyānists and even Zen Buddhists all seemed to find it quite upsetting. It seemed that ethical formalism was creeping into British Buddhism although it had only been going for a few decades. So I let my hair grow longer and longer. After a lecture one evening several people came up to speak to me about the length of my hair, which by now amounted to a couple of inches, and one of them said, 'I don't know why you are growing your hair so long – it is really upsetting everybody. We don't know what it means.'

I found it very interesting that the length of my hair should be a subject of such deep concern to so many people. Even Christmas Humphreys, who was supposed to be very broad-minded, was not, I came to understand, altogether happy about this deviation from the religious proprieties by one whom he had personally admonished to regard himself as the Buddhist equivalent of the Vicar of Hampstead. When I eventually gave up wearing robes, there were some people who were rather pleased – and as with the issue of the hair, their approbation was not always for the right reasons – but there were others who were deeply upset, feeling that this was tantamount to giving up Buddhism.

This whole episode was something of an eye-opener for me, and when I set up the Friends of the Western Buddhist Order I tried to discourage any creeping paralysis of the forms and institutions through which we practise and spread the Dharma. It still happens, of course – people are heard to say, 'Well, this is the way we do things in the FWBO.' But in fact, things in the Buddhist movement I started are generally the way they are because I once thought, 'That's how we'll do things for now.' Within the FWBO, nothing apart from the centrality of Going for Refuge to the Three Jewels is set in stone. There isn't one right way of doing things – there never has been.

Of course in communicating the Dharma one should be responsible about this; one should draw on past experience, and not encourage mere self-expression. And we have already discussed the value of discipline, of rules, in the spiritual life. However, a certain margin of creative variation is not only permissible, but desirable. Every once in a while one needs to re-examine everything with a completely open mind. Maybe one could even go right back to the Buddha's way of doing things – just going from place to place, and talking to people.

The idea that one has to break away from religion and morality as ordinarily understood before one can really start to make any progress on the path is a radical one, even for Buddhists. But it is quite literally what one has to do. One is wasting one's time otherwise. The third fetter is really about fear of breaking the rules. But why is one afraid of breaking the rules? Basically, it is because one doesn't trust oneself. One thinks, 'Well, if I don't observe the rules, who knows what will happen? All hell may break loose.' Yes, perhaps it will.

e. Wrong views

> It is the denial of cause and effect and of action and its result.... Its function is to eradicate the good ...[194]
> *Abhidharmasamuccaya*

This category concerns wrong views regarding actions and their consequences. They are given a category of their own because wrong views of this kind will undermine the spiritual life completely, making any kind of development on the path impossible. In this respect they are, so to speak, the cardinal wrong views. Traditionally there are four: denial of cause, denial of effect, denial of oneself as an ethical agent, and denial of the attainments of the Buddhas and Bodhisattvas.

The first of these, denial of cause, is the wilful refusal to acknowledge any meaningful distinction between good and bad actions – that is, the wilful refusal to recognize the ethical content of actions. This is a wrong view that used to have some currency in some 'beat' Zen circles ('square' Zen being the other extreme of insisting on all the rules, paraphernalia, and rituals of traditional Zen Buddhism). One would assume what one imagined to be the viewpoint of the Enlightened mind which has gone beyond mundane distinctions, including that between good and evil, or skilful and unskilful.

In fact, the Enlightened mind unquestionably perceives the difference between good and evil. If you are Enlightened you will look at compounded existence and perceive what is appropriate to or pertains to it, and this will include the necessary distinction between what is skilful and what is unskilful. Or rather, you will at least seem to others to be recommending skilful courses of action and deprecating unskilful ones. Whether you yourself see things in that way is another matter. What we may be sure of is that an Enlightened one will perceive the ethical implications of our actions far more clearly than we do.

The second of these wrong views, denial of effect, is the wilful refusal to acknowledge any meaningful distinction between good and bad actions in terms of their consequences – specifically karmic ones. This may be a straightforward conclusion arising from the first wrong view, or it may be that no effectual ethical connection between action and experience, karma and *vipāka*, is recognized at all.

Of course, causation is not a straightforward matter, which is why it is better to think in terms of conditionality. In the Indian philosophical tradition, there are two opposing viewpoints with regard to the relationship between cause and effect. The followers of the Sātkāryavāda school of thought, which brought together the Sāṁkhyas and the Advaita-Vedantins, believe that there is essentially no difference between cause and effect, that effect is a transformation of cause, cause in another form. Various illustrations are given in support of this thesis. For instance, one can say that when water freezes, water is the cause, and ice is the effect; that when clay is formed and baked, the clay is the cause, and the pot is the effect; and that when gold ornaments are made, again, the effect is a transformation of the cause. That is the view of the Sātkāryavādins. The opposite viewpoint, the view of the Asātkāryavādins, is that cause and effect are totally distinct. When there is an acorn and then much later there is an oak tree, it seems clear that the tree is not simply a transformation of the acorn, even though the acorn is the cause of the tree. Cause and effect are, according to this view, quite different.[195]

The Buddhist view is that the whole question is artificial, because from a practical point of view it is not necessary to assert either of these positions. Ice arises in dependence upon water; the oak arises in dependence upon the acorn. There is no need to say more than this. Besides, as Nāgārjuna points out, if cause and effect are identical there can be no causation. Similarly, if cause and effect are different, no causation is possible.

The idea of conditionality is effectively the idea of causation employed in modern science. When we use the term cause it should be understood to mean the condition in dependence on which an event is observed to occur. But although there is an event, in the sense of a happening, there is no 'thing' to which something has happened. There is only a process.

From an ethical perspective, the point is that actions have consequences. Unskilful actions of body, speech, and mind do not come from nowhere and do not disappear without leaving a trace. We cannot say that suffering is caused by the *kleśas*, but we can certainly observe that we suffer when we are subject to the *kleśas*.

The third wrong view with respect to actions and their consequences is denial of oneself as an ethical agent: the wilful refusal to recognize that one's relationship with others, as well as with oneself, has an ethical dimension. Our actions affect others, and they affect us too, not only in the immediate future, but with respect to future lives as well. Our past and our future are the product to some degree of our ethical decisions.

The crucial relationship from an ethical point of view is traditionally the relationship with one's mother and father. If one doesn't recognize a special duty or moral responsibility towards them, one may well have lost one's moral bearings altogether (assuming that one's early ethical training did come from one's mother and father). The family in which one grows up, in other words, is said to be the training ground for the maintenance and cultivation of ethical relationships in later life.

The socialization of a child takes time and skill. When it is done well, it produces an ethically aware individual, someone who has a positive attitude towards other human beings, who actually wants to be kind and generous, and who has a positive attitude towards society generally, and can find their place in it. When it is done badly it produces someone who would sell their own grandmother for sixpence, and who has a negative and destructive attitude towards society as a whole – an attitude sometimes quite consciously and irresponsibly instilled in children, with very dangerous long-term results.

Another way of denying that one is an ethical agent is to take the view – perhaps a particularly modern one – that life, even spiritual life, is simply about doing what we feel like doing. Sooner or later, this viewpoint is more or less bound to lead to an over-valuation of the sexual relationship. This is not to say that sexual activity is necessarily unskilful on its own basic level. At the most unrefined mundane level, it is good not to be sexually blocked. There are those whose emotional development is held back by their being sexually repressed, who are unable to free up their emotions at any more subtle level than that of their sexuality. Unless some exceptional spontaneous spiritual experience arises to break through this emotional blockage, straightforward sexual experience may be the answer (which is not to say one cannot be both sexually liberated and thoroughly blocked emotionally – one can, very easily).

The idea that there is nothing to feel guilty about in one's sexuality is for many of us quite new. Because of the atmosphere of guilt that, even subconsciously, still surrounds the issue of sex, Western people sometimes find it difficult to accept sex simply for what it is – just sex. It has to be dignified, it has to be awarded some kind of spiritual validation. If one feels that there is something wrong with sex, one wants it sprinkled with religious rose-water, so to speak, to make it all right. This is perhaps one reason why even quite secular people like to have a church wedding, for example. And it is why some people who would like to be Buddhists refer to their sexual relationship in terms of the Tantra – girlfriends becoming *ḍākinīs*, coupling becoming the union of wisdom and compassion, and so on. They don't want to face the fact that a purely mundane preoccupation occupies a large, perhaps central place in their life, and that a truly spiritual commitment would require a shift in their priorities.

No doubt a sexual experience can reach such a pitch of intensity that one is tempted to make some spiritual claims for it. But there is a simple test to apply here: does faith in the Three Jewels come into it anywhere? Is that intense experience compatible with a simultaneous experience of faith? Is the overall orientation of the emotion involved in that experience in the direction of what the Three Jewels represents – that is, faith in the transcendental? I would suggest that the actual experience of faith is incompatible with any quite defined sexual experience, that it will inhibit and even dissolve the sexual experience. The two cannot occur simultaneously.

The danger is twofold. Firstly, it lies in not recognizing an experience for what it is. That is, as well as not distinguishing the skilful from the unskilful, it involves not distinguishing clearly between lower and higher orders of skilfulness. The danger is that one tries to invest something occupying a lower order of skilfulness with the prestige and mystique of something that belongs to a higher order, in order to justify one's attachment to that less skilful experience.

The fourth of these wrong views, denial of the attainments of the Buddhas and Bodhisattvas,[196] is the wilful refusal to recognize the possibility of liberation from compounded existence – and not just in the abstract. It is the wilful refusal to recognize the concrete reality of the Buddhist ideal as embodied in historical and even contemporary figures. It is to disbelieve that anyone has in the past or the present achieved a level of development that is qualitatively different from ordinary human existence, such as to represent an irreversible shift in their being towards an ever clearer and more compassionate realization of the true nature of existence. With this wrong view one immediately limits the range of one's own vision.

This attitude is probably more prevalent among ex-Protestants than among ex-Catholics because Catholics have at least been brought up with the concrete possibility of the attainment of sainthood embodied in the lives of historical individuals right up to the present day. Protestants, however, through their objection to the worship of saints, lost the notion of sanctity as representing a different and higher level of human development. The whole idea of attaining a particular level of sanctity that is recognized as marking one off from ordinary human goodness is regarded as rather suspect in a Protestant society.

Ex-Protestants tend to think in terms of 'Believe and you will be saved.' If they do accept the possibility of some kind of transformation they tend to think of it as a dramatic, even sensational group experience (mediated, perhaps, by an evangelical preacher). They don't tend to think in terms of spiritual evolution. If they take up meditation, they think of it as a way of being at peace with oneself, of being happy and comfortable with oneself on one's own level, not as a way of moving towards the permanent attainment of a state far beyond that level. Those who resist the possibility of radical change are really looking to reinforce their existing attitude, their existing way of life. If they take up meditation it is for the same reason that most people go to church – to partake of whatever consolation and emotional positivity they can find there, to enable them to carry on with mundane life.

The whole idea that one may develop into a substantially better kind of human being can be undermined by the assumption, widely current today, that no one is better than anyone else. The fact that you are more aware, more positive, more kind, more thoughtful, more energetic than other people, is not supposed actually to make you a better person than others. After all, it may be argued, other people have not had your advantages. You are not more developed; you are differently developed. One of the reasons that festivals celebrating the attainment of Buddhas and Bodhisattvas like Śākyamuni or Padmasambhava are so important is that they overturn this wrong view by drawing our attention not only to the path to Enlightenment but also to actual exemplars of the attainment of its goal.

This analysis of the various categories of wrong view does not exhaust the subject by any means. The *Brahmajāla Sutta* of the Pāli Canon, for example, deals with sixty-two wrong views. This is the first *sutta* of the collection known as the *Dīgha-Nikāya*, which is the first *nikāya* of the Sutta Piṭaka (the whole body of *suttas*), which in turn is the first *piṭaka* of the Pāli Canon. This may be coincidental – after all, the Pāli Canon had to start with something – but one would like to suppose that the compilers of the oral tradition knew what they were about in this as in other matters. The suggestion is that one has to get these wrong views out of the way before one can have access to the rest of the Dharma – before, that is, one can commence the spiritual life at all. The *Brahmajāla Sutta* is the 'great net' in which all wrong views are caught – that is, all the wrong views that were current in India at that time among both Buddhist and non-Buddhist spiritual practitioners. No doubt we could fish up a lot more that we have to contend with today.

One of these sixty-two wrong views is the notion that the universe is the creation of Īśvara, or God. To us, this rejection of the idea of a creator god is one of the defining ideas of Buddhism as a world religion, but in fact the Buddha at no point goes into it in any great detail, simply because it does not seem to have been a very popular view in his time. In a sense, the question is dealt with in the first two of the fourteen inexpressibles: the view that the world is eternal and the view that the world is not eternal. The belief that the universe was created by God – or indeed the belief that it started by chance or necessity – represents one extreme view; the other is the view that the universe is eternal. One might think that one of these views has to be right, but Buddhism rejects all of them.

The reason for this is that – according, at least, to the Yogācāra perspective – wherever there is the perceiving mind, there must be an object. Every attempt to account for the beginning of the universe, for example, is based on the assumption that one can rewind the spool of the universe in one's mind and eventually come to a point where the mind is not confronted by an object. But this is not possible; it is a wrong view to think so. The Yogācārin might say that the question of whether the universe is eternal or not eternal is unanswerable precisely because the question assumes (incorrectly) that there is a *mind-independent* universe to which the attributes 'eternal' or 'not eternal' might be attached.

To use a traditional analogy, one could take the question 'Is the horn of a rabbit big or small?'[197] The horn of a rabbit cannot be big or small because there is no horn of a rabbit to have such attributes. A non-existent entity cannot have attributes! Likewise with the question 'Is the (mind-independent) universe eternal or not eternal?' The (mind-independent) universe cannot be eternal or not-eternal because there is no (mind-independent) universe to have the attributes 'eternal' or 'not-eternal'. Thus, the question is 'unanswerable', because it involves an unwarranted assumption. In modern logical terms, this is an example of the informal fallacy called the 'complex question'.

9

FACTORS OF INSTABILITY

THE FOLLOWING twenty negative emotions are the *upakleśas*. Guenther calls them the proximate factors of instability – that is, they hang around the six *kleśas* as subordinate forms of them. If the *kleśas* are the root defilements, the *upakleśas* could be called the branch defilements. Another way of looking at them would be to call them more complex forms, or developments, of the *mūlakleśas*.

We are given a good many more negative mental events than positive ones, and no doubt one could extend the list considerably – more so, at least, than in the case of the positive mental events. It may even be that we have developed fresh and virulent strains of negative mental events in the time since the Abhidharma was first compiled. However, we may take some comfort from the fact that a small number of positive mental events will suffice to counteract a larger number of negative ones. Much of the importance of this list lies simply in its identification of the demons we create for ourselves. There will probably be some we didn't even realize existed. But once identified, they cease to be demons and become just problems to be worked with.

1. INDIGNATION OR RAGE (*KRODHA*)

> It is a vindictive intention which is associated with anger when the chance to hurt is near at hand. Its function is to become the basis of taking hold of a knife, killing, and preparing to strike.[198]
>
> *Abhidharmasamuccaya*

Krodha is a further development of *pratigha*. Essentially it means 'readiness to strike'; it is the immediate intention to do harm on the arising of an opportunity to do so – for example, if a stick, knife, or other weapon lies to hand. If this mental event is present in one's mind, as well as bearing the intention to harm, one has now fixed on the means to carry it out. Whether or not one actually does so is another matter, though it seems that *krodha* can be interpreted as including the actual deed. Perhaps it is most useful to identify three critical stages in this deteriorating mental state: hatred (the general intention to do harm), rage (the immediate intention to inflict specific harm), and fury (the actual infliction of harm).

As already discussed, experiencing one's anger can be a necessary stage in becoming integrated; anger should not be unconsciously blocked off as this can lead to alienation from the sources of one's energy. This is basic therapeutic wisdom, and it is all well and good. But we must now emphasize another, more important consideration to bear in mind with regard to this sort of negative mental event.

If we were to continue with the psychotherapeutic angle, we might describe rage and fury in terms of psychological tension. When one conceives of the means by which one may express one's rage, it is as if something snaps and one experiences a sudden release of tension. One has let off steam. One has probably even freed up energy. But here we are concerned not with psychology but with ethics. What is under discussion is the immediate intention to inflict suffering on someone else – a much more critical issue than whether or not one is becoming more integrated. If we can seriously think of violence towards another person – or even kicking the cat – in terms of our own psychological states, this in itself suggests that we have lost sight of the ethical perspective.

This self-referential approach is sometimes even built into the way people practise the *mettā bhāvanā* (Sanskrit *maitrī*), which is, of course, the most effective counter-agent to hatred, rage, and fury. It seems that some people do this practice not so much as an exercise in wishing that other people should be well and happy, but rather as a means by which to make themselves feel positive. The aim of the practice, however, is not just to feel good oneself, but to develop a positive attitude towards others in order to be able, when occasion offers, to express that positive attitude in action. Obviously one needs to have a psychologically skilful approach, but the psychological is not an end in itself. One cannot hope to develop skilful mental states without considering what one actually ends up doing as the fruit of those mental states. It is useless wishing people well in a purely theoretical way.

This is very much the Mahāyāna approach: to keep one's spiritual practice free from too great a concern with the preciousness of one's own mental states. If one can make sure that one actually does something genuinely altruistic from time to time, or at least takes on some work that is truly beneficial to others, this is the most effective way of keeping the ethical dimension from being crowded out by the psychological.

In my very early days as a Buddhist I wrote a skit which apparently became something of a talking point among the bhikkhus of the day. It was about an irascible and ill-natured gentleman (a more or less imaginary character) who was a great advocate of the *mettā bhāvanā* practice. He edited a Buddhist newspaper, writing all sorts of furious articles which savagely slated pretty well everything and everybody. His telegraphic address was 'Metta, Colombo'. In this little skit I described him sitting on his bed every morning and radiating *mettā* – this being the way the practice used to be described. One morning while he was radiating *mettā* to the four quarters of the globe, the servant boy happened to come in with his morning cup of tea – which the gentleman took after completing his *mettā* radiation – and tripped, dropping the cup and its contents all over the carpet and rather breaking up the meditative atmosphere. In a moment, the gentleman had seized the boy by the scruff of the neck and soundly thrashed him, saying 'You idiot! Can't you look where you're going when I'm radiating *mettā*?'

2. RESENTMENT (*UPANĀHA*)

It is not letting go of an obsession which develops through association with the anger which underlies it.[199]
Abhidharmasamuccaya

In Robert Burns' poem 'Tam o'Shanter', while the eponymous hero is at the pub, his wife waits at home, 'nursing her wrath to keep it warm'.

This is *upanāha*, resentment, brooding over an injury, bearing a grudge. We want to go on being angry; we rather enjoy it, we cultivate it. We even cherish our anger. We won't let go – we refuse just to put up with the fact that we have suffered an injury.

Resentment is a pervasive form of negativity, and its very nature is to hang around situations which people feel helpless to change – a job or a marriage, perhaps – in which one feels put upon or put down or injured in some way. Our resentment gives our ego the sense that when the opportunity arises, it will be able to even the score. Even if there is no likelihood that we will be able to effect any kind of revenge, our resentment still gives us an obscure sense that we are getting our own back, albeit in a very ill-directed and pointless way.

Even though we are the only person really suffering from it, we feel we have a right to our resentment. We look back at a situation that has made us angry, feeling again the anger it has evoked, savouring that feeling, and turning the situation over and over in our mind. Most of us carry around a certain quantum of negativity that can show itself at a moment's notice if someone gets in our way. But if we build upon and work up our irritation or annoyance, that quantum of negativity becomes a steady, well-banked fire of resentment. So resentment needs to be checked in the early stages, like depression or sexual infatuation, because its very nature is to perpetuate itself as a settled mental state. If we don't nip it in the bud, there is very little we can do about it later on. Once we have allowed ourselves to get deeply into it, there isn't any straightforward way of extricating ourselves. Resentment is cumulative; it gathers a quiet momentum of its own. If we don't bring it out in the open when we first become aware of what is going on, it can become so strong that we may be afraid of taking the lid off at all. We may feel that we have lost control of it altogether and that if we start to express our feelings we may end up doing actual injury to the object of our resentment. It may be that the other person is not even aware of our resentment, so again we can be afraid of the effect of revealing our true feelings.

It has to be said that resentment is a notable feature of many marriages. A certain pattern of behaviour is established early on, and niggling dissatisfactions grow up in that hot-house atmosphere over many years until one is eaten up with resentment. And yet one's spouse may be totally unaware of the problem, fondly imagining that one loves them. I have known some older women particularly who have found it almost impossible to practise meditation on account of their feelings of resentment, accumulated over decades.

So resentment can become a crippling affliction. We need to be prepared to let go of it, even if it may be uncomfortable from an egoistic point of view to do so, and to let go of the idea that there is any point to it whatsoever. If we really can't let go, we are going to need to tackle it directly with the other person or persons involved, even though this may also be an uncomfortable experience. If the situation is really difficult to handle, we may need to ask for the help of a third party.

3. SLYNESS-CONCEALMENT (MRAKṢA)

It is to perpetuate a state of unresolvedness because of its association with dullness and stubbornness when one is urged towards something positive. Slyness-concealment has the function of preventing one from making a clean break with it and feeling relieved.[200]
Abhidharmasamuccaya

Mrakṣa is sometimes translated as 'hypocrisy'. However, hypocrisy usually suggests the deliberate and systematic adoption of a mode of behaviour in order to conceal one's real intentions, whereas *mrakṣa* implies a context in which one has at least professed to set out on the spiritual path and in which one has quite a deep involvement with the spiritual community. *Mrakṣa* will arise only when one has committed oneself – more especially when one has publicly committed oneself – to certain ethical and spiritual standards that one shares with other members of the spiritual community.

At that point one may discover that there is something in one's life which is incompatible with one's spiritual commitment, but which one is unwilling to give up. It becomes a sore and sensitive area that one is not prepared to discuss with anybody, especially not with one's spiritual friends. Yes, you feel guilty; you know that what you are doing is unskilful. But you are determined to hang on to this pet weakness. You don't come clean and confess it because you would then be openly confronting the fact that you were doing something unskilful – and you would also be urged by your friends to give it up, so as to clear the path to more positive states.

'It is to perpetuate a state of unresolvedness' because in concealing one's fault from others one is also in a sense concealing it from oneself, in that one is not really facing up to its implications, which are that it is obstructing the realization of the positive. One is sort of hoping to muddle through somehow. Thus it is not unconnected with *vicikitsā*, doubt and indecision. One may even start to rationalize one's unskilful behaviour, find all sorts of arguments to justify it. Because one is avoiding clarity, one's state of mind becomes duller and duller. One's friends may be aware that there is something wrong, that one is not making progress for some reason, and they may try to get one to bring one's difficulty out into the open. But one stubbornly pretends that there's nothing the matter.

As long as there is this sacred area of one's life that is off-limits as far as one's friends are concerned, one is effectively closing oneself off from them. One becomes increasingly out of touch – not because of one's unskilful activity (otherwise we should all be out of touch with each other most of the time) but because one insists on holding back from communicating, to those who are supposed to be one's friends, something that is evidently a very pressing problem. The longer one puts off coming clean with one's friends, the more difficult it becomes to do it, and the stronger becomes one's commitment to one's pet weakness. So this *upakleśa* of slyness-concealment, once it becomes entrenched, is one of the most problematic to deal with.

The danger is that one will eventually break off contact with one's spiritual friends altogether, in favour of people who are less demanding. At this point, the most important thing is to feel that your spiritual friends are on your side, that they are not against you. If they really are your friends, they will do their best to maintain contact even though you may be getting quite defensive and isolated as a result of your secrecy and feelings of guilt.

The principal antidote to slyness-concealment is confession of faults. Ideally we should be open with our friends all the time, and anything obstructing communication should be cleared up at once, so confession should be an everyday practice. But what is confession? It is not just admission or acknowledgement of what we have done. It is true that in a legal context admission and confession are more or less interchangeable expressions; they are interchangeable, however, only if they are both taken to have only a psychological significance. But confession in a spiritual context is primarily not a psychological but an ethical act. If we confess to a spiritually unskilful action there is obviously a psychological element there, inasmuch as we are referring to a mental attitude, something pertaining to our own psyche. But there is more to it than this. Indeed, the psychology of the Abhidharma as a whole is not just about psychology. Although it does involve becoming a healthy human being, it is also about developing beyond that level.

When we confess to an unskilful action we are confessing to a failure to live up to our own ideals. We are invoking a norm, a set of ethical and spiritual ideals that we have accepted for ourselves, and that we share with other members of the spiritual community. These ideals are not imposed upon us. There is no veiled threat behind them that if we don't try to live by them we'll be in big trouble. It is this, in fact, that makes them truly ethical and spiritual ideals. And it is this also that makes a refusal to confess one's ethical failures so damaging towards one's integrity as an individual.

A general confession – 'I'm afraid I sometimes behave rather badly' – is not enough. To be effective, confession should be very specific, and it should be addressed to someone who understands the seriousness of what we are confessing. If we have any doubt about whether or not to confess something, we need to make a particular point of confessing it, because that doubt is quite likely to be the first stirrings of slyness-concealment. As its name suggests, it is a slippery customer that has to be watched out for carefully.

We should ideally confess to the person we have offended, but if they don't share our ideals, all we can really do is make an *admission* to them. To make our confession in the spiritual sense, we will need to talk to someone else who understands the Buddhist distinction between skilful and unskilful. In this case it is more important to make the confession than to make the admission.

Confession has been an aspect of the relationship between teacher and disciple in the Buddhist tradition from the earliest times. It is customary in any well-ordered monastic situation for the pupil to go to the teacher every morning and evening and confess any unskilful actions they are aware of having committed during those twelve hours, and ask for forgiveness for any that they are not aware of. One says, 'Whatever faults I have committed of body, speech, and mind, please forgive me.' And the teacher says '*Khamāmi, khamāmi,*' 'I forgive, I forgive.'

This practice differs from Catholic confession and absolution in that the teacher doesn't forgive on behalf of God; in fact, he doesn't forgive offences committed against anyone apart from himself. It is a purely personal exchange. One is asking forgiveness for any offences committed against him personally. If, for example, one had committed an offence against the rules of the order, then that would be dealt with by the order as a whole. However, in respect of offences that don't concern him personally, the teacher can, if not forgive, certainly listen to one's confession and advise one what to do, or what practice to take up, to help one avoid repeating that particular fault.

If – as is usual among modern Western Buddhists – one is not in a traditional teacher–disciple situation but part of a spiritual community, confession can still be very much part of one's spiritual life. Spiritual friends (*kalyāṇa mitras*) can help one another a great deal through mutual confession and exploration of how to act more skilfully in future.

There is a Tibetan practice, originally deriving from the Sarvāstivāda School, of confessing to the thirty-five Buddhas of confession, who each preside over a different set of the monastic rules. That is, one confesses to whichever Buddha presides over the set of rules that includes the one that one has transgressed. It is important, though, not to misunderstand this idea of confessing to the Buddhas. When Buddhist texts speak of asking forgiveness of the Buddhas and Bodhisattvas, this is not to say that the Buddhas might not forgive one if one didn't placate them.

After all, what is forgiveness? It is to let someone off the consequences of their action in terms of one's own personal reaction to it. It is to say that in effect the matter is now closed, the slate is wiped clean. No vicious circle of action and reaction, offence and retaliation has been initiated. But as far as the Buddhas are concerned, one's breaking a precept is no offence to them. It is essentially an offence against oneself – because one will be reaping the *vipāka* of one's karma in the future. In that sense one is going to have to forgive oneself. Of course, as already discussed, one should be careful not to be too self-referential; as well as harming oneself through one's action one will in most cases have caused harm to someone else. One cannot forgive oneself on their behalf, so to speak. Nor can one effectively confess to oneself, though it may be a start. If one is truly to overcome slyness-concealment, one needs to confess to those one respects most, as well as to the person one has offended.

4. SPITE (OR DEFENSIVENESS) (*PRADĀŚA*)

It is a vindictive attitude preceded by indignation and resentment, forming part of anger, and its function is to become the basis for harsh and strong words,...

Abhidharmasamuccaya

It is the urge to use harsh words of disagreement due to anger and
resentment when others raise one's shortcomings,...[201]
Yeshe Gyaltsen

Pradāśa is a vindictive mental event that gives rise not to injurious
action but to unskilful speech. Yeshe Gyaltsen goes a little further than
the *Abhidharmasamuccaya* does, linking it with the specific situation of
receiving criticism, and thus suggesting that this *upakleśa* is directly
connected with the previous one. If we are in the grip of slyness-
concealment and we are taxed with our shortcomings, we are likely to
react defensively. Instead of accepting criticism from our friends in a
positive manner, on the basis of trust in their goodwill, we react with
anger and resentment – basically because we know that we are in a
weak position. We bluster: 'I'm not getting angry,' 'It's not me who's
in a sulk!' 'What's your problem?' 'I don't know why you always
misunderstand me,' 'You're just projecting your own anger on to me,'
'Back off, will you – I just need some space to sort myself out,' 'You're
always saying that – why can't you say something positive for a
change?'

We should watch for this word 'always' in these situations – 'always'
comes up a lot when one is reacting in this way. But the fact is that one
doesn't *always* say or do whatever one is said to be doing or saying:
the statement 'You're always doing that' doesn't make sense. What is
meant is really something like 'I'm aware that there's a problem here
that I need to address, but I can't bring myself to be rational about it.'
But instead of being able to say this, one absolutizes the other person's
action, completely identifying them with it. What the expression
'You're always ...' signals is that one's reaction is out of all proportion
to what has been said or done, and one cannot be treated on the
assumption that one is in a rational state of mind.

This is defensiveness. We distract attention from the objective situation by attacking the *bona fides* of the person who points it out, or
playing the injured innocent, or whatever. An element of paranoia can
develop such that we begin to imagine that other people disapprove
of us when they have said nothing at all; we start to react to criticism
that no one has yet thought of except ourselves. Before we create that
kind of rift between ourselves and our friends we have to be prepared
to be open with them, having sufficient confidence in them to be able
to confess our shortcomings.

If you are the person doing the criticizing, it should be done in a
skilful manner, with kindness and encouragement. Nor should there

be any pretence that you yourself are well clear of that particular shortcoming. In fact, it is a good idea to be explicit about this, and say, perhaps, 'I know this failing only too well from my own experience of it – why don't we tackle it together?' If you are not Enlightened, you won't go far wrong if you make this your approach every time, because whatever the fault, it will be yours too, at least to some extent.

If you just say 'Don't be dishonest with yourself,' you are tacitly suggesting that dishonesty is the other person's problem, not something you have to work to overcome yourself. You're on much safer ground if you say 'Let's face it, we aren't always as honest with ourselves as we might be.' This should be said in full consciousness that it really is something you yourself need to work on as well. 'We are simply concerned with the elimination of unskilful mental states; whether they are yours or mine is virtually irrelevant. Let's work together to eliminate unskilful mental states from the world.' This is the Bodhisattva attitude.

It is always easy to see the faults of others, but pointing them out can be an unskilful activity in itself. For example, one may criticize someone as a pre-emptive strike. This can be a stratagem of slyness-concealment: one conceals one's own faults by getting one's criticism in first. In this sort of case there needs to be a responsible person around to disentangle all the mutual recriminations.

It also happens that someone can be made a scapegoat if for one reason or another they aren't very popular. Some people even seem to invite being targeted in this way. If you go around as though you have a notice pinned to your back saying 'Please kick me,' there will always be people who are happy to oblige. Of course, to victimize someone in this way – even in the name of humour – is terribly unskilful.

In the Zen tradition, the teacher himself sometimes picks on an individual quite deliberately – not, of course, a vulnerable person, but someone who is perhaps rather arrogant and pleased with himself – and makes him see himself as no more than a mass of faults. This is a dangerous approach and should be resorted to only by experienced teachers who definitely have that person's welfare at heart, and who can clearly distinguish helping someone to break through from pushing them to break down. Only very robust people with strong natural self-confidence can stand up to that sort of treatment and benefit from it.

5. JEALOUSY (OR ENVY) (*IRṢYĀ*)

It is a highly perturbed state of mind associated with aversion-hatred which is unable to bear other's excellencies by being overly attached to gain and honour.[202]

Abhidharmasamuccaya

This is *irṣyā*. It is either envy, which one feels with regard to something one doesn't have but would like to have, or jealousy, which one feels with regard to something of which one is already in possession.

With envy one feels a sense of poverty in oneself, one feels unfulfilled, one craves whatever one believes will enrich one's life – and one sees someone else who has, or seems to have, what one craves oneself. The result is a mixture of craving and hatred. Envy seems to be a particularly shameful *upakleśa* to have to admit to, because effectively one hates someone either for their happiness or their good qualities, which can only seem perverse. It is also associated with a feeling of poverty and impotence: instead of being galvanized to emulate someone else's achievements, you resent them because they show you up. As Iago says of Cassio in Shakespeare's *Othello*:

He hath a daily beauty in his life
That makes me ugly;[203]

The antidote to envy is simple: it is to practise what the Buddhist tradition calls rejoicing in merits, being happy in the happiness of others, appreciating the good qualities of others. Another antidote is to associate with people who will appreciate one's own qualities. As so very often with negative mental events, the damage is done in childhood. If you find, when people thank you profusely, or make it clear how much they appreciate you, that you feel uncomfortable, or even get upset, what you are finding difficult to handle is probably a sense of lack of appreciation in the past when you were very young, which is triggered by the appreciation you are experiencing in the present. You feel regret and unhappiness at not having been appreciated in the crucial early years. You have basically never learned to take appreciation: in a perverse way, it doesn't seem right. You therefore respond with self-deprecation, which usually signals that you neither deserve nor need appreciation.

It is often said that power corrupts; but lack of power also corrupts. The corruption that comes from lack of power is envy and jealousy, resentment, discontent, disgruntlement, sourness, inadequacy, sterility, and general negativity. This inner corruption can be addressed by questioning who one thinks one really is. We should perhaps look particularly at what we think of as our better self. This is the self that we like to identify with, the self that tries to keep all our other selves in order. It might feel quite comfortable to have that acceptable, respectable self in charge. But what if it's the wrong self in the chair? Is there some powerful self that is undermining the whole show? Is there some other submerged self that is more truly oneself?

According to Nietzsche, real progress begins when one has the courage to baptize the worst in oneself as the best.[204] He is putting it very strongly, but one can see what he means. You baptize, even sanctify or consecrate, that unacknowledged, apparently less desirable side of you, your 'worst' side. It's a useful exercise sometimes to ask oneself 'What do I really consider to be the worst thing about myself, what am I really ashamed of?' – and then look at it positively.

Jealousy is of course most often associated with our relationships, particularly sexual ones. Again, it can begin in childhood, perhaps especially for one who, having been an only child, is suddenly ousted from centre stage – as it appears – by the arrival of a second child. The jealousy that arises can be very intense indeed – it can even become murderous – though it may be covered up by an excessive demonstration of affection towards the younger sibling, so that the jealousy turns into over-protectiveness.

This is a very common source of jealousy, but it is by no means the only one. Jealousy seems to stem from a basic insecurity which can arise in any number of ways. If one has no worth in one's own eyes, if one does not feel that one is a lovable person, one will become dependent on someone else's love towards one for all one's emotional security. Instead of one's basic worth as a person being one's own property, so to speak, it is experienced only in the form of someone else's regard.

If, therefore, there is any threat of that person's regard being transferred to someone else, then what is under threat is one's whole value as a person. One risks losing not just someone one loves and values, but one's own value to oneself. If they go they will take away with them one's very identity. Jealousy is the fear of being destroyed, almost. It is in this way that jealousy can give rise to murder. To need love of a romantic or possessive kind is neurotic and should be shaken off in any way one can. It should certainly not be idealized.

To need good will, companionship, and warmth is by contrast quite healthy and positive. On the basis of this need for companionship one can then go further and develop something more, which is spiritual fellowship, Sangha. Of course, there are always going to be people who simply get their healthy human needs met within the healthy human environment of the spiritual community. This is fine; the spiritual community has a great deal to offer people on the ordinary, positive level of just being human, even if they are not ready to go for Refuge to the Three Jewels.

6. AVARICE (OR ACQUISITIVENESS) *(MĀTSARYA)*

> It is an over-concern with the material things in life, stemming from
> over-attachment to wealth and honour,...[205]
> *Abhidharmasamuccaya*

It is not just that one is attached to the things of this world; one holds them to be all that matters. *Mātsarya* is an almost obsessive concern with material things – with power, prestige, wealth, and possessions. The implication of this attitude is that these things have an absolute value, that once one has them one will be able to hold on to them for good. The assumption is that one can make real, solid acquisitions. One's life becomes devoted to the pursuit of these things such that one loses sight of their real value, even in material terms. They become ends in themselves rather than the means of satisfying straightforward human desires.

This attitude of possessiveness and acquisitiveness is often quite transparent, but equally often it flourishes behind a sincere spiritual or at least anti-materialist intent. You get Hampstead hippies and champagne socialists – people who take a very critical attitude towards the society within which they continue to live rather well. There are also people who profess to be very concerned to avoid 'spiritual materialism' while being far less – if at all – exercised about freeing themselves from ordinary materialism. That is, they are very careful not to make their spiritual practice an occasion for attachment, while continuing to live rather comfortable lives.

In all these ways it is possible to do things with the appearance of not doing them. If it were slightly more consciously done one would put these examples under the heading of slyness-concealment, or perhaps the heading of defensiveness: criticizing a weakness that one wants to conceal in oneself. In fact, materialism or possessiveness and acquisitiveness is such a pervasive feature of our society that it can all too easily absorb anti-materialist impulses and make good business enterprises out of them.

The antidote to possessiveness is simple enough: it is generosity. It is also to contemplate the impermanence of material things, our own impermanence, and the fragility and evanescence of our hold upon worldly things.

7. DECEIT (OR PRETENCE) (*MĀYĀ*)

It is a display of what is not a real quality and is associated with both [craving] and [ignorance] by being overly attached to wealth and honour. Its function is to provide a basis for a perverse life-style.[206]
Abhidharmasamuccaya

Māyā literally means a magic show – one sees something that isn't there. This is what pretence amounts to: a sort of trick. One pretends to be what one is not in order to gain wealth or honour – to which one is over-attached. One certainly would have to be over-attached to them in order to perform day in, day out, year in, year out, which is what pretending to be what one is not inevitably involves. One has to be systematic, one can't let the mask slip for a moment. One's whole lifestyle has to be harnessed to the task of keeping the lie going.

However, one has to tread a fine line between being honest about one's weaknesses and simply indulging them. One should never affect to experience positive mental events that are not in fact present in one's experience; at the same time it is truly said that one becomes a Bodhisattva by behaving like a Bodhisattva. The Middle Way here clearly involves openness and confession.

Being recognized as a Buddhist, particularly as an ordained Buddhist, you have to step carefully between these extremes. On the one hand, you are, once ordained, in some sense accountable. You stand there as an ethical individual. You can't say 'Well, everyone fiddles their tax returns, don't they?' Other people know that you are a committed Buddhist. And you know that they know. You therefore can't afford to slip up: you are expected to behave in at least a reasonable, human, considerate, and mindful manner. Even if the rest of the order may let you off lightly, the general public won't. You have, in short, to maintain certain standards.

On the other hand, you have to avoid playing up to other people's projections. You have to make sure that when you are teaching meditation other people don't see you as some kind of meditation master.

When you give a talk you have to make sure that you don't get carried away with your own rhetoric, with your ability to manipulate an audience's emotions. The larger the audience, the easier it is for a practised speaker to make this mass of people do or feel or think precisely what he or she wants; and this is a very dangerous power. You can make them laugh or cry or riot; all that is required is a certain theatrical talent.

Strictly speaking, the theatricality of the actor cannot be categorized under the heading of this *upakleśa*, because an actor would never pretend to be, say, Hamlet, as a matter of actual fact. However, the danger for an actor is that he or she may fall almost inadvertently into a whole series of pretences, not distinguishing clearly between theatre and real life, between the personalities they assume and their own personality. They find themselves putting on a bit of a performance all the time, and gradually their own personality loses any kind of definition. What one can safely say, probably, is that the more completely an actor enters the character he or she is playing, the more pure a medium he or she is for the role, and thus the less there is of exhibitionism in the performance. The less one obtrudes the idea of oneself performing into one's work, the better one's chance as an actor of keeping performance and exhibitionism out of one's personality. The same goes for public speaking. One can pour out one's heart and soul, or one can put on a bit of an act; and one may find it difficult to tell the difference oneself – though one's friends should be able to.

Five different forms of pretence are distinguished by Yeshe Gyaltsen:[207]

a. Hypocrisy: the deliberate and continuous adoption of a way of life that is designed to make you appear to be other than you are.

b. Flattery: feigned admiration of someone to butter them up, followed by extravagant admiration of their property in the hope that they will want to give you some of it.

c. Overpraise: servile accord with someone's views, soft soaping, toadying, boot-licking, in order to get something out of someone.

d. Evaluating by possessions: making others ashamed to enjoy something so that you can enjoy it yourself.

e. Seeking wealth by wealth: You let people know how you are used to being treated and rewarded, the covert message being that they should not disappoint your expectations. The size of the limousine you are driven in signals not how much leg-room you like to have in the back, but how much money you expect to be paid.

8. DISHONESTY (ŚĀṬHYA)

These two, deceit and dishonesty, are counted among the four bleak things referred to in the *Kāśyapaparivarta*.
Yeshe Gyaltsen

I am constantly living
Under the watchful eyes of
The Buddhas and Bodhisattvas
Who have unlimited vision.[208]
Bodhicaryāvatāra

Śāṭhya is a more straightforward form of covering up the truth than *mrakṣa* (slyness-concealment). It is dishonesty resorted to simply for the sake of worldly advantage, whether material or social, whether for wealth or for honour.

The answer to it is equally straightforward: one won't get away with it. Never mind for a moment 'the watchful eyes of the Buddhas and Bodhisattvas'. One's friends and associates, especially if they have some experience of the world, are not taken in to the extent one likes to think. Sometimes the truth comes out in most surprising ways. Certainly a politician can never count on keeping his or her dishonesty from coming to light at some point in the future.

The four bleak things are:

a. To lie to one's teacher, or to any other member of the spiritual community. To deceive someone by telling a lie essentially breaks the link between you. There can be no healthy human relationship without the trust and confidence that arises from a mutual respect for the truth. When one tries to deceive those who are more highly developed than one is oneself, one is closing oneself off to their influence, and to their teaching inasmuch as they embody or represent it. More than that, one is effectively shutting oneself off from the spiritual life, in that one is shutting oneself off from those sources of spiritual inspiration and instruction. It is not as if one has anything to fear from them. If one can't be open and honest with one's teacher and one's spiritual friends, who can one be open with? And the most serious way one can deceive one's teacher or spiritual friends is by trying to mislead them as to one's mental state, or one's spiritual practice.

b. To undermine the skilful intentions of others. This is not just discourage-
ment. For example, we may want to dampen down someone's enthusiasm. This can be an expression of ill will or disgruntlement – we just
want to get at them; or it may be that we feel threatened by their energy
– we're afraid we won't be able to keep up, so our natural reaction is
to want to discourage them. We perhaps invoke the Middle Way – as
if the Middle Way were between enthusiasm and apathy – saying,
'Don't let your enthusiasm carry you away. If you were realistic, you'd
see that your scheme would never work.' So there can be an element
of dishonesty here.

But the second bleak thing is more than this. It is to raise doubts in
the mind of someone who is happily doing something positive and
creative, perhaps by questioning their motivation. Perhaps we are
jealous: we want to bring this person down a peg or two, show them
and others who calls the shots. Sometimes people do this because they
think it shows their own superior insight and psychological penetration, their understanding of human nature. But it's a very cheap form
of wisdom, to interpret a good action in terms of some unconsciously
unskilful motivation, and to present this interpretation as fact. It is easy
to undermine someone's confidence. Even when it is genuine, confidence may not necessarily be very firmly established.

The cheap or pseudo psycho-analytical approach is essentially irresponsible. It is, ethically speaking, unaware. One is so fascinated by
the depth and subtlety of one's psychological analysis that one fails to
consider the possible effect of one's words on the other person. We
think of awareness as being one of the most important characteristics
of the true individual. The Buddhist tradition speaks of four dimensions of awareness: awareness of self, of others, of things, of reality.[209]
But when we take the second of these – awareness of others – we can,
if we are not careful, think of it exclusively in psychological terms. It
is possible to think of being aware of someone as simply seeing what
they're like or how they are as an individual quite separate from
oneself, overlooking the fact that in being aware of someone one is
putting oneself in relationship with that person.

This is where the ethical dimension comes in. The psychological
dimension is useful and necessary, but it is not enough. Even if the
other person is at the centre of one's attention, that in itself is not
necessarily to be truly aware of them. If one is in love with someone,
for example, one may be aware of them all the time – aware, at least,
of one's projection on to them – but oblivious to the real effect on them

of one's words and actions, oblivious as to whether one is helping or harming them.

If one is aware of oneself as an individual and of the relationship between oneself and the other person, one is aware of the effect one has on them and the effect they have on oneself. It follows that one has a certain responsibility for the effect one has on them. Awareness of someone implies the adoption of an ethically responsible attitude towards them. This is the attitude of the Bodhisattva – that one does not separate the needs of others from one's own needs.

c. To say nothing in praise of those who sincerely practise the spiritual life. This is to be dishonest by omission; it is akin to slyness-concealment. By choosing not to draw attention to something skilful and wholesome, one is pretending it isn't there. In referring to particular people who are dedicating their lives to the Dharma, for example, if one doesn't ever mention their most conspicuous feature – that they are noticeably developing as individuals – this is a passive lie. If one sees someone who is evidently making an inspired effort to be clearer and kinder, and if an occasion arises when it would be appropriate to remark on that person's merits and qualities, but one just keeps quiet, making no acknowledgement of them whatsoever, even if it is just to nod in agreement with someone else, then this is a bleak thing. Or, to take a more complex and serious situation, it might happen that someone was being generally slandered and one knew the truth, but said nothing – perhaps because one was afraid of being on one's own with one's opinion. This, again, would be a bleak thing indeed.

d. To praise others insincerely. You may think someone doesn't deserve praise, but you praise them anyway, perhaps because you want something from them, or because everyone else praises them and you're afraid to suffer the consequences of standing up for your own convictions. Alternatively, you may praise someone who you know is worthy of praise, but your heart isn't in it because you bear a secret grudge against them. Or else you 'damn with faint praise': your praise of someone is a backhanded way of slighting them.

These are the four bleak things that drain the life out of one's spiritual practice. But if dishonesty is not in itself quite evidently bleak enough to warn us away from it, the traditional antidote is to remind ourselves that we are 'constantly living under the watchful eyes of the Buddhas and Bodhisattvas'.

If one feels a little uncomfortable about this it may be to do with one's general Christian background: the idea that God, the judge, jury, and executioner, is everywhere, totting up one's sins. But one can drop this idea completely; there is no need to feel that one is stuck with it for ever. If any sense of dread or mistrust arises with respect to the 'Buddhas and Bodhisattvas watching over us', one has to keep reminding oneself that the Buddhas and Bodhisattvas have nothing to do with meting out justice. They do not administer the law of karma. They may see all sorts of unskilful things about you but at the same time they are completely 'with' you. It's not that they are going to approve or indulge your wrongdoing – not at all – but they aren't going to withdraw their compassion. There is no personal disapproval, although this can be very difficult to accept or even imagine.

In a sense, they don't care. In a sense, from their point of view, all these things that seem so important to us are utterly trivial. The Buddhas and Bodhisattvas aren't going to bother themselves with approving of one bit of us and disapproving of another bit. They are concerned to get us out of the whole mess. And part of the mess is – from their very much higher point of view – that we bother ourselves so much about our little skilful habits and our little unskilful ones (though we personally can deal with this part of our mess only after we have bothered ourselves about these things a very great deal). So we have to imagine the Buddhas' and Bodhisattvas' view of us as being quite different from our own or from that of any kind of authority figure – or any kind of 'indulgent uncle' figure, for that matter.

9. MENTAL INFLATION (OR SELF-INTOXICATION) (MADA)

It is joy and rapture associated with passion-lust ...
Abhidharmasamuccaya

An inflated mind is the root of unconcern.
Never treat a poor bhikṣu with contempt
Or you may not find salvation in an aeon.
Adhyāśayasaṁcodanasūtra

Look at the vainglory of your social status and appearance,
Your learning, your youth, and your power as your enemies.[210]
Suhṛllekha

Mada arises when one is so pleased, even infatuated and inflated, with being young and healthy, good looking, and successful, intelligent, well-bred, and so on, that one becomes unmindful. It is not simply the possession of these advantages that is the problem; after all, if one is young and energetic one can direct one's youthful energy in a skilful direction. But if one is intoxicated with one's youth and energy, one is unlikely to be thinking about direction at all.

Mada is a happy and joyful feeling that puts you off your guard. When things are going your way and you feel good about yourself – that is often the time when you start to make mistakes. You lose awareness of the fragility of your vaunted advantages over others and imagine that you can walk on water. Sometimes when someone is at the peak of their career everything suddenly starts to go wrong, because success has gone to their head and they have become careless. One also has to watch for this sort of mental inflation when one is doing something at which one is something of an expert. If you are so sure of your expertise, you may start to skimp on the preparations, stop applying the attention to detail that made you an expert in the first place, and this will soon begin to show. It can certainly happen with one's meditation practice.

If you're in this inflated state you don't bother about other people very much, except to the extent of comparing them unfavourably with yourself. Self-intoxication can manifest as a contempt for others who are old or infirm or ugly or unsuccessful or not as clever as you are, and a disregard for their difficulties. It's a kind of egotism: you feel a satisfaction that you're young and beautiful, and that others are not.

The *Adhyāśayasaṃcodanasūtra*'s warning not to treat the poor bhikṣu with contempt can obviously be seen as being directed at the laity, not to be so intoxicated with worldly pleasures that they look down on the humble bhikṣu. However, if we consider that this is a Mahāyāna text it becomes clear that it is not only the laity who are in danger of despising the bhikṣus. It is the Bodhisattva – the aspiring Bodhisattva – who is being addressed here as well as the ordinary laity. Don't think, it says, that with all your fine notions of saving all sentient beings you can afford to look down upon the ordinary bhikṣu just practising the precepts. You may be in for a fall.

10. MALICE (*VIHIMṢĀ*)

It belongs to the emotion anger, lacks loving kindness, pity, and affection, and has the function of treating others abusively.
Abhidharmasamuccaya

... 'lack of loving kindness' is one's own inclination to treat others abusively. 'Lack of pity' is the inclination to induce others to treat others abusively. 'Lack of affection' is to be pleased when one hears or sees others acting in such a way.[211]
Yeshe Gyaltsen

This is *vihiṁsā*. *Hiṁsā* means 'harm' and *vi-* is an emphatic prefix, so *vihiṁsā* is to inflict extreme harm. It is cruelty, the deliberate infliction of pain and suffering for the sake of the gratification it gives you. It is not just hatred, wanting to harm someone in particular; it is getting a taste for the infliction of harm itself, taking pleasure in the suffering of others. There is an admixture of craving with hatred.

Although this seems to be a very perverse and distorted mental state, it is evidently one that forms a significant component in the make-up of many people's minds. The malice of little boys is almost proverbial – pulling the wings off flies, tormenting cats, and so forth – and it would seem that with most people this element becomes socialized, but not necessarily eliminated. Western culture has a long tradition of staging spectacles of bloodthirsty violence, whether in the Roman arena, in Renaissance art, on the Elizabethan and Jacobean stage, or in modern film and television – not to speak of bear-baiting, bull-fights, and public hangings. Malice clearly finds expression, even just on an imaginative level, in some of the highest and most refined – as well as in the most obviously depraved – manifestations of Western culture. Perhaps it is the gratification by proxy of this dangerous *upakleśa* that effectively keeps it under control from a social point of view.

From an individual perspective, it would seem that people have a stable quantum of negativity that remains more or less the same whatever their circumstances, give or take the occasional mood-swing, and that some people have a bigger quantum of negativity than others. (By the same token, some people seem to have a stable quantum of positivity that remains more or less unaffected by the ups and downs of life.) If one is a Buddhist practising the *mettā bhāvanā*, what does one do with that quantum of negativity once one becomes aware of one's habitual projections of it on to various people or groups of people? One can withdraw those projections, only to find that one's negativity manifests in connection with the people one is living with. Obviously one is going to want to overcome this negativity completely, but as a stepping-stone it may help to find some impersonal object for one's negativity to fix on to. For example, one can direct one's aggression towards ideas or attitudes, say, or spelling mistakes, rather than the people who disseminate them. Or, more simply, one may channel one's aggression into some harmless sporting activity.

Malice is considered in Buddhism to be the worst of all possible mental events to entertain. Hence, if one deliberately decides to see a film, say, that one knows will include the closely observed depiction of people being tortured or killed, one has to reflect on one's motives. Such graphic depictions are simply unnecessary; the issue of violence can be addressed with terrifying immediacy without the necessity for the direct gratification of malice.

11. SHAMELESSNESS (ĀHRĪKYA)

[Āhrīkya] is not restraining oneself by taking one's perversions as one's norm....
[Anapatrāpya] is not restraining oneself by taking others as the norm.[212]
Abhidharmasamuccaya

Āhrīkya and *anapatrāpya* (the next factor) form a pair as the direct opposites of the pair of positive mental events, hrī and *apatrāpya*.

Āhrīkya, shamelessness or lack of self-respect, is not just being un-skilful. It is to perform a habitual unskilful action as if it were good, as if it were a principle by which you stand. You say, perhaps, 'Well yes, I am rather hot-tempered. That's just the way I am, and you'd better get used to it.' The suggestion is that you know that what you are doing is unskilful, you know what the Buddhist ideal truly consists in, but you obstinately refuse to accept the implications of that ideal for your own practice. Your weakness is not to be questioned. Against your better judgement you have drawn a line across the path of your development that has hardened into a basic principle by which you approach everything else. Anything that is incompatible with the bad habit that you have accepted as your norm must be rejected.

It is not even that you're rationalizing your position. It's not as if you're saying that going to the pub every night is your skilful means or that you don't tell people you're vegetarian when they offer to cook for you because you don't want to put them to any trouble. Lack of self-respect is not that you persuade yourself that the unskilful things you want to do are really skilful. Nor is shamelessness to do with just being a bit weak, yielding to external pressures, say. It is when you don't – or rather won't – care that what you do is unskilful. You're going to do it anyway, and that's all there is to it.

12. LACK OF SENSE OF PROPRIETY (ANAPATRĀPYA)

Lack of respect for wise opinion is obviously similar to shamelessness; but whereas shamelessness is resistance to one's own better judgement, lack of respect for wise opinion is resistance to the better judgement of others, a lack of sensitivity to others. In exploring the positive equivalent of this *upakleśa*, we emphasized the importance of not submitting to the assumed verities of conventional opinion, stressing that one should distinguish between 'wise opinion' and simply conventional opinion. However, lack of respect for wise opinion implies not just that we respect the wisdom of certain people and then choose to ignore their opinions. It means that we are not open to the wisdom of others at all. We are not receptive. We don't care what anybody thinks. In discarding respect for conventional opinion, therefore, we should be careful that we are not simply rationalizing a general contempt for others, an arrogant posture of self-sufficiency. The fact is that we have to depend on others for guidance up to a certain point. We cannot make progress at any level unless we cultivate an openness to wiser counsel, a receptivity to the possibility that others may be wiser than ourselves, particularly with regard to our own spiritual needs.

The root of these *upakleśas* is lack of love for oneself. This is why one does not heed one's own ethical perceptions or the opinions of the wise – of other people, that is, who have one's welfare at heart and truly understand one's situation. If one doesn't love oneself, or care for oneself very deeply, one cannot believe that others might care about one's welfare.

It is difficult to recognize that one has a deficiency in self-love – firstly because it generally begins in early childhood in one's experience of one's parents, and secondly because a healthy self-love can easily be confused with various forms of unhealthy self-regard – like selfishness, narcissism, egotism, or solipsism – which actually derive from lack of real self-love.

Again, we find here the importance of asserting the ethical dimension as distinct from the psychological. It is not enough to know oneself in a psycho-analytical way. True self-knowledge must include self-love; you can't be an ethical individual unless you love yourself. This healthy self-love is comparatively rare. People who find it difficult to love themselves are going to find it difficult to receive love from others as well. But usually the way people come round to a positive self-regard is through becoming convinced, eventually, that someone else really does wish them well. It is, I think, very unusual for this to happen in a romantic context; in a sexual relationship the friendship and the element of *mettā* tends to get swamped by attachment and possessiveness.

By healthy self-love is meant self-*mettā* – non-exclusive love, love that cannot be grasped in an egoistic way. Romantic love is grasped at as compensation for lack of self-love. If you are aware that someone also has genuine goodwill for you, you can come to feel genuine goodwill for yourself; but this is quite different from using someone's love to fill the sense of inner emptiness with a temporary substitute for self-love. In the one case you learn to love yourself by being with someone who loves you, who feels *mettā* for you; you come to realize that another person feels that you are genuinely worthwhile, and begin to appreciate your own worth for yourself. In the other case you let the other person love you because you can't do it yourself. They do it for you, and you never learn to love yourself.

Unfortunately, if you feel that only romantic love will fill the aching void inside, you may not be sensitive to *mettā*, which may seem rather cold and impersonal and rarefied. Even if someone is showing real good will and kindness by their actions, you may experience their *mettā* as a lack of interest or concern. If what you are looking for is a strong emotional attachment, then disinterested concern and warmth and kindness, however powerfully felt, will quite possibly not touch you. However, *mettā* is almost certainly what someone who has no shame or no respect for wise opinion needs; because what they are missing is real interest in their own welfare and development.

13. GLOOMINESS (OR STAGNATION) (*STYĀNA*)

It is the way in which the mind cannot function properly and is associated with listlessness.[213]

Abhidharmasamuccaya

Styāna literally means stiffness or stagnation. It is a state of emotional blockage that has hardened into a sort of paralysis. You are bound, costive – nothing is moving at all. Nothing can go out, nothing can come in. It is a chronic physical and mental heaviness to the point of petrifaction. Everything has closed down. It is quite a complex state, emotionally speaking, and likely to be the result of a build-up of a number of negative mental factors over time.

Like many of the other *upakleśas*, stagnation is difficult to get out of by oneself. One almost doesn't want to be helped. When one is resentful, anxious, or depressed for one reason or another, one can get into a state where one says 'There's nothing you can do. I'm finished.' One can no longer even see a way to retrace one's steps or undo the harm one has done oneself without determined and skilful intervention from one's friends. In these extreme and entrenched states there is generally resistance to being helped, but when one is extremely lethargic, one hasn't even got sufficient energy moving around to summon up resistance.

Probably the easiest way to get energy moving again is through the body, through physical exercise. However, this state is a negative *mental* event, even if it expresses itself to some extent in physical terms, so at some point it has to be addressed on a mental or emotional level. One has to look for its real origins, which are probably in the area of unresolved conflict, or blocked or repressed emotion – anger or fear, say. It's a kind of depressive state, a tendency which is easily recognizable in that when one has succumbed to it, one becomes dull, gloomy, and listless, at least for a time. In its fully developed form, however, it is quite unusual.

14. EBULLIENCE (AUDDHATYA)

> It is restlessness of mind which is associated with [craving] that gets involved with things considered to be enjoyable. Its function is to obstruct quietness.[214]
> *Abhidharmasamuccaya*

Auddhatya is a sort of recklessness; an excited, emotional turmoil; hilarity; scattered, unmindful liveliness – with reference specifically to pleasurable objects. You are like a greedy child let loose in a sweetshop, intoxicated by the pleasurable objects you encounter, always in search of a good time. You get so excited, darting from one enjoyable object to another, that you're unable to settle upon any one of them. Young girls in fashionable clothes-shops seem to be in this sort of state sometimes. (The atmosphere in bookshops – with which I am personally rather more familiar – by contrast seems altogether heavier – a heavy atmosphere of greed.) The chief characteristic of this *upakleśa* is an unintegrated, irresponsible, and thus essentially selfish bubbly energy.

Clearly, ebullience is the opposite extreme to the previous *upakleśa*, stagnation, and moderate forms of the pair of them can be seen to alternate in the same person, as in manic depression. Some creative people in particular seem to swing between moods of dull depression and vigorous elation – except that the concentration involved in their creative energy makes this a completely different state from the negative one under discussion here. This is one reason why one needs to be precise in examining mental events; otherwise it is quite possible to confuse a positive mental event with a negative one.

In fact, one might say that creative inspiration in the sense of *prīti* and creative energy in the sense of *vīrya* are the positive counterparts of this *upakleśa*, ebullience. There is a distinguishing psychological element – freed-up energy – which the negative mental event shares with the positive ones. The difference is that *vīrya* is specifically 'energy in pursuit of the good'; it has an essentially ethical reference.

We tend to think of energy, and even *vīrya*, in psychological terms. If one feels full of positive, fairly benign energy, for most of us that'll do. If we can free up our energies, that is enough. We'll settle for that. However, if we accept the whole psychological model of human development as self-sufficient, as an end in itself, we are left with a self-centred, self-indulgent, and thus very limited idea of what we are about.

15. LACK OF TRUST (OR NON-FAITH) (*ĀŚRADDHYA*)

> It is the mind associated with [ignorance] which does not have deep conviction, has lack of [faith], and has no desire for things positive. It provides the basis for laziness.
> *Abhidharmasamuccaya*

> It is a preponderance of dullness which is not conducive to [faith].[215]
> Yeshe Gyaltsen

There is more to non-faith than simply the absence of faith. In this state we are lazy with respect to positive things, with respect to the development of positive mental states. We have no appreciation of the value of those positive things, nor even any very deep conviction about their existence, and therefore no definite drive in their direction or clear volition to realize them.

We don't appreciate the fact that our actions have consequences and we therefore don't make any particular effort to act skilfully and avoid unskilful activity. We don't really understand the value of the Three Jewels and we therefore don't commit ourselves to them, we don't go for Refuge to them. And of course without faith in the transcendental, without faith in the possibility of Enlightenment, we are not going to be interested in them. In this way lack of faith is the link between dullness in the sense of not appreciating what the Dharma really means, and laziness in the sense of not practising the Dharma.

Faith is a very precise mental event. It represents a quite distinctive – one might even say unique – kind of emotion, and it is actually very rare. One may be affected, moved, and inspired by one's experience of Buddhism, but this does not necessarily amount to faith. If, for example, one attends a Buddhist centre regularly, one may find it a very congenial place – warm, friendly, peaceful, colourful; one may appreciate its positive effect on one's mental state; one may be moved and inspired by the possibilities of spiritual development that it opens up. But faith is more than this.

When one wishes to be ordained as a Buddhist, for example – and here I am thinking in particular of my own order, the Western Buddhist Order – one can 'do all the right things', and still be asked to wait. Of course it is natural to wonder what one has to do to be considered ready for ordination. One may well feel that one has done enough to earn promotion. One may even go off the idea of this particular Buddhist order and go to another Buddhist group that will accept one more readily. Or one may reconcile oneself to the situation by persuading oneself that the waiting time is a sort of test, or that people in the order are prejudiced against one for one reason or another.

But the fact of the matter is more straightforward than this. If one seeks ordination as a sort of natural process of promotion within the group, which one can earn by good works, so to speak, one has no real idea of what ordination, or Going for Refuge to the Three Jewels, or commitment, or faith, is really about. This might sound strange, but people can be devoted Buddhists for years without having any idea whatsoever of what faith means. They'll talk in terms of faith and commitment, but they'll use these terms without understanding them at all. It isn't that they have a partial understanding which they can gradually build upon; they haven't any inkling of what these things really mean.

It can be difficult to detect this absence of understanding beneath all the right attitudes and expressions and genuinely positive feelings about the Dharma and the spiritual life. But it's as if a certain faculty is missing, a faculty that one needs if one is to perceive the Three Jewels in such a way that one may be said to have faith in them. And it can take quite a long time to develop this faculty.

It is possible, of course, to confuse faith with pleasure. One can read a book like *The Life of Milarepa* and be inspired by the vicarious experience of all that meditation, all that spiritual practice, all that attainment of higher mental states – but being stirred up in this way does not constitute faith. A book may even inspire one to meditate, but unless this is more than a wish for enhanced or pleasurable experiences in meditation, it is not faith. The pleasures of religious literature can be a sort of indulgence, particularly if one gets through a lot of it at once. The danger is that one ends up consuming books like boxes of chocolates.

The same thing goes for one's Buddhist friends. They may be good company, they may be helpful, they may provide positive support and advice, one may trust them – but to have *faith* in spiritual friends involves an attitude towards them which is qualitatively different from the appreciative pleasure one takes in them as friends. If the positive group revolves around pleasure at some more or less refined level, the spiritual community by contrast revolves around faith.

One could say that faith is the single significant element missing from the purely psychological or therapeutic model of human development. There is a great deal of happiness, energy, pleasure in the positive sense, even joy, to be found in various psychological and therapeutic circles – but no faith. There may sometimes be a spiritual dimension of some kind, but not a transcendental dimension.

As we have already seen in our discussion of *śraddhā* as a positive mental event (see page 120), faith is not to be associated with pleasure at all. Some of the Christian mystics make this point very firmly. They warn that one should carry on with one's contemplations regardless of what they call 'sensible consolations', and that one should not regard the withdrawal of such pleasures of meditation as a sign that one is not making progress. This condition is best known under the term coined by St John of the Cross as the 'dark night of the senses'. (There is, of course, no Buddhist analogy for what he terms the 'dark night of the soul', when the presence of God seems to be withdrawn). Conversely, the fact that one feels good with regard to some allegedly religious or spiritual object does not mean that one necessarily has faith in it.

To awaken the faculty of faith, one needs to bridge the gap between the emotions and the intellect, and to do this it is not enough just to try to balance these two areas of one's experience. The problem lies with our limited conception of what 'intellect' means. Originally, the word meant a higher, intuitive power to see directly into the truth of things. Now that its meaning has been debased into simply the power of reasoning, we are left short of a vital concept.

It is possible to be drawn to the Dharma for intellectual reasons (though such a motivation could never, obviously, be *purely* rational), or through an emotional response, or a combination of the two. But none of this is enough. Faith involves the stimulation of something else, the stirring into life of an imaginal, visionary faculty, which is the total reaction of the whole being when confronted by the Ideal, whether embodied in human form or in the teaching.

Without the operation of this spiritual faculty of the imagination, the emotions and the intellect remain dissociated from each other. In a sense, the imagination, in the sense in which I am using the term, is a separate faculty from reason and emotion, but it operates with them in the form of a psycho-spiritual network – that is, its nature is to unite reason and emotion.

We may begin by becoming involved with Buddhism academically, organizationally, or socially. We have to catch hold wherever we can. But whatever bit we get hold of is not actually Buddhism. It's not that one can get a clear idea of the Dharma, and then all one has to do is introduce a little emotion, a little warmth. No. If one looks at the Dharma rationally and coldly, one will already have a distorted idea of it. In integrating the emotions with the intellect, faith changes the way we see things.

Unfortunately, many people are in the situation of thinking, or even knowing or believing, 'This is what I ought to do,' but not wanting to do it. One should be able to work with this, but if the conflict becomes too extreme, one will need to go right back and address the question: 'How did I come to be the kind of person who knows what is good for me but doesn't feel like doing anything about it?' In order to re-contact one's feelings one has to go back to doing what one really wants to do and work towards one's ideals from that basis.

16. LAZINESS (*KAUSĪDYA*)

It is an unwilling mind, associated with [ignorance], relying on the pleasures of drowsiness, lying down and not getting up. Its function is to obstruct and hinder one in applying himself to positive things.[216]
Abhidharmasamuccaya

While *kausīdya* is generally interpreted in terms of 'drowsiness, lying down and not getting up', we shouldn't come away with the idea that we counteract it simply by being more energetic. It is essentially an unwillingness to apply oneself to positive things, so it may equally well express itself in energetic activity, if that activity is directed towards an unwholesome end. Satan finds work for idle hands. We have already touched on this topic in our discussion of the object-determining mental event *chanda* or eagerness (see page 103).

It would seem that laziness can involve the expenditure of plenty of energy, but it is expended inappropriately – that is, it is not a question of blocked energy so much as active resistance to appropriate activity. We all need to relax from time to time, but for a healthy person to prolong the period of relaxation beyond its natural limits means either that their energy has stagnated – which is *styāna* – or that they are lazy, which is different. Laziness is not an inability to mobilize energy, but an unwillingness to mobilize available energy towards a positive end.

Dr Johnson was very conscious of being a lazy person, and he regretted it bitterly. He made regular resolutions to remedy this defect in his character, but to no avail. He used to write in bed, because he didn't get up till late, and he said that if a sheet he was using blew on to the floor he would write what he had written over again on a fresh sheet to avoid the trouble of getting out of bed to pick it up. However, among many other things he single-handedly compiled his great English dictionary, so he can't have been short on energy; he did manage to do the things he needed to do, despite his laziness.

Laziness is perhaps a weakness that Buddhists particularly need to guard against. I remember seeing a book called *The Lazy Man's Guide to Enlightenment*; this sort of nonsense seems to appeal to people who become interested in Buddhism. Laziness is often what attracts people to the advanced teachings of Zen Buddhism, which emphasize the teaching that the Dharma is a raft, to be left behind once one has crossed the river of saṁsāra.[217] The way these teachings are sometimes presented in the West gives the impression that one can discard the raft before one has bothered to make use of it at all.

Even without such manifestly wrong views, there is a constant danger of settling down wherever one finds oneself comfortable. The spiritual life is so rewarding on all kinds of levels that one can always be tempted basically to stay put. Quite early on one discovers how to operate effectively and happily on a straightforward human level, how to live a happy, healthy life, how to communicate well and so on, and one can think, 'Well, I'll settle for this.' Even if one gets over this stage, even if one is apparently meditating eight hours a day, it can still be that one is just treading water, just enjoying the fruits of one's practice. It's like wallowing in bed just because it's warm and comfortable – you cling on to that half-dreaming state and resist the challenge of the new day.

This is laziness. It is associated with ignorance because what is lacking is vision. What is lacking is a 'divine discontent' – not disgruntlement, but a sense of continual striving towards an ideal, an awareness of the limitations of the mundane (the compounded, the psychological, the hedonic) sufficient to keep taking one beyond oneself.

17. UNCONCERN (OR HEEDLESSNESS) (PRAMĀDA)

It is to persevere in passion-lust, aversion-hatred, and [ignorance] aggravated by laziness. It is not to attend to what is positive and so also is not to protect the mind from those things which cannot provide lasting satisfaction.[218]
Abhidharmasamuccaya

We have seen that one can give way to laziness at any point before Stream-entry. When one stops making an effort in response to the pull of the Unconditioned, one is effectively giving way to the pull of the conditioned. We may have the sense that we want to stay just where we are for a while, but this is impossible. If we aren't moving forward, we're slipping back.

If we persist in this course, there comes a point where we let go completely; we cease to offer any resistance at all to the kleśas and upakleśas. We just don't care any more about what is happening. This is heedlessness or pramāda. It's a sort of lack of responsibility towards oneself. We no longer bother to protect the mind from negative mental events. We let everything slide.

It's like someone who 'lets themselves go', who stops taking care of their appearance. One becomes a spiritual slattern, ethically down at heel. Or it's like someone who just stops bothering to keep their house in repair. There are broken panes of glass in the windows, the roof leaks in several places, doors are coming off their hinges, floorboards are loose, and they don't even try any more to keep dust from gathering and dead leaves from blowing in, and cats and dogs from fouling the place wherever they like. If one could see one's spiritual condition when one no longer bothers about it, this is more or less how it would appear.

If we become heedless out of craving it is like someone who lets their house go to rack and ruin because they sit about all day drinking. Our mind gets so taken up with the objects of our craving that we hardly notice, let alone care, what sort of state of mind we're in.

If we become heedless out of hatred it's as if we're much more concerned to make our neighbour suffer – breaking his windows and trampling on his flower beds – than we are to look after our own property: we are so intent on inflicting harm that we are unconcerned about our own interests.

And if we become heedless out of ignorance we are like someone who is so dull-witted that they don't know any better than to let their house become a shambles. In this case we are simply unaware of the serious consequences of allowing negative mental events to take over our minds. We allow the kleśas and upakleśas to run riot either because we don't think it matters or perhaps because we think that being mindful or watchful is not good for us, or else because it has never occurred to us to consider the question at all.

Just as a house will not keep itself in good repair, so with the mind. One has to watch for the leak in the roof, stains on the carpet need to be cleared up and so on. Likewise one has to guard against ethical and spiritual deterioration. Indeed, the case of the mind is more perilous than this comparison suggests, because it is not just a thing that is subject to disintegration – rather, it is in ever-present danger of being actively invaded. One has to maintain – with the help of one's friends – a constant posture of non-heedlessness.

18. FORGETFULNESS (OR UNRECOLLECTEDNESS OR UNMINDFULNESS) (MUṢITASMṚTITĀ)

It is a flash of awareness in which the mind is not made clear and forgets immediately the positive thing because it is an attention to an emotionally tainted object.
Yeshe Gyaltsen

It functions as the basis of distraction.[219]
Abhidharmasamuccaya

If one is experiencing muṣitasmṛtitā, one adverts to a positive object, but very fleetingly, because the mind is immediately pulled away from it by other, purely negative, factors. It is not simply forgetfulness – one can be forgetful of anything, positive or negative. Here, the object is a positive one. The mind happens to alight on a positive object but we don't properly appreciate the nature of that positive object. It makes a very weak impression, so that our attention is at once snatched away.

This is what happens – according to the *Tibetan Book of the Dead* – when we have a glimpse of the clear light of Reality in the *bardo* and our consciousness is unable to sustain this vision. On a more basic level it also happens in meditation. Meditation is essentially easy: all one has to do is sit down and concentrate on one's breathing. That's it. If one were a balanced, happy, and integrated person one would be able to become more and more absorbed in the breath without any trouble. So it's not that it's difficult to concentrate on the breathing. The difficulty is to keep one's attention from being drawn away by distractions – i.e. negative mental events. So in a sense, *muṣitasmṛtitā* is forgetfulness of oneself.

Forgetfulness is the inability to retain the impression of the positive. If you read a book while you're in a negative state of mind, for example, it won't make any impression at all. You may pass the words across your mind but they just don't register, they don't mean anything to you – whereas at another time they might sink in very deeply. Negative emotions have such a hold over us that we can't fix the attention on anything positive long enough to begin to come under its influence. So we forget all about it. Clearly the counter-agent to this *upakleśa* is mindfulness.

19. INATTENTIVENESS (OR PURPOSELESSNESS) (*ASAMPRAJANYA*)

It is an emotionally tainted discriminating awareness which lacks watchfulness with regard to the activities of body, speech, and mind and is not associated with carefulness.... This inattentiveness becomes the foundation for falling from one's level of being ...[220]
Yeshe Gyaltsen

This is the negative mental event which consists in the lack of *samprajanya*, usually translated as 'mindfulness of purpose'. If one does not stay continually aware of one's purpose and aim in life – which for a Buddhist is ultimately the attainment of Enlightenment – one will succumb to *asamprajanya*, which could be described as a sort of neurotic introspection with no clear purpose or point. One can be aware in some degree of what is going on in one's own mind, one can even have a measure of faith in the possibility of attaining to higher states of being, but if one isn't fully mindful – that is, if one isn't watchful with regard to one's mental states, one's speech, and one's actions – one will 'fall from one's level of being' to a lower level of existence through the process of karma and rebirth.

If one does not bring one's activities of body, speech, and mind into line with one's discriminating awareness and one's faith – that is, if one's approach is purely psychological – one will come to grief. If one is careless or cavalier with regard to ethics, no amount of discriminating awareness will save one. The point is that it is possible to examine and analyse one's mental states without actually being mindful or watchful with regard to them any more than to one's speech and physical actions. If one is preoccupied with one's mental states in this unhealthy, even neurotic way to such an extent that one doesn't heed the ethical implications of those mental states in terms of one's actions of body, speech, and mind, there is bound to be an overall deterioration in one's level of being.

This is because one's level of being is determined by one's volitional actions, by whether they are skilful or unskilful, not by whether or not one feels good while performing those actions. Unfortunately, there is a tendency in the West to be far more concerned about the complexities of one's inner psychological states than about the much simpler questions of how to live an ethical life. One may perhaps fear, for example, that giving up some unskilful activity may disrupt the free flow of one's energies: it may well do this, but one should then be able to redirect that energy into a more skilful activity.

It is true that Buddhist ethics are ethics of intention, but this does not mean that they are simply about how we feel; rather, they are about our intentions with regard to objective situations. If we are to act skilfully, we need to focus our attention on the objective situation rather than on ourselves and how we feel about what we are doing. It may be reasonable to expect to get something out of what we do, at least occasionally, but the paradox is that we are going to get something out of it only to the extent that our focus is not on getting something out of it.

20. DESULTORINESS (OR DISTRACTION) (*VIKṢEPA*)

It is to be a scatter-brain and belongs to the categories of [greed, hatred, and ignorance]. Its function is to obstruct one from

becoming free of [greed].²²¹
Abhidharmasamuccaya

Vikṣepa literally means a sort of tossing of the mind. You toss and turn, you stagger or flounder from one thing to another. There are traditionally six varieties of this *upakleśa*,²²² though one could no doubt think of others. And in fact, according to Yeshe Gyaltsen, not all the six varieties he lists are really variants of this *upakleśa*; the first, he says, is indeterminate, and the last is actually positive, while of the other four it is really the second and third on the list that we should focus on as being of the essence of this particular negative mental event.

a. Desultoriness qua *desultoriness:* One is distracted from one's meditation through sense perception of one kind or another: a fly lands on one's arm, one smells something, one hears something. When one is not particularly concentrated, whatever it is cannot but impinge upon one's consciousness and distract one, if only momentarily. When one *is* concentrated, there can be a sound going on, say, but one's reception of it is inhibited by one's state of concentration. One may be aware of a very subtle, muffled noise, but it is not definite enough to cause one's mind to go towards it. One becomes aware of what one has heard, one names or identifies it, only when one comes out of the state of concentration.

b. Desultoriness regarding the without: One drifts away from one's concentration on the real nature of compounded things and become distracted by their illusory qualities. This kind of distraction occurs in the context of insight practice and refers specifically to the mind being drawn to the opposite of what one is trying to realize. For example, one may be reflecting or meditating on the impermanence of something but become unable to fix one's mind on that object in such a way as to penetrate into its impermanence, because one starts relishing it as if it were permanent. Or – to take a rather shocking example – one may be practising the *aśubha bhāvanā*, fixing one's mind on the inherent unloveliness of compounded things by contemplating a corpse; but then one's mind may drift off to think of other bodies that are very much alive and really rather lovely. In ways such as this one can lose sight of the real characteristics of the object of concentration and start grasping its unreal characteristics.

c. Desultoriness regarding the within: One becomes distracted in meditation through getting caught up in various negative mental states.

One becomes more and more involved and fascinated with one's inner experience, with one's subjective states of mind, instead of becoming more and more deeply absorbed in the object of one's meditation. It is a mental restlessness.

d. Desultoriness regarding defining characteristics: One is distracted by the opinions of others as to what meditation practice one should be doing. Not being firm enough in one's purpose, one has to rush off and try every new method one hears about. In this way one drifts from one method of practice to another. This kind of distraction comes from lack of confidence, from being unduly influenced by the recommendations of others. It also comes from placing too much faith in the particular method; that is, one clings to the idea that if one could only find the right method of practice all one's difficulties would be over.

e. Desultoriness of inappropriate action: One is drawn to practices based on perverse or topsy-turvy views, and one takes up these activities, one after another, with a conceited sense that one is getting into something positive. The perverse or topsy-turvy views meant here are those expressed in a list called the four *viparyāsas*, the four perversities; they are to take the perishable as imperishable, the painful as pleasant, the impure as pure, and the devoid of self as possessing self.[223] So one drifts from one pseudo-positive thing to another, from one personal growth therapy to another, from one 'deep and meaningful' experience to another. All the time one thinks that one is getting somewhere; one thinks that one's life is becoming more and more rich and significant. As one guzzles one 'profound life-changing experience' after another one gathers an inflated idea of one's own psychological and spiritual development.

f. Desultoriness by rationalization: One is distracted from the highest ideals by intermediate attainments. Thus the popular Mahāyāna view is that the ideal of the Arhant can become a distraction from the Bodhisattva ideal, that one can settle for a limited form of Enlightenment for oneself alone. In fact, it's more that one can become distracted by the limited progress to be made in one's practice of the Dharma when one makes a point of going it alone – i.e. leaving the Sangha Refuge out of one's practice. This is essentially about the positive taking one away from the even more positive. To take another example, the first *dhyāna* is a thoroughly positive state of mind, but it becomes a distraction if one doesn't move on from it to the even more integrated states represented by the higher *dhyānas*. All the *dhyānas* are equally positive inasmuch as they are all positive and not negative, just as all shades of blue are blue inasmuch as they are all blue and not red or yellow. But of course some blues are bluer than others, and likewise some *dhyānas* represent a greater degree of integration than others.

10

UNCLASSIFIABLE MIND

THESE LAST FOUR mental events, the *aniyatas* – torpor, worry, initial application of mind, and sustained application of mind – are essentially unclassifiable; that is, they cannot be classed as necessarily positive, or negative, or neutral, or object-determining or whatever.

1. DROWSINESS (OR TORPOR) (MIDDHA)

> ... during the night sleep is appropriate for increasing the ability of the body to attend to positive tasks;... The negative aspect of sleep which is emotionally tainted makes one dread positive tasks which must be done.[224]
> Yeshe Gyaltsen

Middha is like the kind of state one is in after a heavy meal. It's primarily a physical state, but it does of course have mental repercussions, and these may be either positive or negative depending on circumstances. If the mind is in a drowsy state it may drift either way. As for an Enlightened mind, according to the Theravādin tradition, the Arhant is liable to torpor, *middha*, but not to its mental equivalent, *thīna*.[225]

The state of torpor or drowsiness does obviously involve a loss of energy; because one is in a hazy, even passive state, one drifts in the

direction of one's natural inclination, whether that is positive or negative. In meditation it may involve withdrawing inward, away from the
object of meditation. One might think that meditation is all about
withdrawing inward anyway, but in fact it involves all one's energies
going out towards a single object 'out there'. The state of torpor is the
opposite of this, because it takes one back into oneself.

The sleep state, though, cannot be said to involve the loss of energy.
It is a recuperative state. One may feel drowsy, go to sleep, and as a
result bounce out of bed ready and happy to get on with something
positive. Alternatively, unfortunately, one may wake up with a freshly
renewed negative state of mind, or a negative state consisting in a
disinclination to wake up at all.

Of course, the differences between people are particularly evident
when it comes to sleep patterns. Some people need more sleep than
others. Some like to get up early, while others seem to be naturally late
risers and are more active late at night. Some people take longer to
emerge from sleep than others; they may be a little slower in their
reactions, a little less sharp or wakeful. One particular sleep pattern is
not in itself more virtuous than another. And even within one's own
pattern one may sometimes need to make allowances. If one has been
overactive and one's system needs a rest, there may be a natural and
healthy reluctance to get out of bed. There is certainly no particular
virtue in needing less sleep than other people. In deciding how much
sleep one needs, one just has to take into consideration one's constitution, temperament, and age. Having taken all that into account, one
should be able to rise from sleep with a healthy and optimistic inclination to get on with positive activity.

Of course, to sleep is to dream – and dreaming is one way of staying
in touch with the imaginative part of one's mind. If one is preoccupied
with abstract ideas to the exclusion of more imaginative mental activity, it's as though a whole side of one dies away. Take Charles Darwin,
for example. Of course he was by no means an uncreative or sterile
collector of scientific data, and as a young man he had a vivid appreciation of poetry; but when after twenty-five or thirty years of intense
scientific work he turned one day to his Shakespeare, he discovered to
his dismay that he was completely unable to enjoy poetry. He had
simply lost that faculty, and apparently he never regained it.

This one-sidedness is represented in the writings of William Blake
by what he calls the Spectre, which is reason split off from feeling
(whereas feeling split off from intellect he calls the Emanation).

According to Blake, the prime examples of the Spectre were to be found in the scientific and philosophical community of his day; he cited Bacon, Locke, and Newton. In other words, science and philosophy do not express the whole person. The natural expression of the integrated human being is the Imagination, which is only realized when Spectre and Emanation come together.

When one takes up the spiritual life, one needs to engage one's emotions with one's spiritual practice, and integrate one's intellectual with one's emotional life. It is characteristic of someone who is governed by Blake's Spectre (and this seems a most appropriate term) that they can think their way quite effectively around anything, even feelings – which means that they find it easy to go through the motions. If one is of this type, rather than trying to work away at developing one's emotional side, one might do best to lie around for a while doing nothing – dozing, sleeping, dreaming even – until real feelings start floating up. Then one can move on to working at developing those feelings, perhaps through making a connection with the arts or with devotional practice.

It can be useful to study Blake, especially the so-called Prophetic Books, because they cannot be reduced to a cut-and-dried system; they contain contradictions that cannot be reconciled. This is, indeed, part of their message: that the Spectre cannot have everything under its control. In trying to sort out the tangle of Blake's symbolism, the Spectre defeats itself: if you want every symbol and every statement to have one definable meaning and one definable relationship to every other symbol and statement, you are going to get very frustrated. But if you just plunge into the poetry and absorb its direct emotional impact, the general drift of Blake's meaning is quite clear.

I had a similar experience when I first started exploring the Tantric disciplines. I very much wanted to fit them all into a neat, overall synthesis, but I found that this just couldn't be done. However you arrange the material, there are always loose ends trailing all over the place. In the end I concluded that this was in some sense intentional. You can never get an overall view of the Tantra. But if you accept that you can only ever have a partial view of it, and that you get this view by engaging with the material rather than by standing back from it, you can at least get a precise *feel* for it. One might go as far as to say that nothing that is thoroughly amenable to rational analysis will satisfy us for long. A language, for example, needs to be rich in ambiguities in order to serve our needs fully.

So although torpor, drowsiness, dreams, and sleep may well represent negative mental states in the form of dullness and laziness, they are also our most direct connection with a whole realm of experience that we ignore at our peril. They represent a perspective that we need to maintain especially within the context of the Abhidharma, in which we find an attempt to rationalize the Buddha's teaching, to make it all hang together in an orderly fashion, to reduce it to its 'essentials' by removing all the 'extraneous' elements of biography, history, myth, and poetry. Useful as this exercise may be, particularly in certain details – such as in this analysis of mind and mental events – we must constantly bear in mind the limitations inherent in the whole approach of the Abhidharma.

In the autobiography of Geshe Rabten, who studied and wrote extensively on Abhidharma topics, it is striking that, in trying to describe to Westerners what a Tibetan monastery was like, he chose the image of a factory, evoking a picture of the machinery of the monastery whirring away and turning out monks, and everybody very busy on the production line. That Geshe Rabten should choose this little image, as so often with small details, is very telling.

It is a useful practice to meditate or recite devotional verses or repeat mantras just before going to sleep; in this way one can prolong awareness into the sleep state, and one's dreams are then more likely to have spiritual significance. One can have valuable experiences in dreams that are simply not accessible in the waking state. It seems that a lot goes on in dreams that doesn't proceed parallel with one's waking life but takes a direction of its own. Our dream experience may touch, even burst through, our waking life at times, but it has, in a sense, a life of its own. It's as though the life dominated by one's waking consciousness is only a narrow segment of one's total life. A lot is happening on other levels, or other dimensions, of one's being, beyond even what one normally thinks of as one's individuality. Perhaps one is even living a quite different life on some other level – even in another world, in a sense – of which, with one's conscious mind, one is not aware. 'It' is no more aware of 'you' than 'you' are aware of 'it', but they are somehow both aspects or dimensions of 'you' in the broader sense, and they may very occasionally cross paths. What one has to guard against is taking one's stand on rational consciousness and from there appropriating that other realm of experience by trying to analyse it, explain it, understand it, translate it into completely rational terms. By controlling it in this way one avoids having to experience it. In a way asking what dreams, symbols, and myths 'mean' is beside the point.

Having said that, I can remember receiving a very clear message from my own dreams at one time. Many years ago I used to have a recurring dream of a woman scolding me. She wasn't anybody I knew, and I couldn't make out what she was complaining about, but she was very angry. Sometimes I would meet her; sometimes she would just be on the telephone. At first I was rather puzzled by these dreams, because I wasn't on bad terms with any particular woman. But finally I realized what it was about. She was my imagination, my creativity, if you like, and she was protesting that she wasn't getting enough attention. So I learned from this – I eased up on the Abhidharma and picked up a volume of poetry from time to time – and I haven't heard from her now for very many years.

The more one looks at the stable ego the more it is seen to disintegrate. It's just a very weak thread of waking consciousness artificially holding together a large bundle of disparate materials. In the case of the ordinary person the unifying factor is the physical body – the only relatively stable component of our experience – so for all practical purposes one's body is who one is. This is why the Buddha said on one occasion that to identify with the body is a less serious error than to identify with the mind. The implication is that to think of the mental and emotional roller-coaster that is the mind as the locus of one's sense of an unchanging self is clearly absurd, but one might be forgiven for thinking of one's body as oneself.

However, if one can develop some awareness of the multi-dimensional nature of consciousness one can begin to get one's everyday sense-consciousness into perspective. Then when one dies – to risk using an image which is just as utilitarian as Geshe Rabten's factory but which may help to make things clear – it's like a man who is involved in a number of different businesses, one of which has folded. On the level of that little business there is total failure, but within the totality of all his interests and operations, it's not so important. He'll probably be able to open another business and transfer the staff there.

2. WORRY *(KAUKṚTYA)*

Its function is to obstruct the mind from becoming settled.[226]
Abhidharmasamuccaya

Worry can be positive if one can do something to allay it, and if it leads one to do something useful and appropriate about it; if, that is, it is a spur to appropriate action. It can act as a useful message from one's subconscious mind that one has overlooked something. In the case of Milarepa, for example, worry and regret about the very serious karmic consequences of his previous evil actions drove him to seek Enlightenment in that very lifetime, as the only alternative to being reborn in the hell realms.

If, on the other hand, there is nothing you can do about what you're worried about, or the time has passed for doing anything about it, or if your worry effectively undermines what you are doing to allay it, it is negative, it's anxiety. If Milarepa had continued to worry after realizing what he had to do, or had worried that he wasn't going to be able to attain Enlightenment, such worrying would have been pointless and harmful. If in the middle of the night you think, 'Oh, I don't think I locked the front door,' that is perhaps appropriate worry. But if you go downstairs, check the door, go back to bed, then continue to worry about whether you checked it properly, that is inappropriate worry, or anxiety.

Freud explains anxiety as arising when one is trying to keep the lid on powerful feelings that one regards as negative. You don't allow yourself to experience those feelings so far as to acknowledge them properly, but at the same time you can't exclude them altogether, so you feel a sort of diffuse, floating anxiety all the time which attaches itself to particular situations. This happens because you are not acknowledging some factor in your life that is very important to you, and that bubbles up despite all your efforts to keep the lid on. Again, we are dealing here with the split between the rational and the emotional. The problem comes when we worry about external, 'objective' things without addressing the emotional source of our anxieties, whatever that might be.

Having done all one can reasonably do in a given situation, one should be able to sit back and forget all about it. If one finds oneself continuing to worry that something may go wrong, this may be because one hasn't fully accepted the fact that something *may* go wrong. Sometimes we want more certainty than life by its very nature is able to give. In the end we feel uncertain because life is uncertain, although we don't want to accept this fact. We can never have complete certainty; we can't be certain beyond all doubt that we will live until lunchtime. All we can do is go on with our life in the absence of any complete certainty.

3 & 4. SELECTIVENESS AND DISCURSIVENESS (OR INITIAL APPLICATION OF MIND; SUSTAINED APPLICATION OF MIND)

[Initial application of mind] is a rough estimate of the thing under consideration and [sustained application of mind] is an exact investigation of it.[227]
Yeshe Gyaltsen

These two mental events – *vitarka* and *vicāra* – occasionally get mentioned separately, but they are usually referred to as a pair, especially in connection with the first and second *dhyānas*. As we have already seen (see page 187), they represent the kind of mental activity that is present in the first *dhyāna* and absent in the higher *dhyānas*. In simple terms, they are 'thinking of' and 'thinking about'. Traditionally they are likened to seizing a pot with one hand – *vitarka* – and scouring it round with the other – *vicāra*. On the one hand one has got a mental hold of the object without knowing anything about it; on the other, one investigates it in detail.[228]

These two mental events may be positive – as when you bring a friend to mind and consider their good qualities; or they may be negative – as when you bring to mind some attractive object and think how nice it would be to possess it. Thus *vitarka* and *vicāra* are variable mental events; they may be positive, negative, or neutral.

However, in the context of the Abhidharma's analysis of mind and mental events, one might ask whether there is any real distinction to be drawn between *vitarka* and mind. Can we not say that *vitarka* is mind and *vicāra* is mental events in general? As we know by now, mind is defined as that which perceives an object – no object, no mind – while *vitarka* is defined as an actual apprehension of the object. But where perception of the object ends and apprehension of the object begins would be difficult to say – though there must be some difference, otherwise *vitarka* would be classified as mind, not as a mental event. It is not as if this apprehension is 'recognition' because recognition is a separate mental event – *saṁjñā*. Really one would think that *vitarka* as a mental event should be superfluous, because what seems to be the function of *vitarka* is performed well enough by mind.

The difference would seem to be that *vitarka* is just one of the functions of mind, inasmuch as the object of *vitarka* is a mental object, whereas the mind perceives perceptual objects in general – that is, objects of ordinary sense perception as well as objects of mental or 'categorical' perception. Furthermore, the objects of perception of the mind in the higher *dhyānas* are not possible objects of *vitarka*; so it would seem that *vitarka* represents just the coarser-grained element of mind.

Thus even in the Abhidharma we find loose ends. There isn't really a definite fixed number of separate entities; there are all sorts of overlaps between mental events. In this case we seem to have a complete overlap of one by another, *vitarka* by mind viewed as a mental event. So, after all, we shouldn't take the idea of mind and mental events too literally. Mind isn't distinct from mental events. They are all – and the Mahāyāna teachers of the Abhidharma stress this, as we have seen – operational concepts.

CONCLUSION

MAKING THE MOST OF ANALYSIS

Those who do wrong actions become the helpers of Anaṅga (Cupid)
And become degenerate by the clouds of stupidity
Which are the waves of this degenerate age, and thus
They become inflated by seeing this degeneration as the best possible
world.[229]

This is one of the sequence of verses with which Yeshe Gyaltsen ends
his exploration of mind in Buddhist psychology. A legend recounted
in one of the Hindu Purāṇas explains how this figure of Anaṅga –
which means 'limbless' or 'bodyless' – got his name.[230] Once upon a
time – indeed, for thousands of years – the god Śiva was engaged in
his austerities, completely oblivious to what was happening in the
world. And during this period the world was being troubled by a
terrible demon. The gods held a council to decide what to do about it,
and eventually a great rishi told them that the demon could be destroyed only by a son of Śiva. At first this seemed to be more of a
theoretical than a practical resolution of the difficulty, because, of
course, Śiva was immersed in his solitary meditations in the Himalayas
and thus in no mood to beget a son. Anyway, the gods decided to do
what they could, and they deputed Kāmadeva, the Hindu god of love
(like the Greek Cupid) to seek out Śiva and shoot one of his flowery

arrows at him. So Kāmadeva set off and found Śiva. He was just drawing his bow when Śiva suddenly, for an instant, emerged from his contemplation, opened his third eye, and threw out a great flame that consumed the little love-god to nothing.

Ever since then, Kāmadeva has been invisible. But although we can't see him, he's still in business just as before. We are not even aware of when he is up to his tricks – so we have to be on our guard. It is very easy to be fascinated by the mundane, and rather more difficult to be fascinated by the transcendental. In the Buddhist tradition this difficulty is recognized; there is, indeed, a sort of sublimated form of Kāmadeva in the figure of Kurukullā, the Bodhisattva representing the fascination aspect of Enlightenment, Enlightenment as the beautiful.

In doing wrong actions we are playing into the hands of Ananga – that is, we are often not really aware of our unskilfulness. We become 'degenerate by the clouds of stupidity' upon which we attempt to establish our lives. One might suppose that during the twentieth century we have jettisoned what seemed to many people to be the facile optimism, the enthusiastic faith in human progress, of the Victorian age. Not a bit of it. It is nowadays generally held that libertarian, egalitarian, socially progressive, technologically advanced, liberal democracies represent an ideal to which the rest of the world should aspire. However, one could certainly take the view that these 'ideal' societies actually represent a plunging degeneration, without any clarity of values or sense of community. So yes, unfortunately, we do see this degeneration as the best possible world. And at the heart of this degeneration is muddle over what is skilful and what is unskilful, what is positive and what is negative.

Even when we conclude that the way forward, for ourselves and for the world, is to follow a spiritual path, we may still be muddled when it comes to determining the nature of spiritual development. The Abhidharma's analysis takes place within an overall context of spiritual practice, which is, of course, about self-development. But the very notion of self-development can undermine itself if it is interpreted too narrowly. It is true that Buddhism emphasizes the importance of being concerned for oneself as well as for others, but it also emphasizes the importance of being concerned for others as well as for oneself. One may have to overcome a tendency to see the spiritual life as being to do with the negation of the self; but at some point one needs to see it as basically about devoting oneself to the welfare of others – and looking after oneself as well, incidentally.

Yes, one needs to discover the importance to one's self-development of one's relationships with other people. One needs to realize the importance within one's programme of self-development of being kind and generous towards other people. It is at least a start to realize that time and energy spent looking after other people's development does not mean time lost with regard to one's own. That is at least something. Some people don't even get that far: they think that any time spent on behalf of others is lost as far as their own spiritual development is concerned. But having brought the existence of other people into consideration, one has to move on from regarding other people and what one does for them as simply a means towards one's own spiritual ends. Other people, one has to realize, have a value of their own.

Perhaps one starts practising the *mettā bhāvanā* with a view to getting into higher states of consciousness, becoming a better person, even gaining Enlightenment. One takes other people as objects for the development of one's *mettā*: one wishes other people well so that one will become a better, happier person. But the practice only works if one really does become concerned about the welfare of others; and when that happens one loses interest in one's original reason for doing the practice. One's own personal development can no longer be a separate issue from the spiritual welfare of other people.

It is within the framework of the dichotomy between self and other that all our thought and experience takes place. As far as ordinary experience goes, this dichotomy is irreducible. We cannot talk our way round it. So on the level of empirical, relative reality, we need a double approach. As reality has bifurcated into subject and object, we have to approach it not only via the self, but also via the other.

In fact, it could be said that the best way to approach reality is via the other, because we naturally approach it from the point of view of the self anyway. It comes naturally to us to feel that we count, and perhaps that our nearest and dearest count, but that others hardly count at all. By helping others one begins to register that others are just as real and just as important as one is oneself, and one engages in something which one can be certain will be helping to break down the subject–object dichotomy.

However you try to approach ultimate reality it is always *you* doing it; and as long as you are trying to attain it for yourself, you will fail in this endeavour. There is no possibility of you yourself attaining to ultimate reality. Only you plus others can do it. *Prajñā* (wisdom) is the culmination of the self-oriented approach, *karuṇā* (compassion) is the culmination of the others-oriented approach, and in non-dual reality these two necessarily coalesce.

If, therefore, one's approach to the realization of ultimate reality is with a view to realizing it for oneself, if it is – with all the benevolent feeling for others in the world – essentially for one's own benefit, then there is no breaking down of the dichotomy of subject and object, and therefore no realization. To put it very simply, it is not enough to feel unselfish – one has to *be* unselfish, which means acting unselfishly. This is the only way to break down the barrier between subject and object. Self and other have to become interchangeable as the source of motive for one's actions. One realizes as a matter of *fact* that there is no difference between self and other. This is the vision of the Bodhisattva: that there is no nirvāṇa for oneself (however benevolent one may feel towards others) at all. Hence the importance of the traditional practice of dedicating one's merits, which involves wishing that any merit one has gained from one's actions may benefit not just oneself but all beings. Whenever one does something positive, one needs to make sure one isn't trying to appropriate the benefits for oneself; otherwise those benefits will in a sense be frittered away.

One may think, 'Surely it's best to look after myself first. Then, when I have a bit more experience and understand other people's needs better, I can move on to looking after them as well.' But one can just as easily turn the argument round: why not look after others first? Then, when one has a bit more experience and understands one's own real needs better, one can move on to looking after oneself as well. One can't go wrong with this approach. As long as one is doing things for others, or doing useful things with no thought of self-gratification, one can be sure that one is taking steps towards the real aim of any kind of spiritual practice.

If we value the psychological too much and the ethical not enough, the spiritual life becomes a sort of refined, pseudo-spiritual, hedonic aestheticism. Of course, refining and concentrating one's experience is inherent in spiritual practice; but is one refining one's experience of the self–other dichotomy, or is one simply refining one's experience of selfhood? If one is bent on refining one's subjectivity in the context of an awareness of the dichotomy, all well and good. But if one is concerned with increasingly more refined experiences of oneself while becoming resentful about other people somehow getting in the way of one's enjoyment of or devotion to those refined experiences, clearly something has gone awry.

One cannot refine oneself out of the mundane world altogether; there always has to be something that is being refined. For example, in one of the monasteries of Tibet in the old days there was, so I have heard, an enormous vat in which they brewed tea every day for all the hundreds of monks. In fact, tea had been brewed in the same vat for about six hundred years, since the days of Tsongkhapa. And every day they left a little bit at the bottom, so that every monk in every generation had an infinitesimal drop of the very tea Tsongkhapa himself had partaken of. By this process, however diluted Tsongkhapa's tea became, it was still there. The same is basically true for compounded existence. One cannot refine it out of existence. One has to make an existential leap – throw out the last drop of tea.

There is of course the ideal of aesthetic appreciation in a higher, contemplative, objective sense: through delighting in something for its own sake, one loses oneself in the object. But this needs to be distinguished from a subjective aesthetic appreciation in the sense of enjoying an object, at however subtle a level, for one's own individualistic gratification – which cannot, by itself, lead to liberation. One may say that *samādhi* represents the most refined levels of this purely subjective pleasure. But on its own, without transcendental insight, *samādhi* cannot produce Enlightenment: the culmination of the spiritual life is not just some great wonderful experience for oneself.

One does not attain an ideal of objective aesthetic appreciation in which one achieves a dissolution of the self in the object without practical reference to the ethical dimension. In a way one could say that one can't dissolve oneself in contemplation of the object without dissolving others in that object too, and one can do that only by devoting oneself to others. Really, what we are trying to dissolve is the subject–object dichotomy itself. The one value of ultimate reality must be approached from two directions: from wisdom and from compassion.

So one should be concerned neither just with oneself, nor just with others, but with self *and* others. It's impossible to have one without the other; they are interconnected. Any unselfish act is the expression of some kind of apprehension or experience or realization of this reality, at the very least an aspiration towards that understanding.

Being unselfish basically involves taking on responsibilities. Of course, most people take on major responsibilities by becoming parents, and develop a measure of unselfishness. But if some people choose not to take on domestic responsibilities in order to follow the spiritual path, it would be a big mistake to take from this the notion that the spiritual life involves avoiding responsibility. Quite the opposite. In the same way that one makes time for one's meditation practice, one should make time for disinterested activity on behalf of others – that is, responsibilities. It is a good idea not to be too particular about exactly what jobs one takes on to do; a choosy attitude will obviously undermine the whole project of breaking down the subject–object dichotomy. And to float around with no responsibilities at all, with no sense that what one does should be in some way for others' benefit, is for most people quite dangerous.

Taking on responsibilities means not just agreeing to do things for people, but also carrying out what one has agreed to do at the time one agreed to do it. It means keeping one's word. If one doesn't keep one's word, and if others are inconvenienced thereby, it means one is not really aware of other people, it means a lack of responsibility – which means a lack of ethical identity. Very often people give their word very lightly and easily because they know that they aren't going to be very particular about keeping it – so that their word is not really their word. Then come the blustering excuses: 'Look, I didn't say I'd definitely do it; I said I'd do it if I could – I just haven't got round to it yet. I've had a lot on.'

It also happens that the person who has to do something is not the person who agreed to do it. We can be so unintegrated that when we volunteer to do something, it is just a part of us that volunteers – the part of us that happens to be uppermost at the time, the part that wants a bit of attention and approval, the part that wants to be slapped on the back for being such a good sport. This part of us probably does want to do what we have volunteered to do. But once we have had the attention and sense of self-worth we wanted, this part subsides and disappears. When the time comes for doing whatever it is we said we would do, some other part of us is uppermost, a part that isn't interested in what we volunteered for but has other interests entirely.

To show willing is fine so long as everyone knows that that's all one is doing, but it isn't really good enough if others are led to believe that what one is volunteering to do is actually going to get done. Unfortunately, some people seem to think that being willing is, morally speaking, tantamount to actually doing, or that one should get some credit for offering, even if one doesn't quite manage to get round to fulfilling that offer. This is not the attitude of the ethical individual. The ethical individual is aware and responsible and integrated, which means that they are concerned about others, and act in a way that reflects that concern. Only an integrated person can be trusted, only an integrated person has an ethical identity.

The list of mental events we have been exploring here is not exhaustive. Indeed, it may be that the ancient people of India had different emotional emphases from our own, and that we need to seek to identify further mental events, appropriate to the particular emotional colouring we have developed in more recent times. But what should be clear from an examination of the traditional analysis of mind and mental events is that by becoming more aware of precisely how the mind works and how the activity of the mind is expressed in actions of speech and body, we can move with more direction and focus in our spiritual practice. We can become more aware of our mental states and the actions of speech and body that arise out of them and in turn give rise to further mental states. We can identify mental events as being helpful or hindering, and can move to build on them or counteract them more swiftly and accurately.

Whatever we have come to understand in the course of studying the Abhidharma must be practically applied, both in meditation and in other situations. But the real purpose of the Abhidharma analysis of the mind and mental events is to bring us to an understanding, an experience, of ourselves. This understanding is to perceive that those ever-changing and developing mental events actually constitute in themselves what we usually think of as the self. It is to watch one's whole idea of one's self dissolve in the continuous flow of mental events.

But, to balance this, we need to move beyond a narrow concern with our personal mental states towards a realization of our true nature through a wholehearted and authentic engagement with the interests and concerns of others. Only in this way will we begin to approach the perspective of the Enlightened Mind.

APPENDIX

THE FIFTY-ONE MENTAL EVENTS (*CAITTA*)

Translations are those used by Sangharakshita in the text. Alternative translations from J. Hopkins, *Meditation on Emptiness*, are given in square brackets. The Sanskrit equivalent is shown in italics.

THE FIVE OMNIPRESENT MENTAL EVENTS (*SARVATRAGA*)
1. Feeling-tone (*vedanā*)
2. Recognition or conceptualization [discrimination] (*saṁjñā*)
3. Directionality of Mind [intention] (*cetanā*)
4. Contact (*sparśa*)
5. Egocentric demanding [mental engagement] (*manaskāra*)

THE FIVE OBJECT-DETERMINING MENTAL EVENTS (*VINIYATA*)
1. Interest [aspiration] (*chanda*)
2. Intensified interest which stays with its object [belief] (*adhimokṣa*)
3. Inspection (or mindfulness or recollection) (*smṛti*)
4. Intense concentration [stabilization] (*samādhi*)
5. Appreciative discrimination [knowledge] (*prajñā*)

THE ELEVEN POSITIVE MENTAL EVENTS (*KUŚALA*)
1. Confidence-trust (or faith) (*śraddhā*)
2. Self-respect (or shame) (*hrī*)
3. Decorum (or respect for wise opinion) [embarrassment] (*apatrāpya*)
4. Non-attachment (*alobha*)

5. Non-hatred (*adveṣa*)
6. Non-deludedness [non-ignorance] (*amoha*)
7. Diligence (or energy in pursuit of the good) [effort] (*vīrya*)
8. Alertness (or tranquillity) [pliancy] (*praśrabdhi*)
9. Concern (or non-heedlessness) [conscientiousness] (*apramāda*)
10. Equanimity (*upekṣā*)
11. Non-violence [non-harmfulness] (*avihiṁsā*)

SIX BASIC EMOTIONS (*MŪLAKLEŚA*)

1. Cupidity-attachment [desire] (*rāga*)
2. Anger (*pratigha*)
3. Arrogance [pride] (*māna*)
4. Lack of intrinsic awareness [ignorance] (*avidyā*)
5. Indecision [doubt] (*vicikitsā*)
6. Opinionatedness [afflicted view] (*dṛṣṭi*)

THE TWENTY PROXIMATE FACTORS OF INSTABILITY (*UPAKLEŚA*)

1. Indignation (or rage) [belligerence] (*krodha*)
2. Resentment (*upanāha*)
3. Slyness-concealment [concealment] (*mrakṣa*)
4. Spite (or defensiveness) (*pradāśa*)
5. Jealousy (or envy) (*irṣyā*)
6. Avarice (or acquisitiveness) [miserliness] (*mātsarya*)
7. Deceit (or pretence) (*māyā*)
8. Dishonesty [dissimulation] (*śāṭhya*)
9. Mental inflation (or self-intoxication) [haughtiness] (*mada*)
10. Malice [harmfulness] (*vihiṁsā*)
11. Shamelessness [non-shame] (*āhrīkya*)
12. Lack of sense of propriety [non-embarrassment] (*anapatrāpya*)
13. Gloominess (or stagnation) [lethargy] (*styāna*)
14. Ebullience [excitement] (*auddhatya*)
15. Lack of trust (or non-faith) (*āśraddhya*)
16. Laziness (*kausīdya*)
17. Unconcern (or heedlessness) [non-conscientiousness] (*pramāda*)
18. Forgetfulness (or unrecollectedness or unmindfulness) (*muṣitasmṛtitā*)
19. Inattentiveness (or purposelessness) [non-introspection] (*asamprajanya*)
20. Desultoriness (or distraction) (*vikṣepa*)

THE FOUR VARIABLES (*ANIYATA*)

1. Drowsiness (or torpor) [sleep] (*middha*)
2. Worry [contrition] (*kaukṛtya*)
3. Initial application of mind [investigation] (*vitarka*)
4. Sustained application of mind [analysis] (*vicāra*)

NOTES AND REFERENCES

1 Herbert V. Guenther and Leslie S. Kawamura (trans.), *Mind in Buddhist Psychology: A Translation of Ye-shes rgyal-mtshan's 'The Necklace of Clear Understanding'*, Dharma, Berkeley 1975, p.xvi. That the translation is the work of both scholars should be understood wherever Guenther's name is mentioned.

2 The term is *maggam bhāveti*. See Nyanatiloka, *Buddhist Dictionary*, Buddhist Publication Society, Kandy 1988, p.169, 'The Progress of the Disciple'.

3 *Dhammapada* verse 183.

4 See *Mind in Buddhist Psychology*, p.xxiv.

5 See *The Sāṁkhyakārikās of Iswara Krishna: An Exposition of the System of Kapila*, trans. John Davies, Susil Gupta (India) Ltd., Calcutta 1957.

6 Buddhaghosa, *Visuddhimagga (The Path of Purity)*, trans. Pe Maung Tin, Pali Text Society, London 1975.

7 The seven books of the Theravāda Abhidhamma are available in translation from the Pali Text Society. The books of the Sarvāstivāda Abhidharma are less accessible. The original Sanskrit texts are no longer extant, and while Chinese versions do exist, they have not yet been translated into any European language. The most accessible and most famous source for the Sarvāstivāda Abhidharma is the *Abhidharmakośa*,

which has been translated in full into French and English.

8 The Buddha first taught the five *skandhas* very soon after his Enlightenment, as part of his teaching to his first five disciples. See *Vinaya Piṭaka* ('The Book of the Discipline'), vol.iv (*Mahāvagga*), trans. I.B. Horner, Pali Text Society, London 1982, pp.20–1; or Bhikkhu Ñāṇamoli, *The Life of the Buddha*, Buddhist Publication Society, Kandy 1992, pp.46–7.

9 H.V. Guenther, *Philosophy and Psychology in the Abhidhamma*, Shambhala, Berkeley and London 1976, p.146.

10 This distinction is made clearly in the *Nyāyānusāra* of Saṁghabhadra, which is extant only in Chinese. For a partial English translation and analysis see C. Cox, *Disputed Dharmas: Early Buddhist Theories of Existence*, International Institute for Buddhist Studies, Tokyo 1995. For a discussion of the *prajñaptisat-dravyasat* distinction in Abhidharma texts, see Paul Williams, *Journal of Indian Philosophy* 9, 1981, pp.227–57.

11 *The Life of the Buddha*, op. cit., p.270.

12 The *Abhidharmasamuccaya* is not yet available in English translation. However, there is a translation into French: *Le compendium de la super-doctrine (philosophie) (Abhidharmasamuccaya) d'Asaṅga*, translated and annotated by Walpola Rahula, École française d'extrême-orient, Paris 1971.

13 See Vasubandhu, *Abhidharmakośabhāṣyam*, English translation by Leo M. Pruden from the French translation by Louis de La Vallée Poussin, Asian Humanities Press, Berkeley 1988–1990, four volumes.

14 See Plato's *Parmenides*. For the 'negative dialectic' of Parmenides and the 'positive dialectic' of Plato see *Proclus' Commentary on Plato's Parmenides*, translated by Glenn R. Morrow and John M. Dillon, Princeton University Press 1987, pp.40–7.

15 Published in English as *Mind in Buddhist Psychology*, op. cit.

16 Hsüan Tsang, *Ch'eng Wei-Shih Lun: Doctrine of Mere-Consciousness*, trans. Wei Tat, Ch'eng Wei-Shih Lun Publication Committee, Hong Kong 1973.

17 The path of five stages, to which Dr Guenther devotes the greater part of his introduction to *Mind in Buddhist Psychology*, is outlined in Vasubandhu's *Abhidharmakośa*. See also Edward Conze, *Buddhist Thought in India*, Ann Arbor Paperbacks, Michigan 1967, pp.175–7.

18 The four right efforts were taught by the Buddha as the sixth limb of his Noble Eightfold Path, as recorded in various contexts in the Pāli Canon; see, for example, *Dīgha-Nikāya* 22.

19 Both these meditation practices were taught by the Buddha; for his teaching of the mindfulness of breathing, see *Majjhima-Nikāya* 22; for the *mettā bhāvanā*, see the *Mettā Sutta* (*Sutta-Nipāta* i.8, verses 143–52) or the *Kālāma Sutta*, (*Aṅguttara-Nikāya* i.188–93).

20 The four bases of psychic power, or more literally 'roads to power', have their origin in the Pāli Canon (the Pāli is *iddhipāda*); see, for example, *Saṁyutta-Nikāya* li.2. The order in which they are delivered varies.

21 According to the Pāli Canon, the Buddha spoke of these five spiritual faculties just after his Enlightenment; see *Saṁyutta-Nikāya* xlviii.57; or *The Life of the Buddha*, op. cit., p.35. See also Sangharakshita, *A Survey of Buddhism*, Windhorse, Birmingham 1999 (forthcoming), p.315ff.

22 Paul Williams, *Mahāyāna Buddhism*, Routledge, London and New York 1989, p.209.

23 Gam-po-pa, *The Jewel Ornament of Liberation*, trans. H.V. Guenther, Rider, London 1959, chapter 21, 'Buddha Activity'.

24 *Mind in Buddhist Psychology*, pp.3–4.

25 See Bhagavan Das, *Science of the Emotions*, Theosophical Publishing House, Adyar, Madras 1924, p.218; or Sangharakshita, *The Religion of Art*, Windhorse, Glasgow 1988, p.94.

26 It is worth noting, however, that according to some Mahāyāna Buddhists, including Gelukpas, Buddhas in their *dharmakāya* aspect are *literally* omniscient, being said directly to cognize *all* phenomena all the time. See, for example, J. Hopkins, *Meditation on Emptiness*, Wisdom, London 1983, pp.188ff. and Paul Williams, *Mahāyāna Buddhism*, Routledge, London and New York 1989, p.180.

27 For traditional life stories of the 'Six Ornaments of India' see, for example, *Tāranātha's History of Buddhism in India*, translated from the Tibetan by Lama Chimpa and Alaka Chattopadhyaya, Motilal Banarsidass, Delhi 1990.

28 Various translations are available. See for example D.J. Kalupahana, *Nāgārjuna: The Philosophy of the Middle Way*, State University of New York Press 1986; B. Bocking, *Nāgārjuna in China: A Translation of the Middle Treatise*, Edwin Mellen , Lewiston 1995; K.K. Inada, *Nāgārjuna*, Hokuseido, Tokyo 1970.

29 Śāntideva, *Bodhicāryavatāra*, trans. Kate Crosby and Andrew Skilton, Oxford University Press, Oxford 1996.

30 For an English translation, see *The Precious Garland and the Song of the Four Mindfulnesses*, trans. J. Hopkins et al., George Allen and Unwin, London 1975.

31 See *Laṅkāvatāra Sūtra*, trans. D.T. Suzuki, Routledge, London 1932, p.239.

32 For an account of Milarepa's life see *The Life of Milarepa*, trans. Lobsang P. Lhalungpa, Shambhala, Boston and London 1985.

33 Henry Vaughan, *Silex Scintillans*, 'The Retreat'.

34 William Wordsworth, 'Ode: Intimations of Immortality'.

35 See Traherne, *Centuries of Meditations*.

36 According to Buddhist tradition a *kalpa* is the time taken for a world system to evolve and involve; a *kalpa* is divided into four *asāṁkheyya-kalpas* (Pāli *asankheyya-kappas*). See *A Survey of Buddhism*, op. cit., p.60.

37 See, for example, *Sutta-Nipāta* iv.229.

38 *Dhammapada*, verses 1–2.

39 For a fuller account of karma and rebirth see Sangharakshita, *Who is the Buddha?* Windhorse, Birmingham 1995, chapter 7.

40 *Mind in Buddhist Psychology*, p.5.

41 ibid., p.6.

42 ibid., p.6.

43 See W.M. McGovern, *Manual of Buddhist Philosophy*, Kegan Paul, London 1923, p.166.

44 For more on Pure Land Buddhism see *A Survey of Buddhism*, op. cit., pp.374ff.

45 *Philosophy and Psychology in the Abhidhamma*, op. cit, p.146.

46 There are a great many Jātakas – literally 'birth stories' – giving accounts of the Buddha's previous lives. See Sangharakshita, *The Eternal Legacy*, Tharpa, London 1985, pp.55–61.

47 See S. Foster Damon, *Blake Dictionary*, Thames and Hudson, London 1973, p.341 and p.195.

48 See D.Y. Paul, *Philosophy of Mind in Sixth Century China*, Stanford University Press, Stanford 1984.

49 For more on the mandala of the five Buddhas see, for example, Vessantara, *Meeting the Buddhas*, Windhorse, Birmingham 1994, pp.67–126.

50 See *Madhyānta-vibhaṅga: Discourse on Discrimination Between Middle and Extremes*, ascribed to Bodhisattva Maitreya, trans. Th. Stcherbatsky, Firma KLM Private Limited, Calcutta 1992, chapter 2. See also *Seven Works of Vasubandhu, the Buddhist Psychological Doctor*, Stefan Anaker (trans. and ed.), Motilal Banarsidass, Delhi 1984, pp.191ff. See also *A Survey of Buddhism*, op. cit., pp.408f.

51 See *Saṁdhinirmocana Sūtra*, published as *Buddhist Yoga*, trans. Thomas Cleary, Shambhala, Boston and London 1995.

52 For Yeshe Gyaltsen's account of this, see *Mind in Buddhist Psychology*, pp.15–16.

53 ibid., p.16.

54 See, for example, *Mahāsatipaṭṭhāna Sutta, Dīgha-Nikāya* 22 (ii.303).

55 *Mind in Buddhist Psychology*, p.9.

56 Published as *Madhyānta-vibhaṅga: Discourse on Discrimination Between Middle and Extremes*, op. cit., pp.113–4.

57 On facticity and haecceity, see *Mind in Buddhist Psychology*, p.9.

58 ibid., p.10.

59 ibid., p.10.

60 See ibid., pp.xxv–xxvi.

61 See ibid., p.xxvi.

62 J. Hopkins, *Meditation on Emptiness*, Wisdom, Boston 1996, p.236.

63 *Mind in Buddhist Psychology*, p.11.

64 *Philosophy and Psychology in the Abhidhamma*, op. cit, p.146.

65 *Mind in Buddhist Psychology*, p.12.

66 Milton, *Paradise Lost*, Book 1, lines 254–5.

67 *Mind in Buddhist Psychology*, p.14.

68 See Anuruddha, *Abhidhammatthasaṅgaha (Compendium of Philosophy)*, trans. Mrs Rhys Davids, Pali Text Society, London 1910, p.29.

69 *Mind in Buddhist Psychology*, p.18.

70 See ibid., p.18.

71 ibid., p.19.

72 See Spinoza, *Ethics*.

73 *Mind in Buddhist Psychology*, p.20.

74 William Blake, *MS Note-Book*, p.99, 'Several Questions Answered'.

75 See Epicurus' *Sovran Maximus*, quoted in *Diogenes Laertius: Lives of Eminent Philosophers*, trans. R.D. Hicks, Cambridge, Mass. and London 1979, vol.ii, p.665: 'It is impossible to live a pleasant life without living wisely and well and justly, and it is impossible to live wisely and well and justly without living pleasantly.'

76 See Lama Anagarika Govinda, *The Psychological Attitude of Early Buddhist Philosophy*, Rider, London 1961, p.117.

77 *Mind in Buddhist Psychology*, p.21.

78 The *mettā bhāvanā* meditation practice has five stages. In the first stage one cultivates a feeling of goodwill, of loving kindness, towards oneself, then in the second, third, and fourth stages extends this warm feeling to a friend, a 'neutral person', and an 'enemy'. In the fifth and final stage, referred to here, one further extends this feeling of *mettā* to include, progressively, the people and other beings around one, then throughout the universe.

79 Tennyson, 'In Memoriam'.

80 *Mind in Buddhist Psychology*, p.22.

81 ibid., p.23.

82 ibid., p.23.

83 See ibid., p.23.

84 See ibid., pp.24–5.

85 See *Visuddhimagga* iii.21.

86 One of the few canonical references to the twelve positive *nidānas* is to be found in the *Saṁyutta-Nikāya*, trans. Mrs C.A.F. Rhys Davids, *Book of the Kindred Sayings* vol.ii, p.27, Pali Text Society; quoted in *A Survey of Buddhism*, op. cit., pp.139–40. For more on the spiral path generally see Sangharakshita, *What is the Dharma?*, Windhorse, Birmingham 1998, chapter 7.

87 For the Nyāya School's views on ontological absence, see B.K. Matilal, *The Navya-Nyāya Doctrine of Negation. The Semantics and Ontology of Negative Statements in Navya-Nyāya Philosophy*, Harvard University Press, Cambridge 1968.

88 *Mind in Buddhist Psychology*, p.26.

89 See *Aṅguttara-Nikāya (Book of the Gradual Sayings)*, Pali Text Society, vol.iii, p.145. Also see Nārada Thera, *Manual of Abhidhamma*, Vajirārāma Publications, Colombo 1956, p.85; and Anuruddha, *Abhidhammatthasaṅgaha (Compendium of Philosophy)*, op. cit., pp.43–5.

90 *Mind in Buddhist Psychology*, p.25.

91 For more about the three doors to Enlightenment, see *What is the Dharma?*, op. cit., p.66.

92 See Anuruddha, *Abhidhammatthasaṅgaha (Compendium of Philosophy)*, op. cit., p.30.

93 *Mind in Buddhist Psychology*, p.26.

94 These ten precepts have numerous canonical sources; see, for example, the *Kūṭadanta Sutta*, *Dīgha-Nikāya* 5, and the *Sevitabba-asevitabba-sutta*, *Majjhima-Nikāya* 114. See also Sangharakshita, *The Ten Pillars of Buddhism*, Windhorse, Birmingham 1996, pp.22–31.

95 *Dhammapada* verse 80.

96 *Mind in Buddhist Psychology*, p.27.

97 ibid., p.28.

98 Hsüan Tsang, *Ch'eng Wei-Shih Lun: Doctrine of Mere-Consciousness*, op. cit., p.159.

99 Nyanatiloka, *Buddhist Dictionary*, Buddhist Publication Society, Kandy 1988, p.112.

100 *Mind in Buddhist Psychology*, p.29.

101 ibid., pp.29–30.

102 See *The Jewel Ornament of Liberation*, op. cit., p.183.

103 The three levels of wisdom are enumerated in, for example, *Dīgha-Nikāya* 16:iii.219. See also page 134.

104 *Mind in Buddhist Psychology*, p.31.

105 ibid., p.32.

106 In his *Buddhist Dictionary*, Nyanatiloka notes that there are six *anussatis* often described in the *suttas* of the Pāli Canon: recollection of the Buddha, the Dharma, the Sangha, morality, liberality, and heavenly beings. A further four are listed less frequently: mindfulness of death, of the body, of breathing, and of peace. See Nyanatiloka, *Buddhist Dictionary*, Buddhist Publication Society, Kandy 1988, pp.20–2.

107 Interestingly, according to the Pāli Abhidhamma *cittass'ekaggata* (the Pāli equivalent of *samādhi*) is an omnipresent mental event rather than an object-determining one; here is a key difference between the Theravāda Abhidhamma and the Sarvāstivāda Abhidharma.

108 *Mind in Buddhist Psychology*, p.35.

109 Hsüan Tsang, *Ch'eng Wei-Shih Lun: Doctrine of Mere-Consciousness*, op. cit., p.379.

110 *Mind in Buddhist Psychology*, p.35.

111 *Some Sayings of the Buddha*, trans. F.L. Woodward, Oxford University Press 1973, pp.136–7.

112 *Mind in Buddhist Psychology*, p.36.

113 ibid., p.37.

114 The *viparyāsas* are listed in *Aṅguttara-Nikāya* viii.20. See also *What is the Dharma?*, op. cit., pp.127–8.

115 See *Mind in Buddhist Psychology*, p.37.

116 For more information on the seven *bodhyaṅgas* see *What is the Dharma?* op. cit., pp.131ff.

117 Buddhist meditation practices are broadly of two kinds: *śamatha*, calming meditation, and *vipaśyanā*, insight meditation. *Śamatha* practices such as the mindfulness of breathing and the *mettā bhāvanā* give one a positive and calm basis upon which to approach more reflective insight practices such as the one described here.

118 *Mind in Buddhist Psychology*, p.38.

119 Hsüan Tsang, *Ch'eng Wei-Shih Lun: Doctrine of Mere-Consciousness*, op. cit., p.389.

120 ibid., p.388.

121 *Mind in Buddhist Psychology*, p.39.

122 See ibid., p.40.

123 ibid., p.41.

124 William Wordsworth, 'Lines composed a few miles above Tintern Abbey', lines 95–9.

125 *Mind in Buddhist Psychology*, p.43.

126 See *Aṅguttara-Nikāya* ii.7.

127 *Mind in Buddhist Psychology*, p.42.

128 Lama Anagarika Govinda, *Foundations of Tibetan Mysticism*, Century, London 1987, p.230.

129 *Mind in Buddhist Psychology*, p.42.

130 See Nārada Thera, *Manual of Abhidhamma*, op. cit., pp.93–4.

131 Alexander Pope, *Imitations of Horace*, 'Epilogue to the Satires', Dialogue 2, lines 208–9.

132 Hsüan Tsang, *Ch'eng Wei-Shih Lun: Doctrine of Mere-Consciousness*, op. cit., p.395.

133 *Mind in Buddhist Psychology*, p.43.

134 Hsüan Tsang, *Ch'eng Wei-Shih Lun: Doctrine of Mere-Consciousness*, op. cit., p.395.

135 ibid., p.397.

136 See Śāntideva, *Bodhicāryāvatāra*, trans. Kate Crosby and Andrew Skilton, Oxford University Press, Oxford 1995, chapter 6, 'Perfection of Forbearance', verses 48–9.

137 *Mind in Buddhist Psychology*, p.44.

138 ibid., p.44.

139 Hsüan Tsang, *Ch'eng Wei-Shih Lun: Doctrine of Mere-Consciousness*, op. cit., p.397.

140 For more about the twelve classes of literature, see Sangharakshita, *The Eternal Legacy*, Tharpa, London 1985, pp.9–19.

141 *Mind in Buddhist Psychology*, p.47.

142 This distinction originates in the *Aṅguttara-Nikāya* of the Pāli Canon; see Nyanatiloka, *Buddhist Dictionary*, op. cit., pp.25–6.

143 The term *apratiṣṭhita nirvāṇa* was probably introduced by the Yogācārin tradition. For an excellent account of this 'non-abiding nirvāṇa' see Paul Williams, *Mahāyāna Buddhism*, Routledge, London 1989, pp.181–4. The *apratiṣṭhita nirvāṇa* appears in various Yogācāra texts. It is, for example, the topic discussed in the ninth chapter of Asaṅga's *Mahāyānasaṅgraha*. See G.M. Nagao, *Mādhyamika and Yogācāra: A Study of Mahāyāna Philosophies*, trans. L.S. Kawamura, State University of New York Press 1991, pp.23–34.

144 *Mind in Buddhist Psychology*, p.50.

145 William Blake, *Milton* preface, 'And did those feet in ancient time'.

146 See *The Threefold Lotus Sūtra*, trans. Bunno Kato et al., Weatherhill/Kosei, New York and Tokyo 1978, pp.58–9.

147 See Note 86 above.

148 *Mind in Buddhist Psychology*, p.53.

149 ibid., p.54.

150 See *Mahāparinibbāna Suttanta*, *Dīgha-Nikāya* 16 (ii.156).

151 S. Dasgupta, *An Ever-expanding Quest of Life and Consciousness*, Orient Longman, New Delhi 1971, pp.189–92.

152 *Dhammapada* verse 21.

153 *Mind in Buddhist Psychology*, p.55.

154 ibid., pp.57–8.

155 See, for example, the *Nidānakathā*, translated as *The Story of Gotama Buddha (Jātaka-nidāna)*, trans. N.A. Jayawickrama, Pali Text Society, Oxford 1990, p.87.

156 See *Majjhima-Nikāya* 55.

157 See *Laṅkāvatāra Sūtra*, trans. D.T. Suzuki, Routledge, London 1932, p.217.

158 See *Mind in Buddhist Psychology*, p.58.

159 See ibid., p.59.

160 The four *saṅgraha-vastus* are mentioned several times in the Pāli Canon (i.e. as the *saṅgaha-vatthus* in Pāli). See for example *Dīgha-Nikāya* iii.152. They also occur in numerous Mahāyāna texts: see, for example, *The Holy Teaching of Vimalakīrti*, trans. Robert A. Thurman, Pennsylvania State University Press 1976, p.150; see also Sangharakshita, *The Inconceivable Emancipation: Themes from the Vimalakīrti-nirdeśa*, Windhorse, Birmingham 1995, p.50. For an excellent account see H. Dayal, *The Bodhisattva Doctrine in Buddhist Sanskrit Literature*, Motilal Banarsidass, Delhi 1978, pp.251–9.

161 *Mind in Buddhist Psychology*, p.60.

162 See ibid., p.62.

163 See *Majjhima-Nikāya* 117; or *The Life of the Buddha*, op. cit., p.225.

164 *Mind in Buddhist Psychology*, pp.63–4.

165 ibid., p.65.

166 'The great secret of morals is love; or a going out of our own nature, and an identification of ourselves with the beautiful which exists in thought, action, or person, not our own. A man, to be greatly good, must imagine intensely and comprehensively; he must put himself in the place of another and of many others; the pains and pleasures of his species must become his own.' P.B. Shelley, 'A Defence of Poetry' (*Selected Prose Works of Shelley*, Watts and Co., London 1915, p.87).

167 *Mind in Buddhist Psychology*, p.66.

168 See *Visuddhimagga* iii.101–2.

169 *Mind in Buddhist Psychology*, p.68.

170 Anon., in W.G. Hiscock, *The Balliol Rhymes*.

171 H.C. Beeching, in ibid.

172 *Mind in Buddhist Psychology*, p.72.

173 See Bryan Magee, *The Philosophy of Schopenhauer*, Oxford and New York 1997, p.170 et seq.

174 See Sangharakshita, *Wisdom Beyond Words*, Windhorse, Glasgow 1993, pp.188–9.

175 See *A Survey of Buddhism*, op. cit., pp.490–5.

176 *Mind in Buddhist Psychology*, p.74.

177 See *What is the Dharma?*, op. cit., chapter 6.

178 See, for example, the *Aṭṭhakavagga* (The Chapter of the Eights) from the *Sutta-Nipāta*. This chapter is one of the oldest sections of the Pāli Canon. One of its main themes in that the wise man relinquishes *all* views. For a translation, see *The Rhinoceros Horn and Other Buddhist Poems*, trans. K.R. Norman, Pali Text Society, London 1985, pp.129–58.

179 *Mind in Buddhist Psychology*, pp.74–5.

180 ibid., p.75.

181 See ibid., p.76.

182 See *Majjhima-Nikāya* 72, trans. Bhikkhu Ñāṇamoli and Bhikkhu Bodhi, Wisdom, Boston 1995, *Aggivacchagotta Sutta*, 'To Vacchagotta on Fire', pp.590–4.

183 The Pali Text Society's Pāli–English dictionary (Oxford 1995, p.521) says that a *manomayakāya* 'can be created by great holiness or knowledge; human beings or gods may be endowed with this power'. The dictionary cites *Dīgha-Nikāya* i.17,77,186; *Vinaya* ii,185; *Majjhima-Nikāya* i.410; *Saṁyutta-Nikāya* iv,71; *Aṅguttara-Nikāya* i,24; iii,122,192; iv,235; v,60.

184 *Mind in Buddhist Psychology*, p.77.

185 This was an aspect of the Buddha's first teachings after his Enlightenment. See *Vinaya*, book 4 (*Mahāvagga*), chapter 1; or *The Life of the Buddha*, op. cit., p.42.

186 *Mind in Buddhist Psychology*, p.77.

187 See Candrakīrti's commentary on Nagarjuna's *Madhyamakakārikā*, xiii.8. See also Sangharakshita, *Wisdom Beyond Words*, op. cit., p.128.

188 See *Itivuttaka* 111.

189 See Bhikshu Thich Thien Chan, *The Literature of the Personalists (Pudgalavādins) of Early Buddhism*, Vietnam Buddhist Research Institute, 1997.

190 See Edward Conze, *Buddhist Thought in India*, Ann Arbor Paperbacks, Michigan 1967.

191 For a more recent reference, see Paul Williams, *Altruism and Reality*, Curzon, London 1997, pp.238–9.

192 *Mind in Buddhist Psychology*, p.78.

193 See Sangharakshita, *The Taste of Freedom*, Windhorse, Birmingham 1997, pp.19–22.

194 *Mind in Buddhist Psychology*, p.79.

195 The Sāṁkhya philosophers are generally identified as the 'Satkāryavādins', in that they hold that the effect is (pre-)existent (*sat*) in the cause. The causal operation simply makes manifest the already existing unmanifest effect. The Nyāya-Vaiśeṣika philosophers are generally identified as the 'Asatkāryavādins'. For these thinkers, the effect is not (pre-)existent (*asat*) in the cause. The causal operation brings into being an effect which previously did not exist at all. See, for example, S.N. Dasgupta, *A History of Indian Philosophy*, Motilal Banarsidass, Delhi 1991, vol.1, pp.257–8, 320. See also D.J. Kalupahana, *Causality: The Central Philosophy of Buddhism*, University Press of Hawaii, Honolulu 1975.

196 See *Mind in Buddhist Psychology*, p.80.

197 See, for example, *Laṅkāvatāra Sūtra*, op. cit., pp.46–8.

198 *Mind in Buddhist Psychology*, p.82.

199 ibid., p.83.

200 ibid., p.84.

201 ibid., p.84–5.

202 ibid., p.85.

203 *Othello*, Act 5, Scene 1, lines 19–20.

204 See Nietzsche, *Beyond Good and Evil*, chapter 4, aphorism 116.

205 *Mind in Buddhist Psychology*, pp.85–6.

206 ibid., p.86.

207 See ibid., p.87.

208 ibid., p.88.

209 See Sangharakshita, *Vision and Transformation*, Windhorse, Glasgow 1990, pp.132–46.

210 *Mind in Buddhist Psychology*, p.89.

211 ibid., pp.89–90.

212 ibid., p.90.

213 ibid., p.91.

214 ibid., p.92.

215 ibid., p.93.

216 ibid., p.94.

217 The parable of the raft originates in the Pāli Canon. See *What is the Dharma?*, op. cit., pp.13ff.

218 *Mind in Buddhist Psychology*, p.94.

219 ibid., p.95.

220 ibid., p.96.

221 ibid., p.96.

222 See ibid., p.97.

223 For more detail, see Sangharakshita, *The Three Jewels*, Windhorse, Glasgow 1991, p.82.

224 *Mind in Buddhist Psychology*, p.100.

225 Interestingly, though, in Theravada Abhidhamma *thīna* (sloth / tiredness) and *middha* (sleepiness / torpor) are both listed as negative mental events. See, for example, Anuruddha's *Abhidhammatthasaṅgaha*.

226 *Mind in Buddhist Psychology*, p.101.

227 ibid., p.102.

228 See *Visuddhimagga* iv.91.

229 *Mind in Buddhist Psychology*, p.113.

230 See Sister Nivedita and Ananda Coomaraswamy, *Myths of the Hindus and Buddhists*, Harrap, London 1914, p.296.

FURTHER READING

Asaṅga's *Abhidharmasamuccaya* is not available in English. There is a French version translated and annotated by Walpola Rahula: *Le compendium de la super-doctrine (philosophie) d'Asaṅga*, École française d'extrême-orient, Paris 1971.

Asaṅga, *The Summary of the Great Vehicle*, translated from the Chinese of Paramātha by John P. Keenan, Numata Center for Buddhist Translation and Research, Berkeley Calif. 1992.

Paul J. Griffiths et al. (trans.), *The Realm of Awakening*, a translation and study of the tenth chapter of Asaṅga's *Mahayanasaṅgraha*, Oxford University Press 1989.

Vasubandhu's *Abhidharmakośa(bhāṣya)* is available as *Abhidharmakośabhāṣyam*, English translation by Leo M. Pruden from the French translation by Louis de la Vallée Poussin, Asian Humanities Press, Berkeley Calif. 1988–90, (4 vols.)

Ganganatha Jha. (trans.), *The Tattvasaṅgraha of Shāntarakṣita: With the Commentary of Kamalashīla*, 2 vols., Motilal Banarsidass, Delhi 1986.

NĀGĀRJUNA'S *MADHYAMAKAKĀRIKĀ*
Various translations are available, for example:
D.J. Kalupahana, *Nāgārjuna: The Philosophy of the Middle Way*, State

University of New York Press, Albany 1986.
B. Bocking, *Nāgārjuna in China: A Translation of the Middle Treatise*, Edwin
Mellen, Albany 1995.
J.L. Garfield, *The Fundamental Wisdom of the Middle Way*, OUP, Oxford 1995.
K.K. Inada, *Nāgārjuna*, Hokuseido, Tokyo 1970.

RATNĀVALĪ
For an English translation see:
J. Hopkins et al (trans.), *The Precious Garland and the Song of the Four
Mindfulnesses*. George Allen and Unwin, London 1975.

ABHIDHARMA
Nyanaponika Thera, *Abhidhamma Studuies: Researches in Buddhist
Psychology*, Buddhist Publication Society, Kandy 1976.
W.F. Jayasuriya, *The Psychology and Philosophy of Buddhism: An Introduction to
the Abhidhamma*, Buddhist Missionary Society, Kuala Lumpur 1976.
Lama Anagarika Govinda, *The Psychological Attitude of Early Buddhist
Philosophy and its Systematic Representation According to Abhidhamma
Tradition*, Motilal Banarsidass, Delhi 1991.
H.V. Guenther, *Philosophy and Psychology in the Abhidharma*, Motilal
Banarsidass, Delhi 1991.
Nayanatiloka Mahāthera, *Guide Through the Abhidharma-Piṭaka*, Buddhist
Publication Society, Kandy 1971.

SOME OF TSONGKHAPA'S PRINCIPAL WRITINGS
Great Exposition of the Stages of the Path (Lam rim chen mo)
Partial translation by A. Wayman, *Calming the Mind and Discerning the Real*,
Columbia, New York 1978.
Partial translation by E. Napper, *Dependent-Arising and Emptiness*, Wisdom,
London 1989.
*Essence of the Good Explanations, Treatise Discriminating What is to be
Interpreted and the Definitive (drang ba dang nges pa'i don rnam par ba'i bstan
bcos legs bshad snying po)*. Translation by Robert Thurman, *Tsong Khapa's
Speech of Gold in the Essence of True Eloquence*, Princeton University Press,
Princeton 1984.
Great Exposition of Special Insight (lhag mthongchen mo). Translation by Alex
Wayman, *Calming the Mind and Discerning the Real*, Columbia University
Press, New York 1978.
Great Exposition of Secret Mantra (sngags rim chen mo). Chapter 1: translation
by Jeffrey Hopkins, *Tantra in Tibet*, George Allen and Unwin, London

1977; Chapters 2 and 3: translation by Jeffrey Hopkins, *Yoga of Tibet*, George Allen and Unwin, London 1981.

The Three Principal Aspects of the Path (lam gtso rnam gsum). Translation by Geshe Wangyal, *The Door of Liberation*, Lotsawa, New York 1978, pp.126–60. Translation by Jeffrey Hopkins and Geshe Sopa, *Practice and Theory of Tibetan Buddhism*, Grove, New York 1976, pp.1–47. See also the translation by Jeffrey Hopkins (including commentary by the Dalai Lama), in Tenzin Gyatso, *Kindness, Clarity, and Insight*, Snow Lion, Ithaca NY 1984, pp.118–56.

Praise of Dependent-Arising (rten 'brel bstod pa). Translation by Geshe Wangyal, The Door of Liberation, Lotsawa, New York 1978, pp.117–25.

Ocean of Reasoning, Explanation of (Nāgājuna's) 'Fundamental Treatise on the Middle Way Called "Wisdom"'. Translation of chapter 2 in Jeffrey Hopkins, *Chapter Two of Ocean of Reasoning by Tsong-ka-pa*, Library of Tibetan Works and Archives, Dharamsala 1974.

YOGĀCĀRA

P. Williams, *Mahāyāna Buddhism: The Doctrinal Foundations*, Routledge, London 1989, pp.77–95.

S. Anaker, *Seven Works of Vasubandhu, the Buddhist Psychological Doctor*, Motilal Banarsidass, Delhi 1984.

P. Griffiths, *On Being Mindless: Buddhist Meditation and the Mind-Body Problem*, Open Court, La Salle 1986, pp.76–106.

G.M. Nagao, *Mādhyamika and Yogācāra: A Study of Mahāyāna Philosophies*, L.S. Kawamura (trans.), State University of New York Press, Albany 1991.

J.D. Willis, *On Knowing Reality*, Columbia University Press, New York 1979.

Chhote Lal Tripathi, *The Problem of Knowledge in Yogacara Buddhism*, Bharat-Bhararti, Varanasi 1972.

Traditional life stories of Nāgārjuna, Āryadeva, Asaṅga, Vasubandhu, Candrakīrti, Dignāga, etc:

Lama Chimpa and Alaka Chattopadhyaya (trans.), *Tāranātha's History of Buddhism in India*, Motilal Banarsidass, Delhi 1990.

INDEX

The Windhorse symbolizes the energy of the enlightened mind carrying the Three Jewels – the Buddha, the Dharma, and the Sangha – to all sentient beings.

Buddhism is one of the fastest-growing spiritual traditions in the Western world. Throughout its 2,500-year history, it has always succeeded in adapting its mode of expression to suit whatever culture it has encountered.

Windhorse Publications aims to continue this tradition as Buddhism comes to the West. Today's Westerners are heirs to the entire Buddhist tradition, free to draw instruction and inspiration from all the many schools and branches. Windhorse publishes works by authors who not only understand the Buddhist tradition but are also familiar with Western culture and the Western mind.

For orders and catalogues contact

WINDHORSE PUBLICATIONS
11 PARK ROAD
BIRMINGHAM
B13 8AB
UK

WINDHORSE PUBLICATIONS INC
540 SOUTH 2ND WEST
MISSOULA
MT 59801
USA

WINDHORSE PUBLICATIONS
P O BOX 574
NEWTON
NSW 2042
AUSTRALIA

Windhorse Publications is an arm of the Friends of the Western Buddhist Order, which has more than sixty centres on five continents. Through these centres, members of the Western Buddhist Order offer regular programmes of events for the general public and for more experienced students. These include meditation classes, public talks, study on Buddhist themes and texts, and 'bodywork' classes such as t'ai chi, yoga, and massage. The FWBO also runs several retreat centres and the Karuna Trust, a fund-raising charity that supports social welfare projects in the slums and villages of India.

Many FWBO centres have residential spiritual communities and ethical businesses associated with them. Arts activities are encouraged too, as is the development of strong bonds of friendship between people who share the same ideals. In this way the FWBO is developing a unique approach to Buddhism, not simply as a set of techniques, less still as an exotic cultural interest, but as a creatively directed way of life for people living in the modern world.

If you would like more information about the FWBO please write to

LONDON BUDDHIST CENTRE
51 ROMAN ROAD
LONDON
E2 0HU
UK

ARYALOKA
HEARTWOOD CIRCLE
NEWMARKET
NH 03857
USA

KAMALASHILA

MEDITATION:

THE BUDDHIST WAY OF TRANQUILLITY AND INSIGHT

A comprehensive guide to the methods and theory of Buddhist meditation, written in an informal, accessible style. It provides a complete introduction to the basic techniques, as well as detailed advice for more experienced meditators seeking to deepen their practice.

   The author is a long-standing member of the Western Buddhist Order, and has been teaching meditation since 1975. In 1979 he helped to establish a semi-monastic community in North Wales, which has now grown into a public retreat centre. For more than a decade he and his colleagues developed approaches to meditation that are firmly grounded in Buddhist tradition but readily accessible to people with a modern Western background. Their experience – as meditators, as students of the traditional texts, and as teachers – is distilled in this book.

304 pages, with charts and illustrations
ISBN 1 899579 05 2
£12.99/$25.95

ANDREW SKILTON

A CONCISE HISTORY OF BUDDHISM

How and when did the many schools and sub-sects of Buddhism emerge? How do the ardent devotion of the Pure Land schools, the magical ritual of the Tantra, or the paradoxical negations of the Perfection of Wisdom literature, relate to the direct, down-to-earth teachings of Gautama the 'historical' Buddha? Did Buddhism modify the cultures to which it was introduced, or did they modify Buddhism?

   Here is a narrative that describes and correlates the diverse manifestations of Buddhism – in its homeland of India, and in its spread across Asia, from Mongolia to Sri Lanka, from Japan to the Middle East. Drawing on the latest historical and literary research, Andrew Skilton explains the basic concepts of Buddhism from all periods of its development, and places them in a historical framework.

272 pages, with maps and extensive bibliography
ISBN 0 904766 92 6
£9.99/$19.95

ALSO FROM WINDHORSE

P.D. RYAN

BUDDHISM AND THE NATURAL WORLD:
TOWARDS A MEANINGFUL MYTH

P.D. Ryan takes a fresh look at our relationship with the living world and offers a radical analysis of our consumerist attitudes. Applying the Buddha's fundamental message of non-violence to these crucial issues, he draws out a middle way between destructiveness and sentimentality: a way which recognizes the truth of the interdependence of all life and places universal compassion at the very centre of our relationship with the world.

In *Buddhism and the Natural World* Ryan emphasizes the importance of living in accord with this truth – and reminds us of the Buddha's insistence that to do so calls for nothing less than a revolution in consciousness.

144 pages
ISBN 1 899579 00 1
£6.99/$13.95

RICHARD P. HAYES

LAND OF NO BUDDHA:
REFLECTIONS OF A SCEPTICAL BUDDHIST

Witty, honest, and thought-provoking, Richard Hayes casts a critical eye over modern society and the teachings of Buddhism as they flow into the West. Written with the perspective that comes from more than twenty years of study and practice, *Land of No Buddha* examines the pitfalls awaiting those who search for the truth. A sceptical Buddhist, Hayes nevertheless proposes the radical path of the Buddha – becoming free from self-indulgent passions and delusions – to those seeking genuine wisdom, not just slogans to stick on the bumpers of their cars.

288 pages
ISBN 1 899579 12 5
£9.99/$19.95